Learn French with The Adventures of Nono

HypLern Interlinear Project
www.hyplern.com

First edition: 2025, June

Author: Jean Grave
Translation: Kees van den End
Foreword: Camilo Andrés Bonilla Carvajal PhD

ISBN: 1989643108

kees@hyplern.com
www.hyplern.com

Learn French with The Adventures of Nono

Interlinear French to English

Author
Jean Grave

Translation
Kees van den End

HypLern Interlinear Project
www.hyplern.com

The HypLern Method

Learning a foreign language should not mean leafing through page after page in a bilingual dictionary until one's fingertips begin to hurt. Quite the contrary, through everyday language use, friendly reading, and direct exposure to the language we can get well on our way towards mastery of the vocabulary and grammar needed to read native texts. In this manner, learners can be successful in the foreign language without too much study of grammar paradigms or rules. Indeed, Seneca expresses in his sixth epistle that "Longum iter est per praecepta, breve et efficax per exempla[1]."

The HypLern series constitutes an effort to provide a highly effective tool for experiential foreign language learning. Those who are genuinely interested in utilizing original literary works to learn a foreign language do not have to use conventional graded texts or adapted versions for novice readers. The former only distort the actual essence of literary works, while the latter are highly reduced in vocabulary and relevant content. This collection aims to bring the lively experience of reading stories as directly told by their very authors to foreign language learners.

Most excited adult language learners will at some point seek their teachers' guidance on the process of learning to read in the foreign language rather than seeking out external opinions. However, both teachers and learners lack a general reading technique or strategy. Oftentimes, students undertake the reading task equipped with nothing more than a bilingual dictionary, a grammar book, and lots of courage. These efforts often end in frustration as the student builds mis-constructed nonsensical sentences after many hours spent on an aimless translation drill.

Consequently, we have decided to develop this series of interlinear translations intended to afford a comprehensive edition of unabridged texts. These texts are presented as they were originally written with no changes in word choice or order. As a result, we have a translated piece conveying the true meaning under every word from the original work. Our readers receive then two books in just one volume: the original version and its translation.

The reading task is no longer a laborious exercise of patiently decoding unclear and seemingly complex paragraphs. What's more, reading becomes an enjoyable and meaningful process of cultural, philosophical and linguistic learning. Independent learners can then acquire expressions and vocabulary while understanding pragmatic and socio-cultural dimensions of the target language by reading in it rather than reading about it.

Our proposal, however, does not claim to be a novelty. Interlinear translation is as old as the Spanish tongue, e.g. "glosses of [Saint] Emilianus", interlinear bibles in Old German, and of course James Hamilton's work in the 1800s. About the latter, we remind the readers, that as a revolutionary freethinker he promoted the publication of Greco-Roman classic works and further pieces in diverse languages. His effort, such as ours, sought to lighten the exhausting task of looking words up in large glossaries as an educational practice: "if there is any thing which fills reflecting men with melancholy and regret, it is the waste of mortal time, parental money, and puerile happiness, in the present method of pursuing Latin and Greek[2]".

Additionally, another influential figure in the same line of thought as Hamilton was John Locke. Locke was also the philosopher and translator of the Fabulae AEsopi in an interlinear plan. In 1600, he was already suggesting that interlinear texts, everyday communication, and use of the target language could be the most appropriate ways to achieve language learning:

> ...the true and genuine Way, and that which I would propose, not only as the easiest and best, wherein a Child might, without pains or Chiding, get a Language which others are wont to be whipt for at School six or seven Years together...[3]

---

1 "The journey is long through precepts, but brief and effective through examples". Seneca, Lucius Annaeus. (1961) Ad Lucilium Epistulae Morales, vol. I. London: W. Heinemann.

2 In: Hamilton, James (1829?) History, principles, practice and results of the Hamiltonian system, with answers to the Edinburgh and Westminster reviews; A lecture delivered at Liverpool; and instructions for the use of the books published on the system. Londres: W. Aylott and Co., 8, Pater Noster Row. p. 29.

3 In: Locke, John. (1693) Some thoughts concerning education. Londres: A. and J. Churchill. pp. 196-7.

Who can benefit from this edition?

We identify three kinds of readers, namely, those who take this work as a search tool, those who want to learn a language by reading authentic materials, and those attempting to read writers in their original language. The HypLern collection constitutes a very effective instrument for all of them.

1. For the first target audience, this edition represents a search tool to connect their mother tongue with that of the writer's. Therefore, they have the opportunity to read over an original literary work in an enriching and certain manner.
2. For the second group, reading every word or idiomatic expression in its actual context of use will yield a strong association between the form, the collocation, and the context. This will have a direct impact on long term learning of passive vocabulary, gradually building genuine reading ability in the original language. This book is an ideal companion not only to independent learners but also to those who take lessons with a teacher. At the same time, the continuous feeling of achievement produced during the process of reading original authors both stimulates and empowers the learner to study[1].
3. Finally, the third kind of reader will notice the same benefits as the previous ones. The proximity of a word and its translation in our interlinear texts is a step further from other collections, such as the Loeb Classical Library. Although their works might be considered the most famous in this genre, the presentation of texts on opposite pages hinders the immediate link between words and their semantic equivalence in our native tongue (or one we have a strong mastery of).

---

1 Some further ways of using the present work include:

1. As you progress through the stories, focus less on the lower line (the English translation). Instead, try to read through the upper line, staying in the foreign language as long as possible.
2. Even if you find glosses or explanatory footnotes about the mechanics of the language, you should make your own hypotheses on word formation and syntactical functions in a sentence. Feel confident about inferring your own language rules and test them progressively. You can also take notes concerning those idiomatic expressions or special language usage that calls your attention for later study.
3. As soon as you finish each text, check the reading in the original version (with no interlinear or parallel translation). This will fulfil the main goal of this

collection: bridging the gap between readers and original literary works, training them to read directly and independently.

Why interlinear?

Conventionally speaking, tiresome reading in tricky and exhausting circumstances has been the common definition of learning by texts. This collection offers a friendly reading format where the language is not a stumbling block anymore. Contrastively, our collection presents a language as a vehicle through which readers can attain and understand their authors' written ideas.

While learning to read, most people are urged to use the dictionary and distinguish words from multiple entries. We help readers skip this step by providing the proper translation based on the surrounding context. In so doing, readers have the chance to invest energy and time in understanding the text and learning vocabulary; they read quickly and easily like a skilled horseman cantering through a book.

Thereby we stress the fact that our proposal is not new at all. Others have tried the same before, coming up with evident and substantial outcomes. Certainly, we are not pioneers in designing interlinear texts. Nonetheless, we are nowadays the only, and doubtless, the best, in providing you with interlinear foreign language texts.

Handling instructions

Using this book is very easy. Each text should be read at least three times in order to explore the whole potential of the method. The first phase is devoted to comparing words in the foreign language to those in the mother tongue. This is to say, the upper line is contrasted to the lower line as the following example shows:

Et	il	regarda	autour	de	lui	;	mais	personne	ne	se
And	he	looked	around	of	him	;	but	no one	not	herself

montrait.
showed

The second phase of reading focuses on capturing the meaning and sense of the original text. As readers gain practice with the method, they should be able to focus on the target language without getting distracted by the translation. New users of the method, however, may find it helpful to cover the translated lines with a piece of paper as illustrated in the image below. Subsequently, they try to understand the meaning of every word, phrase, and entire sentences in the target language itself, drawing on the translation only when necessary. In this phase, the reader should resist the temptation to look at the translation for every word. In doing so, they will find that they are able to understand a good portion of the text by reading directly in the target language, without the crutch of the translation. This is the skill we are looking to train: the ability to read and understand native materials and enjoy them as native speakers do, that being, directly in the original language.

Et	il	regarda	autour	de	lui	;	mais	personne	ne	se
And	he	looked								self

montrait.
showed

In the final phase, readers will be able to understand the meaning of the text when reading it without additional help. There may be some less common words and phrases which have not cemented themselves yet in the reader's brain, but the majority of the story should not pose any problems. If desired, the reader can use an SRS or some other memorization method to learning these straggling words.

Et il regarda autour de lui ; mais personne ne se montrait.

Above all, readers will not have to look every word up in a dictionary to read a text in the foreign language. This otherwise wasted time will be spent concentrating on their principal interest. These new readers will tackle authentic texts while learning their vocabulary and expressions to use in further communicative (written or oral) situations. This book is just one work from an overall series with the same purpose. It really helps those who are afraid of having "poor vocabulary" to feel confident about reading directly in the language. To all of them and to all of you, welcome to the amazing experience of living a foreign language!

Additional tools

Check out shop.hyplern.com or contact us at info@hyplern.com for free mp3s (if available) and free empty (untranslated) versions of the eBooks that we have on offer.

For some of the older eBooks and paperbacks we have Windows, iOS and Android apps available that, next to the interlinear format, allow for a pop-up format, where hovering over a word or clicking on it gives you its meaning. The apps also have any mp3s, if available, and integrated vocabulary practice.

Visit the site hyplern.com for the same functionality online. This is where we will be working non-stop to make all our material available in multiple formats, including audio where available, and vocabulary practice.

Table of Contents

Chapter	Page

Le désir
The desire

Nono est un petit garçon de neuf ans, intelligent, tapageur, mais pas
Nono is a little boy of nine years (old) intelligent rowdy but not

mauvais diable cependant. Comme tous les enfants, il a bien quelques
(a) bad devil however Like all the children he has well some

moments de vivacité et de turbulence où il fait enrager ses parents
moments of vivacity and of turbulence where he makes enrage his parents

; des instants où son petit être, en pleine expansion, se répand en
; -of the- moments where his little being in full expansion itself spreads in

bonds et cris de joie, ne choisissant pas toujours le moment favorable
leaps and cries of joy not choosing -not- always the moment favorable

pour leur donner libre cours, se dépensant en espiègleries, sans
for them to give free course themselves spending in shenanigans without

s'occuper si les parents sont d'humeur à le supporter.
himself to occupy whether the parents are of mood to it support
to take care   in a mood

Seulement, ce qui gâte un peu son bon naturel, c'est un entêtement
Only this which spoils a bit his good nature that is a stubbornness

obstiné dont il n'y a pas moyen de le corriger. Entêté, non
obstinate of which it not there has -not- means of it to correct Stubborn not
                      there is no

pas comme une mule, non pas comme deux chèvres, mais bien comme
-not- like a mule not -not- like two goats but well like

dix mille cochons.
ten thousand pigs

Lorsqu'une fois il s'est mis dans la tête de ne pas vouloir faire
When one time he himself is put in the head of not -not- to want to do
         himself has

quelque chose, c'est fini, il n'y a plus moyen de rien lui
some thing it is finished it not there has no longer means to anything him
              over   there is no

2

faire faire : réprimandes, coups, raisonnements, douceurs, promesses, rien
make do : reprimands blows reasonings sweets promises nothing

n'a prise sur lui. En lui-même, il reconnaît qu'il a tort, surtout
-not- has take on him In him self he recognizes that he has wrong especially
has grip Inside is

lorsqu'on lui fait comprendre que s'il ne sait pas être agréable
when one him makes understand that if he not knows how -not- to be pleasant

aux autres, les autres ne feront rien pour lui faire plaisir.
to the others the others not will do anything for him to make pleasure
to make him happy

Je ne veux pas dire que Nono soit roué de coups ; c'est un moyen
I not want -not- to say that Nono be rolled of blows ; that is a means
don't given a beating

dont les parents usent assez souvent contre les enfants obstinés ; car
which the parents use rather often against the children obstinate ; because

il est plus facile de lancer une calotte que de donner une raison, et
it is more easy to launch a cap than to give a reason and
easier slap

trop souvent les parents ont recours à ce moyen. S'ils étaient obligés
too often the parents have recourse to this means If they were forced

de donner la raison de leurs ordres, ils seraient forcés d'avouer
-of- to give the reason of their orders they would be forced of to confess

qu'ils n'en ont pas d'autre que leur simple caprice, et d'autre droit
that they not of it have -not- of else than their simple whim and -of- else right
have nothing no other

que d'être les plus forts. Lorsqu'on est de mauvaise humeur, c'est une
than of to be the most strong When one is of bad mood it is a
strongest in a bad

détente de pouvoir la passer sur quelqu'un qui ne peut répondre.
relaxation of power it to pass on someone who not can answer

Mais les parents de Nono, s'ils ne sont pas tout à fait à l'abri
But the parents of Nono if they not are -not- all to made at the shelter
absolutely

de ce travers ; si, par instants, ils ont la main quelque peu leste,
of this crossing ; if by moments they have the hand some bit nimble
a little loose

ils n'abusent cependant pas trop de ce moyen de réprimande, et
they not abuse However -not- too (much) of this means of reprimand and

3

se　　donnent　parfois　la　peine　de　faire　entendre　raison　au
-themselves-　give make　sometimes　the　trouble　of　to make　hear　reason　to the

petit　obstiné,　en　lui　faisant　comprendre　que　nous　ne　pouvons
little　obstinate (boy)　in　him　making　understand　that　we　not　can

raisonnablement　nous　attendre　à　ce　que　les　gens　soient　aimables
reasonably　ourselves　expect　to　this　that　the　people　are　friendly

envers　nous　qu'à　condition　de　l'être　nous　mêmes　à　leur　égard.
towards　us　that at　(the) condition　of　it being　ourselves　same　to　their　respect
to them

Nono　reconnaît　qu'il　a　tort　de　s'obstiner　dans　ses　refus,　mais
Nono　recognizes　that he　has is　wrong　of　-himself- to persist　in　his　refusals　but

il　considère　comme　un　point　d'honneur　de　ne　pas　revenir　sur　ce
he　considers　like　a　point　of honor　of　not　-not-　to return　on　this

qu'il　a　dit　—　surtout　lorsque　c'est　un　refus　d'accomplir　une　chose
that he　has　said　—　especially　when　it is　a　refusal　of to accomplish　a　thing

qu'on　lui　demande　de　faire.　—　Pour　qu'il　revienne　à　de　meilleurs
that one　him　requests　of　to do　—　For　that he　returns　to　-of-　best

sentiments,　le　mieux　est　de　le　laisser　bouder　dans　son　coin,　et
feelings　the　better　is　of　him　to let　sulk　in　his　corner　and

d'attendre　que　la　réflexion　l'amène　à　des　sentiments　plus　sociables.
of to wait　that　the　reflection thought　him leads　to　-of the-　feelings　more　sociable

Si　les　parents　sont,　assez　souvent,　mal　disposés,　les　enfants,　de　leur
If　the　parents　are　enough　often　badly　disposed　the　children　from　their

côté,　ont　aussi　leurs　moments　désagréables.　Chez　les　parents,　les　soucis
side　have　also　their　moments　unpleasant　With　the　parents　the　worries

du　ménage,　les　inquiétudes　sur　le　travail ;　à　l'atelier,　le　patron
of the　household　the　worries　about　the　work ;　at　the workshop　the　boss

a　été　injuste,　on　n'a　pas　pu　lui　dire　carrément　ce　que　l'on
has　been　unfair　one　not has　-not-　been able　him　to say　straight directly　this　that　it one

pensait,　on　rentre　à　la　maison　de　mauvaise　humeur ;　et　c'est　la
thought　one　returns　to　the　house　with　(a) bad　mood ;　and　it is　the

femme et les gosses qui écopent.
woman and the kids who pay the price

Lorsqu'ils sont dans cette fâcheuse situation d'esprit, il arrive aux parents
When they are in this annoying situation of spirit it arrives to the parents
happens

de donner, sans s'en apercevoir, leurs ordres d'un ton très
of to give without oneself of it to notice their orders with a tone very

impératif. Nono, lui, est très froissé de ce ton, même lorsqu'il serait
imperative Nono him (he) is very hurt of this tone even when he would be

le plus disposé à accomplir ce qu'on lui demande ; ce n'est alors
the most disposed to accomplish this that one him requests ; this not is then

qu'en rechignant qu'il obéit.
that while grudging that he obeys
that in reluctance

Bien souvent aussi, lorsqu'il ne comprend pas toujours la nécessité d'un
Well often also when he not understands -not- always the need of an

ordre, — après tout, à neuf ans, on ne peut pas en connaître autant
order — after all at nine years one not can -not- of it to know as much

que ses parents, — il suffirait d'un mot d'explication, mais les parents
as his parents — it would suffice with a word of explanation but the parents

sont trop habitués à croire que les enfants doivent obéir sans
are too accustomed to believe that the children have to obey without

discuter, et parce que, très souvent, ils ne savent pas s'en
to discuss and because that very often they not know -not- oneself of it
discussion

faire comprendre, ils s'imaginent que les enfants sont dépourvus
to make understand they -themselves- imagine that the children are lacking

de toute compréhension, aussi ne se donnent-ils pas la peine de
-of- all comprehension also not themselves give they -not- the trouble of

raisonner. « Un enfant doit obéir à ses parents sans discuter », cela
to reason A child must obey -to- his parents without to discuss that
discussion

dispense de toute explication.
exemption of all explanation

Aussi, voilà bien des occasions de gronderies et de tiraillements,
Also see there well of the opportunities of scoldings and of tuggings
disagreements

comme vous voyez.
as you see

On a fait, jusqu'ici, beaucoup de livres pour apprendre aux enfants
One has made up to here much of books for to teach to the children
by now many books

qu'ils doivent être sages, obéissants ; mais, malheureusement, ce sont
that they have to be wise obedient ; but unfortunately these are

les parents qui les écrivent, et on a oublié d'en faire pour
the parents who them write and one has forgotten of them to make for

recommander aux parents de ne demander aux enfants que des
to recommend to the parents of not to ask to the children (other) than -of- the

choses à portée de leur âge et de leur raisonnement ; il arrive que
things at (the) bearing of their age and of their reasoning ; it arrives that
the weight happens

la plupart des pères et des mères ne connaissent pas du tout
the largest part of the fathers and of the mothers not know -not- of the all
at

leur métier de parents.
their trade of parents

Espérons qu'on en écrira quelques-uns pour leur apprendre à être
Let's hope that one of it will write some for them to learn to be

raisonnables à l'égard de leurs enfants. Peut-être un des enfants qui
reasonable at the regard of their children Maybe one of the children who

me lit en ce moment, se rappellera-t-il, lorsqu'il sera grand, les
me reads in this moment himself remembers he when he will be big the
adult

choses qui lui auront semblé les plus injustes dans la conduite de
things which him will have appeared the most unrighteous in the behaviour of

ses parents à son égard, et se mettra-t-il à écrire ce livre ; à
his parents to his respect and himself will he set to write this book ; at

moins qu'il ne trouve mieux de le leur faire remarquer
least that he not finds better of it them to make notice
if he something better

de suite. Seulement, en ce cas, je ne suis pas très certain qu'il ne
of following Only in this case I not am -not- very certain that it not
right now

serait — would be
pas — -not-
plus — more
prudent — sensible
à — for
lui — him
d'essayer — of to try
d'en — of them
faire — to make
un — a
conte. — tale
Le — The

moindre — least
qu'il — that it
pourrait — could
lui — him
en — of it
arriver, — arrive
serait — would be
de — of
se — himself
faire — to make
traiter — treat

d'effronté, — of cheeky
d'enfant — of child
sans — without
cœur — heart
qui — who
ose — dares
critiquer — criticize
la — the
conduite — behaviour
de — of
ses — his

pauvres — poor
parents. — parents
Le — The
conte — tale
serait — would be
beaucoup — much
plus — more
amusant — fun
à — to
écrire — write
que — than

les — the
stupidités — stupidities
qu'on — that one
leur — them
donne — gives
comme — like
compositions — compositions essays
à — at
l'école, — the school
les — the

parents — parents
en — of it
seraient — would be
plutôt — rather
amusés — entertained
; — ;
et — and
s'ils — if they
n'étaient — not were
pas — -not-
trop — too
bêtes, — beasts dumb

ils — they
saisiraient — would seize would grasp
peut-être — maybe
la — the
leçon — lesson
sans — without
se — themselves
fâcher. — to annoy to become angry

Du — From the
côté — side
de — of
l'enfant, — the child
c'est — this is
une — an
autre — other
histoire — history
: — :
il — it
est — is
bien — well
dur — hard
de — of

quitter — to leave
le — the
livre — book
que — that
l'on — -it- one
tient — holds
pour — for
aller — to go
chercher — search
quatre — four
sous — nickels
de — of

beurre — butter
ou — or
un — a
litre — litre
de — of
pommes de terre — apples of earth potatoes
; — ;
justement — exactly (when)
on — one
en — of it
était — was
au — at the

passage — passage
le — the
plus — most
intéressant — interesting
: — :
au — at the
moment — moment
où — where
le — the
héros — hero
du — of the
livre — book

vient — comes
d'être — of to be
pris — taken
par — by
des — -of the-
brigands, — robbers
ou — or
est — is
sur — on
le — the
point — point
de — of
faire — to make

naufrage — shipwreck
; — ;
on — one
ne — not
voudrait — would like
pas — -not-
l'abandonner — him to abandon
dans — in
une — a
position — position
aussi — so

critique. — critical
Ou — Or
bien — well
encore — still
on — one
est — is
très — very
actionné — actuated
à — to
une — a
émouvante — moving
partie — part

de — of
cache-cache — hide and seek
avec — with
ses — his
camarades — comrades
; — ;
la — the
mère — mother
est — is
très — very
mal — badly at a very bad time
venue — come
de — of

vous déranger pour vous envoyer chercher deux sous de sel, ou vous
you to bother for you to send to search two nickels of salt or you
to get

faire remonter pour laver la vaisselle. Aussi, il arrivait à Nono de ne
to make go up for to wash the dishes Also it arrives to Nono of not
happens

pas exécuter toujours promptement les ordres reçus, et de se les
-not- to execute always promptly the orders received and of himself them

faire répéter bien des fois, avant de les exécuter, non sans
to make repeat well of the times before of them to carry out not without
a good number of

murmurer et traîner fortement ses pieds à terre en signe de
muttering and dragging strongly his feet on earth in sign of
the ground

mécontentement. C'est que, hélas ! il n'y a personne de parfait, et
dissatisfaction It is that alas ! it not there has person of perfect and
there is no one perfect

les bons petits enfants — comme les parents sans défauts du reste —
the good small children — like the parents without defects of the rest —

n'existent que dans les livres qu'on leur fait lire pour leur
not exist (other) than in the books that one them makes read for them
do not exist

apprendre à être bien sages.
to learn to be well wise

Il arrive aussi quelquefois, à notre jeune héros, de se battre avec son
It arrives also sometimes to our young hero of himself to fight with his
happens

grand frère Alexandre — qu'on est habitué d'appeler Titi — et avec sa
big brother Alexander — that one is used of to call Titi — and with his

sœur Cendrine. Son frère Titi est beaucoup plus âgé que lui, mais
sister Cendrine His brother Titi is much more aged than him but
older

n'a guère plus de raison ; aussi, il leur arrive de se disputer
not has hardly more -of- reason ; also it them arrives of themselves to dispute
argue

comme deux chiffonniers.
like two rag-gatherers

Cendrine n'est que d'un an plus âgée que lui ; elle aussi, est taquine
Cendrine not is than of a year more old than him ; she also is (a) tease
is only one year older

à ses moments. Mais comme Nono est le plus jeune, on exige de sa
at her moments But like Nono is the most young one requires of his

sœur qu'elle cède aux fantaisies de monsieur ; nécessité dont elle
sister that she yields to the fantasies of (the) gentleman ; (the) need of which she
{her littler brother}

n'est pas, du reste, très convaincue, et qu'elle est moins disposée
not is -not- of the rest very convinced and that she is (even) less disposed
for the

encore à subir.
still to undergo

On commence par se chamailler un peu ; on s'arrache les jouets, et
One begins by himself to bicker a bit ; one pulls the toys and

puis, ma foi ! les poings se mettent de la partie, jusqu'à ce que
then my faith ! the fists themselves put of the part up to this that

quelques paires de calottes, impartialement distribuées, viennent mettre la
some pairs of caps impartially distributed come to put the
slaps

paix entre les belligérants.
peace between the belligerents

Il y a bien un autre petit frère, Paulo, mais il est si jeune, un
It there has well an other little brother Paulo but he is so young a
There is indeed

an à peine, que ce n'est guère possible de se disputer avec lui, et
year at pain that it not is hardly possible of oneself to dispute with him and
barely to argue

on est très content de l'avoir, au contraire, car il ne finit
one is very satisfied of to see him on the contrary because he not finishes

jamais sa bouillie et ses gâteaux ; avec lui il y a toujours quelques
ever his porridge and his cakes ; with him it there has always some
there are

miettes à attraper.
crumbs to catch

Mais, somme toute, les parents de Nono aiment leurs enfants ; leurs
But sum all the parents of Nono love their children ; their
in summary

défauts tiennent des préjugés, des habitudes qu'ils ont trouvées
shortcomings have -of the- prejudices, -of the- habits that they have found

9

établies, qu'ils ont prises avec l'éducation qui leur a été donnée,
established that they have taken with the education which them has been given
received from

et non de leur caractère qui est plutôt celui de la bonté.
and not from their character which is rather the one of the goodness

Nono, s'il est têtu, n'est pas un mauvais diable, il aime ses
Nono himself he is stubborn not is -not- a bad devil he loves his

parents et, — surtout lorsqu'il a quelque chose à leur demander —
parents and — especially when he has some thing to them ask —

sait trouver des câlineries qui ne manquent jamais leur effet et
knows to find -of the- caresses which not miss ever their effect and

ont, plus d'une fois, fait rire le père en dedans, alors que,
have more than one time made laugh the father on (the) inside then that
since

pour la forme, il faisait les gros yeux.
for the form he made the big eyes
for appearances sake acted surprised

À part les fichus quarts d'heure dont nous avons parlé, on a
At side the lousy quarters of (an) hour of which we have spoken one has
Apart from

d'assez bons moments à la maison, et les bourrasques sont vite
-of- enough good moments at the house and the squalls are quickly

oubliées, car personne n'y apporte de méchanceté.
forgotten because person not there brings -of- wickedness
no one there

Au moment où nous faisons connaissance avec la famille, Nono vient
At the moment where we make acquaintance with the family Nono comes

d'être d'une sagesse exemplaire. — Il y a longtemps qu'il désire que
of to be with a wisdom exemplary — It there has (a) long time that he wishes that
It has been

son père lui achète un livre de contes, avec de belles images ! —
his father him bought a book of (fairy)tales with -of- beautiful images ! —

ses notes de la semaine à l'école sont excellentes ; il s'est
his notes of the week at the school are excellent ; he himself is

acquitté avec promptitude, et sans murmurer, — en dedans seulement
acquitted with promptness and without muttering — on (the) inside only

pour ne pas en perdre l'habitude — des commissions qu'on lui a
for not -not- of it to lose the habit — of the commissions that one him has

demandé de faire ; aussi, son père lui a promis de sortir avec
asked of to make ; also his father him has promised of to go out with

lui le lendemain — puisque ce sera dimanche — de lui faire visiter
him the following day — since this will be Sunday — of him to make visit

les boutiques où il pourra choisir un objet qui lui plaise. — Pas
the shops where he will be able to choose an object who him pleases — Not

trop cher, car les parents de Nono sont des ouvriers, et les
too expensive because the parents of Nono are -of the- workmen and the

riches dépensent tellement d'argent à leurs futilités, que les ouvriers
rich spend so much -of- money to their trivialities, that the workmen

n'en ont presque plus pour acheter ce qu'il faut à leurs
not of it have almost (any)more for to buy this that it is necessary for their
that is needed

enfants. Mais cette fois-ci le père veut faire bien les choses, il
children. But this time here the father wants to make well the things he

promet de consacrer au moins quarante sous aux achats de Nono
promises of to devote at -the- least forty nickels to the purchases of Nono

!
!

Et Nono, le cœur plein d'espoir, est allé se coucher se
And Nono the heart full of hope is gone himself lay down himself
has

promettant monts et merveilles pour le lendemain. Pendant que sa
promising mountains and wonders for the following day During that his

mère le borde dans son lit :
mother him tucks in in his bed :

— Dis donc, mère, combien ça coûterait-il un livre de contes, comme
— Say then mother how much that would it cost a book of (fairy)tales like

celui que m'avait prêté Charles, avec de belles images ?
the one that me had loaned Charles with -of- beautiful images ?

« Combien ça coûterait-il » n'est peut-être pas d'accord avec la
How much that would cost it not is maybe -not- of agreement with the
in agreement

syntaxe, mais comme un enfant de neuf ans n'est pas tenu de parler
syntax but as a child of nine years not is -not- held of to speak

aussi bien qu'un académicien, si ça ne vous fait rien, nous écrirons
as well as an academic if that not you does nothing bothers we will write

comme parle notre héros.
as speaks our hero

— Père, fait la mère, ton garçon demande combien coûterait un livre
— Father made the mother your boy asks how much would cost a book
said

de contes, avec de belles images coloriées ?
of (fairy)tales with -of- beautiful images colored ?

— Je ne sais pas. Une pièce de trois ou quatre francs, au moins.
— I not know -not- A piece of three or four franks at the least

— Mère, fait Nono, en lui jetant les deux bras autour du cou, et
— Mother made Nono in her throwing the two arms around of the neck and
said

en l'attirant pour l'embrasser, j'ai vingt sous dans ma tirelire, je les
in her pulling for to kiss her I have twenty nickels in my piggy bank I them

donnerais bien à père pour qu'il m'en achète un, si tu voulais y
would give well to father for that he me of it bought one if you wanted there

ajouter ce qui manquerait. Tâche de décider père ?
add this which would miss Try of to persuade father ?

— Tu sais bien demander, mais seras-tu toujours sage ?
— You know well to ask but will you be always wise ?
good

— Je te le promets, fait le garnement, en redoublant ses caresses.
— I you it promise made the scamp in redoubling his caresses
said

— Tu promets, tu promets, tu n'es pas chiche de promettre, mais
— You promise you promise you not are -not- stingy of to promise but

tu ne les tiens pas toujours, tes promesses !
you not them hold -not- always your promises !

— Tu verras, mère, je serai sage, je ferai tes commissions.
— You will see mother I will be wise I will make your commissions
good will do as you say

— Allons, dors ! nous verrons cela demain. Nous demanderons à père.
— Go sleep ! we will see that tomorrow We will ask -to- father

»

Et là-dessus, deux bons gros baisers sur les yeux, avec recommandation
And there upon two good big kisses on the eyes with recommendation

de ne pas trop remuer pour ne pas se découvrir.
of not -not- too stir for not -not- himself to uncover

Et Nono, le nez fourré sous la couverture, est en train de
And Nono, the nose stuffed under the cover is in (the) process of
blanket

réfléchir à tous les livres qu'il a vus, se demandant celui auquel
to think to all the books that he has seen himself asking the one to which
of

il devra donner la préférence. Il en veut un avec des gravures,
he will give the preference He of it wants one with -of the- engravings

de belles images coloriées. Son imagination lui retrace tout un océan
with beautiful images colored His imagination him recounts all an ocean

de volumes, parmi lesquels il ne sait où reposer sa préférence.
of volumes, among which he not knows where to rest his preference

Cela peu à peu finit par devenir vivant et animé : Peau d'Âne,
That bit by bit finishes by to become alive and animated : Skin of Donkey

Don Quichotte, Ali-Baba, le Chaperon-Rouge, l'Oiseau Bleu dansent une
Don Quixote Ali baba the Red riding hood the Bird Blue dance a

sarabande effrénée autour de lui. C'est au milieu d'un
zarabanda unrestrained around of him It is at the middle of a
{Spanish dance in triplet time}

peuple de fées, de génies, de lutins, d'enchanteurs, de gnomes, de
people of fairies of genies of sprites of enchanters of gnomes of

farfadets, d'oiseaux fabuleux, de fleurs fantastiques qu'il s'endort,
sprites of birds fabulous of flowers fantastic that he himself sleeps in
falls asleep

perdant la notion du réel.
losing the notion of -the- reality

Sa mère est en butte aux fureurs de la fée Carabosse ; son père
His mother is in mound -to- the furies of the fairy Carabosse ; his father

13

tient prisonnier l'enchanteur Abracadabra et le force à fabriquer, pour
holds prisoner the enchanter Abracadabra and the force to make for

Nono, un livre dont les personnages, dans les illustrations, parlent et
Nono a book of which the characters in the illustrations talk and

remuent. Sa sœur Cendrine et son frère Titi sont changés en petits
move His sister Cendrine and his brother Titi are changed in small

cochons roses par la fée Mélusine, et lui, Nono, est chargé de les
pigs pink by the fairy Mélusine and he Nono is charged of them

garder, de les conduire à la glandée et de les empêcher de
to keep of them to lead to the acorn field and of them to prevent of

se sauver sous peine d'être lui-même changé en chauve-souris.
themselves to save under pain of to be him self changed in bald-mouse
(a) bat

Premières aventures
First adventures

Lorsque Nono s'éveilla, il faisait grand jour. Mais, chose étonnante, au
When Nono himself awoke it made large day But thing amazing at the
awoke was broad daylight in

lieu de se trouver dans son lit, il était couché sur un gazon épais,
place of himself to find in his bed he was laid down on a lawn thick
lying

rempli de fleurettes élevant leurs corolles au-dessus de l'herbe verte.
filled with flowers raising their corollas above of the grass green
petals

Le soleil éclairait cet endroit, faisant étinceler les couleurs florales,
The sun lit this place making sparkle the colors floral
of the flowers

miroiter les ailes diaprées des innombrables insectes qui voltigeaient
sparkle the wings multicolored of the countless insects which fluttered

à travers ses rayons d'or, ou couraient affairés parmi les brins
-at- through its rays of gold or ran busily among the strands

d'herbe. Le ciel, d'un azur profond, était sans nuages.
of grass The sky with an azure deep was without clouds

Nono s'était soulevé sur son coude, et, les yeux écarquillés par
Nono himself was raised on his elbow and the eyes wide open by
himself had of

l'étonnement, il regardait tout autour de lui, ne se rappelant pas
the astonishment he watched all around of him not himself recalling -not-

avoir jamais visité ce lieu.
to have ever visited this place

L'air était doux et léger ; mille parfums s'échappaient des
The air was sweet and light ; (a) thousand parfums themselves escaped from the

pétales entr'ouverts des mille et une fleurs champêtres qui
petals slightly opened from the thousand and one flowers pastoral which

tapissaient le gazon. Dans les arbres, dans les buissons, sous les taillis,
carpeted the lawn In the trees in the bushes under the thickets

15

une multitude d'oiseaux faisaient entendre les gazouillis les plus variés.
a multitude of birds made hear the chirps the most varied

Quelques-uns, prenant leur essor, traversaient l'espace d'un vol léger,
Some taking their flight crossed the space with a flight light

se poursuivant jusqu'à terre avec des pépiements courroucés,
each other pursuing up to earth with -of the- tweets wrathful
the ground

se disputant, par jeu, quelque graine, ouvrant le bec et les ailes
each other disputing by game some seed opening the beak and the wings

pour se défendre, se dressant sur leurs ergots, pour
for themselves to defend themselves raising on their spurs for
paws

s'arracher le grain disputé, se dérobant mutuellement leur
each other to tear away the grain disputed themselves stealing mutually their

proie à plusieurs reprises, jusqu'à ce qu'un dernier larron, aux
prey at several times up to this that a last thief at the

mouvements plus prestes, au vol plus rapide, vînt mettre fin à
movements more nimble at the flight more rapid came to put (an) end to

la dispute en s'enfuyant avec l'objet du litige, réconciliant ainsi
the dispute in himself fleeing with the subject of the litigation reconciling thus

les adversaires dans une commune déception.
the opponents in a common disappointment

La sécurité avec laquelle ils semblaient se jouer dans ce bocage,
The security with which they appeared themselves to play in this hedgerow

le vol tranquille de ceux qui cherchaient leur pâture, tout démontrait
the flight quiet of those who were looking for their food all demonstrated

qu'ils devaient vivre là en toute sécurité, n'ayant jamais été traqués
that they must live there in all security not having ever been hunted

ni par l'homme, ni par aucun autre être malfaisant.
neither by -the- man nor by any other being evil

Pour mieux se rendre compte où il était, Nono s'était levé sur
For better himself render account where he was Nono himself was raised on
himself had

son séant. Lorsqu'il lui sembla être bien éveillé il se mit debout,
his behind When he himself seemed to be well awake he himself put upright

humant	l'air	avec	délices	;	mais	un	tiraillement	d'estomac	lui	rappela	la
sniffing	the air	with	delights	;	but	a	twinge	of stomach	him	recalled	the

bonne	soupe	que	sa	mère	lui	faisait	chauffer	tous	les	matins,	et	lui
good	soup	that	his	mother	him	made	warm	all	the	mornings	and	him

fit	chercher	des	yeux,	tout	autour	de	lui,	s'il	n'apercevait	pas
made	search	with the	eyes	all	around	of	him	if he	could see	-not-

quelques	traces	de	sa	maison,	fussent	même	les	petits	cochons	qu'il
some	traces	of	his	house	(if it) were	even	the	small	pigs	that he

se	souvenait	d'avoir	charge	de	garder	dans	son	rêve.
himself	remembered	of to have	charge	of	to keep	in	his	dreams

Mais	nulle	trace	d'habitation	ou	d'êtres	humains	en	ce	lieu	charmant.
But	no	trace	of habitation	or	of beings	human	in	this	place	charming

Et	tout	en	cherchant	à	découvrir	quelqu'un,	Nono	se	demandait
And	all	in	searching	at	to discover	someone	Nono	himself	asked

comment	il	se	trouvait	seul	dans	un	pays	qu'il	ne	connaissait
how	he	himself	found	alone	in	a	country	that he	not	knew

pas.
-not-

Continuait-il	de	rêver	?	Qu'étaient	devenus	ses	parents	?	Du	reste	ses
Continued he	of	to dream	?	What were / What had	become	his / of his	parents	?	Of the / For the	rest	his

idées	étaient	loin	d'être	nettes.	Parce	qu'il	était	encore	mal	éveillé
ideas	were	far	of to be	clear	Because	that he	was	still	badly / hardly	awake

sans	doute	;	mais	les	sorciers,	les	enchanteurs,	hantaient	encore
without	doubt	;	but	the	sorcerers,	the	enchanters,	haunted	still

vaguement	son	imagination,	et	il	n'était	pas	éloigné	de	croire	que
vaguely	his	imagination,	and	he	not was	-not-	removed / far away	from	to believe	that

quelque	génie	malfaisant	ou	quelque	mauvaise	fée	l'avait	emporté	loin
some	genie	evil	or	some	bad	fairy	him had	taken along	far

de	chez	lui,	loin	de	ses	parents,	après	avoir	fait	subir	quelque
from	with him home	far	from	his	parents,	after	to have	made	go through	some

métamorphose	à	ceux-ci	et	à	lui-même.	Et	il	se	tâta	par	tout
metamorphosis	to	these	and	to	him self	And	he	himself	patted	by on	all

le corps, pour s'assurer qu'il n'était pas changé en singe ou en
the body for himself to ensure that he not was -not- changed in monkey or in

quelque autre animal aussi laid.
some other animal also ugly

Mais non, il était bien toujours le même, avec son habillement habituel.
But no he was well always the same with his clothing habitual

— Voyons, se disait-il, je me suis bien endormi hier soir chez
— See himself said he I me am indeed fallen asleep yesterday evening with
have

mes parents. Comment se fait-il que je me réveille dans un pays
my parents How itself makes it that I myself wake up in a country

inconnu ? Est-ce que, réellement, il existerait des fées qui peuvent
unknown ? Is it that actually it exist of the fairies who can
there

vous enlever comme cela, sans que vous vous en aperceviez ! Si
you take away like that without that you yourself of it notice ! If

c'en est une qui m'a enlevé, elle ne va pas tarder à se
this of it is one who me has taken away she not goes -not- to delay to herself

montrer, j'imagine.
show I imagine

Et il regarda autour de lui ; mais personne ne se montrait.
And he looked around of him ; but no one not herself showed

Nono était un petit garçon courageux, qui n'avait peur que dans
Nono was a little boy courageous who did not have fear (other) than in
was not afraid

l'obscurité, auquel cas, alors, il chantait tout haut pour se donner
the darkness at the which case then he sung all high for himself to give
in which

du courage. Il était dans une situation qui aurait pu
-of the- courage He was in a situation which would have been able

l'inquiéter. L'absence inexpliquée de ses parents l'aurait, en toute
him to worry The absence unexplained of his parents him would have in all

autre circonstance, certainement fort alarmé. Mais il était, en ce
other circumstance certainly strongly alarmed But he was in this
very much

moment, en une situation d'esprit qui lui faisait accepter cette absence
moment in a situation of spirit which him made accept this absence

comme une chose, sinon comme naturelle, assez plausible tout au
like a thing if not like natural enough plausible all at the

moins. Aussi, loin de s'effrayer en ne trouvant aucune réponse à
least Also far of himself to frighten in not finding any response to

ses appréhensions, il se mit à chercher quelque chemin qui le
his apprehensions he himself put to search some way which him

conduisît à un endroit habité.
conducted to a place inhabited

Quoique jeune, il possédait déjà une certaine dose de raisonnement. Il
Though young he had already a certain dose of reasoning He

se disait qu'un endroit si joli devait certainement attirer des
himself said than a place so pretty must certainly draw -of the-

visiteurs et qu'il n'aurait pas grand chemin à faire pour trouver
visitors and that he would not have -not- large way to make for to find
                                                  a long journey

soit une habitation, soit des promeneurs.
be it a dwelling be it -of the- strollers
                                 people walking for leisure

Un sentier s'étendait devant lui, il le suivit à l'aventure. Ayant
A path itself extended in front of him he it followed to the adventure Having

machinalement, en marchant, mis la main dans sa poche, il en tira
mechanically while moving put the hand in his pocket he of it drew

un petit canif dont son oncle lui avait fait cadeau pour tailler
a little penknife of which his uncle him had made gift for to sharpen
              which   a gift of

ses crayons à l'école. Cette découverte lui donna l'idée de se
his pencils at the school This discovery him gave the idea of himself

couper une baguette dans un des taillis qui bordaient la route ;
to cut a stick in one of the thickets which lined the road ;

l'envie ne se fut pas plus tôt formulée que, déjà, il était à
the desire -not- itself was not more early formulated that already he was (busy) at
the wish   had   barely   when

la besogne. Il eut bientôt une canne dont il se servit pour
the task He had soon a cane with which he himself served for

fouiller | le | sable | en | marchant, | faire | le | moulinet, | ou | décapiter | les
to root in | the | sand | while | moving | to make | the | little mill / it spin around | or | behead | the

hautes | herbes | des | bords | du | sentier.
high | grasses | of the | edges | of the | path

Il | marcha | ainsi | quelque | temps, | sans | avoir | aucune | idée | de | l'endroit
He | walked | thus | some | time | without | to have | any | idea | of | the place

où | pouvait | aboutir | le | sentier | qu'il | suivait. | Il | avait | dû | s'éveiller
where | could | lead | the | path | that he | followed | He | had | had to | himself awake / have awoken

très | tard | dans | la | matinée, | car | le | soleil | commençait | à | être | haut | dans
very | late | in | the | morning | because | the | sun | began | to | be | high | in

le | ciel, | et | ses | rayons, | quoique | tamisés | par | le | feuillage, | ne | cessaient | de
the | sky | and | its | rays | though | sieved | by | the | foliage | not | ceased | of

chauffer | l'atmosphère. | Nono, | que | la | soif | commençait | à | tenailler, | cherchait
to warm | the atmosphere | Nono | that / who | the | thirst | began | to | torment | searched

autour | de | lui | s'il | n'apercevrait | pas | quelques | fruits | pouvant | le
around | of | him | if he | not perceived | -not- | some | fruits | being able | him

désaltérer | en | même | temps | qu'ils | tromperaient | sa | faim.
quench (the thirst) | in | (the) same | time | as they | distracted | his | hunger

Mais | rien, | que | des | arbres | forestiers, | lorsqu'en | traversant | une
But | nothing | (other) than | -of the- | trees | forest / forest trees | when | traversing | a

clairière, | son | attention | fut | attirée | par | une | scène | palpitante | : | un | petit
clearing | his | attention | was | attracted | by | a | scene | thrilling | : | a | little

pinson, | dont | les | pépiements | annonçaient | la | détresse, | se | tenait | sur
lark | of which | the | tweeting | announced | the | distress | itself | kept | on

une | branche, | essayant | de | se | cacher. | Son | corps | était | agité | d'un
a | branch | trying | of | itself | to hide | Its | body | was | agitated | by a

tremblement | convulsif, | ses | yeux | fixés | sur | un | émouchet | qui, | après | avoir
tremor | convulsive | its | eyes | fixed | on | a | goshawk | which | after | to have

plané | un | instant | dans | les | airs, | commençait | à | descendre | en | spirales | de
hovered | a | moment | in | the | air | began | to | descend | in | spirals | -of-

plus | en | plus | serrées | pour | fondre | sur | la | pauvre | bestiole | affolée.
more | in and | more | closed | for | cast (itself) | on | the | poor | beast | distraught

Prompt comme la pensée, Nono leva sa badine et comme l'émouchet
Prompt like the thought Nono raised his switch and as the kestrel
stick

allait atteindre sa proie, d'un coup sec il le jeta à terre la poitrine
went to reach its prey with a strike dry he it threw to earth the chest

brisée.
broken

La peur avait tellement paralysé le pinson qu'il était tombé à terre,
The fear had so much paralyzed the lark that he was fallen to earth
had

le corps agité de petits frissons. Nono le ramassa tout palpitant et
the body agitated of small chills Nono it picked up all palpitating and
beating the heart

le prit délicatement dans ses mains en l'embrassant.
it took gently in his hands in it kissing

Peu à peu l'oiselet se remit de sa frayeur et, par un gazouillis
Bit by bit the little bird itself recovered from its fright and with a warble

plaintif, fit comprendre à son sauveur qu'il désirait reprendre sa
plaintive made understand to his savior that he desired to take again his

liberté.
freedom

Nono ouvrit les mains, l'oiseau agita ses ailes avant de prendre son essor
Nono opened the hands the bird waved its wings before of to take its flight

; puis, joyeux, il s'éleva en l'air, claironnant à son sauveur, en guise
; then happy he itself rose in the air trumpeting to its savior in way
fancy

d'adieu, un chant d'allégresse.
of parting a song of joy

Cet intermède avait fait oublier à notre voyageur la soif qui le
This interlude had made forget to our traveller the thirst which him

pressait ; mais lorsqu'il eut vu disparaître l'oiseau, il la sentit le
pressed ; but when he had seen disappear the bird he it felt him

chatouiller un peu plus fort. Il reprit donc sa marche, continuant à
tickle a bit more strong He continued then his march continuing to

quêter d'un œil inquiet quelque fruit à une branche d'arbre, et
quest with an eye worried some fruit on a branch of tree and
search

surtout si, à travers le gazon, il ne découvrirait pas une source
especially if at through the lawn he not would discover -not- a spring
    on the other side of

fraîche ou il pût se désaltérer à longs traits.
fresh where he could himself drink at long gulps

Mais rien ne se présentait à ses regards déçus, qu'un
But nothing not itself presented to his looks disappointed (other) than an

insecte pris par une patte, empêtré dans les brindilles d'un buisson,
insect taken by a paw entangled in the little branches of a bush
    caught   leg

étalant son ventre noir au soleil, et se démenant désespérément
presenting its belly black at the sun and itself struggling hopelessly

sans arriver à se raccrocher pour reprendre son équilibre et sortir
without to arrive to itself hook loose for to take again its balance and exit

de sa position périlleuse.
from his position perilous

Déjà visiblement fatigué, ses efforts devenaient moins vigoureux et plus
Already visibly tired its efforts became less vigorous and more

espacés. Placée au-dessus, une mésange charbonnière aiguisait son bec
spaced apart Placed above a tit coal sharpened its beak
    great tit

à la branche qui la portait, s'apprêtant à fondre sur cette proie
at the branch which it carried getting ready to throw (itself) on this prey

assurée.
assured

Nono courut au buisson, faisant s'enfuir la mésange, et détacha
Nono ran at the bush making flee the tit and untied

délicatement l'insecte qu'il trouva être un superbe carabe des jardins,
gently the insect that he found to be a superb beetle of the gardens
    beautiful

aux élytres d'un beau vert doré, aux reflets métalliques.
to the elytra of a beautiful green golden to the reflections metallic
with (a sheath) with

Le sauveteur remit à terre l'insecte qui, passant ses pattes de
The rescuer set again on earth the insect which passing its paws of
    the ground

devant sur ses antennes, sembla lui faire un salut de remerciement
in front over its antennas seemed him to make a greeting of thanks

avant de disparaître ensuite dans l'herbe du gazon. Et Nono
before of to disappear subsequently in the grass of the lawn And Nono

reprit sa marche.
continued his march

À l'angle d'un petit sentier obliquant sur la gauche de celui qu'il
To the angle of a little path bearing off on the left of the one that he

suivait, il retrouva son pinson perché sur un des arbres bordant le
followed he found again his lark perched on one of the trees bordering the

chemin. L'oiseau, qui semblait l'attendre, s'envola dans la direction
road The bird which seemed him to await itself flew off in the direction

du nouveau chemin.
of the new road

Nono quitta le sentier qu'il suivait et s'engagea dans celui suivi
Nono left the path that he followed and himself engaged in the one followed
went

par l'oiseau. Mais celui-ci se mit à battre des ailes, s'éleva en
by the bird But that one itself put to beat of the wings rose in

gazouillant, et alla se poster sur un arbre plus loin, semblant
chirping and went himself to post on a tree more far seeming

de nouveau attendre son sauveur.
of new to await his savior
again

— Tu as donc peur de moi ? fit Nono, se parlant plutôt à
— You have then fear of me ? made Nono himself speaking rather to
said

lui-même qu'à l'oiseau.
him self than to the bird

Comme s'il avait compris, celui-ci vint voltiger autour de lui ; toujours
Like if he had understood that one came to flutter around of him ; always
still

méfiant, se posa un instant sur son épaule, pour reprendre ensuite
mistrustful itself set a moment on his shoulder for to take again subsequently

son vol, et aller se poser plus loin.
its flight and to go itself set down more far
farther

Nono	ne	connaissait	rien	de	l'endroit	où	il	se	trouvait ;	il
Nono	not	knew	nothing	of	the place	where	he	himself	found ;	he

suivit	donc	la	bestiole,	indifférent	à	une	route	autant	qu'à	une	autre.
followed	then	the	beast animal	indifferent	to	one	road	as much	as to	an	other

Ils	arrivèrent	ainsi	à	une	clairière,	à	l'extrémité	de	laquelle	un	amas	de
They	arrived	thus	at	a	clearing	at	the end	of	which	a	mass	of

roches	rougeâtres	s'élevaient,	couvertes	de	lichens,	de	mousses	et	de
rocks	reddish	themselves rose	covered	with	lichens	with	mosses	and	with

bruyères.
heather

Sur	une	des	parois	des	rochers,	filtrait	une	petite	source	d'eau	claire
On	one	of the	walls	of the	rocks	filtered	a	little	source	of water	clear

et	vive	qui	descendait	en	cascatelles,	sur	le	flanc	taillé	en	gradins,
and	lively	which	came down	in	little waterfalls	on	the	flank	cut	in	terraces

pour	tomber,	au	pied	d'un	rocher,	dans	une	sorte	de	vasque	naturelle
for	to fall	at the	foot	of a	rock	in	a	kind	of	cauldron	natural

formée	par	le	roc	qu'elle	avait	creusé	et	d'où	elle	s'échappait	en
formed	by	the	rock	that she	had	dug	and	from where	she	escaped	in

un	ruisseau	limpide	qui	serpentait	à	travers	la	clairière	pour	aller
a	stream	clear	which	wound	-at-	through	the	clearing	for	to go

se	perdre	sous	bois.	Un	magnifique	bouleau,	à	l'écorce	argentée,
itself	lose	under	(the) woods	A	splendid	birch	at with	the bark	silver

qui	avait	pris	racine	dans	une	fissure	de	la	roche,	l'abritait	de	son
which	had	taken	root	in	a	rift	of	the	rock	sheltered	with	its

feuillage	délicat,	un	peu	retombant	comme	la	chevelure	d'une	naïade
foliage	delicate	a	bit	falling down	like	the	hair	of a	naiad tree spirit

éplorée.
bereaved

Nono	courut	à	la	fontaine,	où	il	s'agenouilla	pour	puiser	avec	ses
Nono	ran	to	the	fountain	where	he	himself knelt down	for	to draw	with	his

mains	l'eau	dont	il	se	désaltéra	goulûment,	et	qui	lui
hands	the water	with which	he	himself	quenched	greedily	and	which	him

sembla si délicieuse qu'il la trouva la meilleure de toutes les boissons.
seemed so wonderful that he it found the best of all the drinks

— Tout de même, pensa Nono, sans le pinson, je ne serais pas
— All of same thought Nono without the lark I not would be -not-
the would have

venu ici. C'est pour le suivre que j'ai quitté ma première route, et
come here This is for it to follow that I have left my first road and

il le chercha des yeux pour le remercier. L'oiseau avait disparu.
he it sought with the eyes for it to thank The bird had disappeared

Nono se pencha à nouveau vers la source pour boire
Nono himself leaned to new towards the spring for to drink
again

encore une fois de cette eau si fraîche. Enfin rassasié, il allait
still a time of this water so fresh Finally satiated he went
another time

se relever, lorsqu'il aperçut une pauvre abeille qui se débattait au
himself to raise when he saw a poor bee which itself struggled at the
to stand up in the

milieu de la vasque, et que, malgré tous ses efforts, le courant allait
middle of the cauldron and that in spite of all its efforts the current went
little pond

entraîner et submerger dans ses remous. De sa badine qu'il n'avait
to drag and overwhelm in its swirls From his switch that he did not have
stick

pas quittée, Nono sortit la bestiole de l'eau et la posa
-not- left Nono got out the beast from the water and it set
animal

délicatement sur la mousse, où donnait le soleil, pour qu'elle pût
gently on the moss where gave the sun for that she could
shone that it

se sécher, s'attardant à voir ce qu'elle allait faire, malgré les
itself dry lingering to see this that she went to make in spite of the
what it

tiraillements d'estomac que lui faisait éprouver la faim qui, elle,
tugging of (the) stomach that him made experience the hunger which she
rumblings it

n'était pas calmée.
not was -not- subsided

Pendant un moment, l'insecte se traîna lourdement sur la mousse, le
During a moment the insect itself trailed heavily on the moss the

corps alourdi par l'humidité, les ailes froissées par le contact de
body weighed down by the humidity the wings wrinkled by the contact of
the water

l'eau, ayant du mal à se tenir sur les pattes. Puis, lorsqu'elle eut
the water having of the trouble to itself keep on the paws Then when she had
when it

un peu repris la liberté de ses mouvements, elle commença à se
a bit resumed the freedom of its movements she started to itself
it

passer les pattes de derrière sur les ailes afin de les sécher. Enfin,
pass the paws from behind on the wings so of them to dry Finally

lorsqu'elle fut assez forte à son gré, elle prit son vol et s'élança
when she was enough strong to its liking she took its flight and itself launched
when it it

dans l'espace en bourdonnant.
in(to) the space while buzzing

Mais, chose étrange, il semblait à l'enfant étonné que ce bourdonnement
But thing strange it seemed to the child surprised that this humming

prenait forme de langage ! Il lui sembla comprendre que l'insecte lui
took shape of language ! He himself seemed to understand that the insect him

disait : « Tu as eu soif, l'oiseau que tu as sauvé t'a mené à
said : You have had thirst the bird that you have saved you has led to

cette fontaine où tu as pu te désaltérer, et où je
this fountain where you have been able yourself to quench (the thirst) and where I

me serais noyée sans ton secours. Suis-moi, je te guiderai là
myself would be drowned without your help Follow me I you will guide there
would have

où tu pourras te rassasier. »
where you can yourself sate (the hunger)

Nono savait fort bien que les insectes ne parlent pas ; mais il avait
Nono knew very well that the insects not talk -not- ; but he had
don't

tellement lu des livres de contes où l'on faisait parler les
so much read of the books of (fairy)tales where -it- one made speak the

animaux, tellement récité de fables à l'école où l'on faisait parler
animals so much recited of fables at the school where -it- one made speak

non seulement les animaux, mais aussi les insectes les plus infimes,
not only the animals but also the insects the most infinitesimal

jusqu'aux plantes et aux minéraux qui faisaient des discours que bien
up to the plants and to the minerals which made of the speech as well

des êtres humains auraient été incapables de tenir, et dont très
of the beings human would have been unable of to keep and of which very
as the

peu de gens seraient à même de comprendre la sagesse, — lorsque
few -of- people would be -to- even -of- to understand the wisdom — when

ces discours s'avisaient d'être sages — ce qui n'était pas toujours
these speeches themselves advise of to be wise — this which not was -not- always

le cas.
the case

Notre affamé ne fut donc pas étonné outre mesure, non pas
Our famished (boy) not was then -not- surprised besides measure not -not-

d'entendre parler l'abeille — il n'était pas très sûr qu'elle lui eût
of to hear speak the bee — he not was -not- very sure that she (to) him had

tenu ce petit discours, convaincu plutôt que c'était le fruit de son
held this little speech convinced rather that it was the fruit of his

imagination — mais, il aimait à penser qu'elle pouvait le lui avoir tenu.
imagination — but he loved to think that she could it him to have held

Il suivit donc l'abeille tout réconforté ; le vol de l'insecte, du reste,
He followed then the bee all comforted ; the flight of the insect of the rest

lui permettant de le suivre sans fatigue.
him permitting of it to follow without exhaustion

Ils traversèrent ainsi le bois qui commençait derrière les rochers, et
They crossed thus the woods which began behind the rocks and

arrivèrent à un vallon agreste, tout rempli de fleurs des champs.
arrived at a vale rural all filled with flowers of the fields

Toutes les variétés qui, ailleurs, fleurissent à des époques différentes,
All the variations which elsewhere flourish at of the epochs different

se trouvaient là, réunies, en pleine floraison.
themselves found there united in full flowering
bloom

27

Coquelicots étalant leurs pétales d'un rouge éclatant, bleuets d'un
Poppies spreading their petals with a red bright blueberries with a

beau bleu plus sombre s'élevaient à côté pendant que les genêts
beautiful blue more dark themselves raised at (the) side during that the brooms {shrub}

mariaient leurs fleurs d'un suave jaune d'or au violet sombre des
married their flowers with a sweet yellow of gold to the purple dark of the

campanules, au carmin des digitales. Ailleurs, les pâquerettes étalaient
bellflowers to the carmine of the digitalis Elsewhere the daisies spread out

leur disque d'or entouré de blancs pétales, et les saponaires roses
their disk of gold surrounded by white petals and the soapwort pink

donnaient une note plus discrète.
gave a note more discreet

Le serpolet, le fenouil, la menthe, embaumaient l'air de leurs
The thyme the fennel the mint filled with fragrance the air of their

balsamiques senteurs, tandis que dans l'herbe, sous les buissons,
balsamic scents while that in the grass under the bushes

s'épanouissaient violettes et primevères de toutes sortes, que le muguet
blossomed violets and primroses of all kinds that the thrush

ouvrait ses clochettes au doux parfum ; les narcisses, les jonquilles et
opened its bells at the sweet perfume ; the narcisses the daffodils and
with

les jacinthes formaient des tapis diaprés des couleurs les plus
the hyacinths formed of the carpets variegated of the colors the most

diverses, alors que le chèvrefeuille montait à l'assaut des arbres dans
various then that the honeysuckle climbed to the assault of the trees in
as

les branches desquels il s'accrochait, étalant sa floraison aux senteurs de
the branches of which it itself hooked spreading its flowering to the scents of
clung bloom with the

miel.
honey

Nono s'arrêta émerveillé, sans se demander comment il se faisait
Nono stopped marveled without himself to ask how it itself made
marveling was possible

que toutes ces fleurs s'épanouissent en même temps. À neuf ans, on
that all these flowers flourished in (the) same time At nine years one

n'est pas tenu de posséder les connaissances d'un jardinier, et cela ne
not is -not- held of to possess the knowledge of a gardener and that not
expected

le choquait pas plus de les voir, là, pousser sous ses yeux, que
him shocked -not- more of them to see there to push under his eyes than

de le lire dans l'œuvre d'un romancier à la mode.
of it to read in the work of a novelist at the fashion

Jamais notre petit ami n'avait vu tant de fleurs réunies ; ce
Never our little friend did not have seen so many -of- flowers united ; it
had

n'était pas la tentation d'en cueillir un bouquet pour sa mère qui
not was -not- the temptation of them to pick a bouquet for his mother who

lui manquait, mais la peur de voir paraître un jardinier bourru ou
he missed but the fear of to see appear a gardener surly or

quelque gardien non moins hargneux, qui l'empêcherait d'y porter la
some guardian not less aggressive who him would prevent to there carry the

main et le chasserait honteusement. Et puis, il faut bien le dire
hand and him would chase shamefully And then it is necessary well it to say

aussi, la faim surtout, qui le talonnait et lui faisait avoir hâte de
also the hunger especially which him bugged and him made to have hurry of

trouver un endroit où il pût la satisfaire.
to find a place where he could it satisfy

Mais l'abeille, qui avait vu Nono s'arrêter, vint bourdonner plus fort
But the bee which had seen Nono stop came to buzz more strongly

un moment près de lui, et notre affamé reprit inconsciemment sa
a moment near of him and our famished (boy) continued unconsciously his

marche, guidé sur le vol de l'insecte qui se dirigea à l'orée du
march guided on the flight of the insect which itself directed at the edge of the
by

bois, vers un gros arbre autour duquel voltigeaient en grand nombre
woods towards a big tree around of the which fluttered in great number

d'autres abeilles qui s'avancèrent vers l'arrivante.
-of- other bees which themselves advanced towards the arrival

Mais elles ne l'eurent pas plutôt reconnue, qu'elles cessèrent leur
But they not him had -not- rather recognized (than) that they ceased their

bourdonnement de guerre, pour en faire entendre un plus doux,
humming of war for of it to make hear a more sweet

semblant lui souhaiter la bienvenue, et la gronder de les avoir
seeming her to wish the welcome and her to scold of them to have

laissées dans l'inquiétude par suite de sa longue absence.
left in the worry by following of her long absence

Nono les examinait curieusement, les voyant se frotter les
Nono them examined with curiosity them seeing themselves rub the

antennes les unes contre les autres, signes qu'elles répétaient aux
antennas the ones against the others signs that they repeated to the

nouvelles compagnes qui sortaient constamment de la ruche, et quand
new companions who went out constantly from the hive and when

toutes se furent communiqué ce qu'elles avaient appris, elles vinrent
all themselves were communicated this that they had learned they came
had

voltiger autour de Nono, semblant le regarder curieusement, sans
to flutter around of Nono seeming him to look at with curiosity without

chercher à lui faire du mal. Mais ce dernier, qui savait combien
to seek to him do -of the- harm But this last who knew how much

sont douloureuses leurs piqûres, battit prudemment en retraite.
are painful their stings beat carefully in retreat
went

Les abeilles continuaient leur vol autour de lui, parfois elles s'arrêtaient
The bees continued their flight around of him sometimes they stopped

pour frotter leurs antennes contre celles d'une camarade, semblant
for to rub their antennas against those of a comrade seeming

échanger quelque réflexion, puis, à un moment, elles reprirent toutes
to exchange some reflection then at one moment they resumed all
thought

leur vol vers l'arbre qui servait de ruche, pendant que quelques-unes,
their flight towards the tree which served of hive during that some
as

revenant vers le voyageur, reprenaient ensuite leur vol vers la
coming back towards the traveller regained subsequently their flight towards the

ruche, semblant par là l'inviter à les suivre.
hive seeming by there him to invite to them to follow

Mais Nono n'avait garde de comprendre, et se rappelait les
But Nono did not have guard of to understand and himself reminded the

histoires de ceux qui, par trop téméraires, avaient payé d'horribles
stories of those who by (being) too reckless had paid with horrible

souffrances l'imprudence de s'approcher trop près de l'habitation de
sufferings of recklessness of themselves approach too near of the housing of

ces insectes susceptibles. De plus, parmi ce flot mouvant d'insectes, tous
these insects sensitive Of more among this flood moving of insects all
Moreover mass

pareils, de même couleur, il ne reconnaissait plus celle qu'il avait
similar of same color he not recognized (any)more the one that he had

sauvée de l'eau. Il lui sembla être, cette fois-ci, tout à fait perdu
saved from the water It him seemed to be this time all to made lost
entirely

et abandonné, et il se laissa aller, tout découragé, sur un tronc
and abandoned and he himself let go all discouraged on a trunk

d'arbre couché à terre, se demandant anxieusement ce qu'il allait
of (a) tree laid down on earth himself asking anxiously this what he went

devenir.
become

On s'instruit en voyageant
One instructs oneself while traveling

Elles n'étaient pas gaies les réflexions de notre petit ami : En quel
They were not -not- happy the reflections of our little friend : In what
                                  thoughts

pays était-il ? trouverait-il à manger ? Était-il destiné à périr de
country was he ? would he find to eat ? Was he destined to perish of
                would he find anything to eat

faim, ou, nouveau Robinson, serait-il forcé d'accommoder sa vie, loin
hunger or new Robinson would he be forced of to accomodate his life far

de tout semblable ?
from all similar (beings) ?

Robinson, dans son naufrage, avait pu sauver des armes, des
Robinson in his shipwreck had been able to save -of the- weapons -of the-

outils, des vivres, il avait abordé dans une île pourvue de gibier,
tools -of the- rations he had entered in an island provided with game
                landed on

de fruits comestibles ; dans sa promenade Nono, à part les petits
with fruits edible ; in his walk Nono at side the small
                              apart from

oiseaux, n'avait rien vu de mangeable ; comme arme et outil, il
birds not had nothing seen of edible ; as weapon and tool he
        had not seen anything

possédait tout juste un petit canif incapable d'abattre des arbres, de
had all just a little penknife incapable of to fell -of the- trees of

scier des planches et d'attraper un merle au vol.
to saw -of the- boards and of to catch a blackbird at the flight

Et il en revenait toujours au point de départ de ses réflexions :
And he of it returned always to the point of departure of his reflections :

Pourquoi se trouvait-il là tout seul ? Où étaient ses parents, ses
Why himself found he there all alone ? Where were his parents his
        did he find himself

frères, sa sœur ? Décidément, il y avait quelque chose
brothers his sister ? Definitely it there had some thing
                              there was

d'incompréhensible dans son cas.
-of- incomprehensible in his case

Complètement absorbé dans ses réflexions, Nono ne percevait plus
Completely absorbed in his reflections Nono not perceived (any)more

rien de ce qui se passait près de lui, lorsqu'il en fut tiré par
nothing of this which itself passed near of him when he of it was pulled out by

un bourdonnement fort et prolongé que produisait une abeille voltigeant
a humming strong and extended that produced a bee fluttering

autour de lui afin d'attirer son attention.
around of him so of to attract his attention
meaning to attract

Et, nouvel étonnement de Nono, ce bourdonnement, d'abord confus,
And new astonishment of Nono this humming of start confused
initially

indistinct, prenait peu à peu forme de langage et lui devenait
indistinct took bit by bit shape of language and him became

intelligible.
intelligible

— ... « Calme ton chagrin », lui semblait-il entendre, « nous ne
— ... Calm your sorrow him seemed he to hear we not

t'abandonnerons pas. Viens vers mes sœurs, viens que je te présente
you will abandon -not- Come towards my sisters come (so) that I you present

à notre mère, et nous te soulagerons dans ta détresse ».
to our mother and we you will soothe in your distress
will relieve of

Et ayant levé la tête, Nono reconnut sa protégée qui lui faisait
And having raised the head Nono recognized his protegee who him made

des signes, qu'il comprit immédiatement cette fois-ci. L'abeille lui
-of the- signs that he understood immediately this time The bee him

indiquait de se lever et de la suivre.
indicated of himself to raise and of her to follow

Il obéit aussitôt, se leva, suivit sa conductrice qui se dirigeait
He obeyed immediately himself raised followed his driver who herself headed
leader

vers l'arbre qui servait de ruche. Mais au fur et à mesure
towards the tree which served of hive But at the forum and at measure
while

qu'ils s'en approchaient, le vieux tronc perdait sa forme ; ses
that they themselves of it approached the old trunk lost its shape ; its

contours s'atténuaient, son aspect se transformait, et lorsque Nono
contours themselves mitigated its appearance itself transformed and when Nono

n'en fut plus qu'à quelques pas, il avait devant lui un magnifique
not of it was more than at some steps he had in front of him a splendid

palais, placé sur une vaste terrasse à laquelle on accédait par un large
palace placed on a vast terrace at which one acceded by a wide

escalier aux rampes de marbre.
staircase at the / with steps of marble

Une élégante colonnade, formant vestibule, entourait le monument, où
A elegant colonnade forming vestibule went around the monument where

se pressaient la foule des abeilles affairées et remuantes, s'occupant,
itself pressed the crowd of the bees busy and restless dealing

les unes d'aérer les différentes pièces du palais, d'autres de transporter
the ones to aerate the different rooms of the palaces -of- others of to transport

le butin qu'elles rapportaient des champs ; d'autres encore
the booty that they reported / brought back from the fields ; -of- others still

travaillaient à réparer les murs du palais, façonnaient les appartements
working to repair the walls of the palace fashioning the apartments / rooms

aux besoins auxquels elles les destinaient.
at the needs at the which they them destined

Mais chose plus étrange encore, ces abeilles n'étaient plus de
But thing more strange still these bees were not (any)more of

vulgaires insectes : au fur et à mesure que le tronc se
vulgar insects : at the forum and at measure that the trunk itself

transformait en palais, les mouches également grandissaient, se
turned in palace the flies equally grew themselves

transformaient en êtres humains tout en rappelant cependant leur forme
transformed in beings human all in recalling however their shape

primitive, conservant les ailes diaphanes qui leur permettaient de voltiger
primitive keeping the wings diaphanous which them permitted of to flutter

dans l'espace.
in the space

L'abeille qui conduisait Nono subissait la même transformation. Et elle
The bee who led Nono suffered the same transformation And she

voltigeant, Nono gravissant les marches de l'escalier monumental, ils
fluttering Nono climbing the steps of the staircase monumental they

arrivèrent devant une dame assise sous le vestibule en un riche fauteuil
arrived in front of a lady seated under the vestibule in a rich chair

au large dossier. Près d'elle s'empressait la foule des abeilles que
at the wide back Near of her itself hastened the crowd of the bees that
with a which

n'appelaient pas d'autres travaux, lui apportant des coussins pour
not (they) called -not- of other works her bringing -of the- cushions for
was called for other

s'appuyer, une nourriture exquise et parfumée, des boissons à
herself to support a food exquisite and perfumed -of the- drinks at

l'odeur délicieuse.
the scent wonderful

Son visage était empreint d'une très grande douceur. Elle fixait Nono
Her face was imbued with a very great softness She fixed Nono

d'un air de bonté aimable, lui faisant signe d'approcher.
with an air of goodness pleasant him making sign of approaching

Et comme Nono n'osait s'avancer :
And as Nono did not dare himself to advance :

— Je te fais donc peur, mon enfant ? dit-elle d'une voix suave et
— I you make then fear my child ? said she with a voice sweet and

mélodieuse.
melodious

Chez son père, Nono avait bien entendu dire que les rois, les reines, les
With his father Nono had well heard say that the kings the queens the

empereurs et les impératrices n'étaient pas faits d'une pâte autre que
emperors and the empresses were not -not- made from a dough other than

celle du commun des mortels, et n'en différaient que par le
that of the common -of the- mortals and not of it differed than by the

costume ; mais, à l'école, on les entretenait tant de leurs actes, de
costume ; but at the school one them maintained so much of their acts of

leur puissance, leur attribuant tant d'action sur les événements, sur les
their power them assigning so much of action on the events on the

destinées des peuples, qu'il ne pouvait pas ne pas s'imaginer
destinies of the peoples, that he not could -not- not -not- himself imagine

qu'ils ne fussent d'une essence supérieure. Et comme il avait aussi
that they not were of a essence superior And like he had also

entendu dire que les abeilles étaient gouvernées par une reine, il ne
heard say that the bees were governed by a queen he not

douta pas un seul instant qu'il ne fût devant cette redoutable
doubted -not- a single moment that he not was in front of this frightening

personne.
person

— Oh ! non, madame la reine, s'empressa-t-il de répondre.
— Oh ! no madam the queen himself hastened he of to answer

— Qui t'a dit que j'étais reine ? fit la dame en souriant.
— Who you has said that I was queen ? made the lady while smiling
said

— Oh ! madame, ça se voit bien, fit l'enfant qui s'enhardissait.
— Oh ! madam that oneself sees well made the child who growing bolder
said

— Ah ! Et à quoi t'en es-tu aperçu ?
— Ah ! And by what you of it are you perceived ?
have you

— Parce que je vois toutes les autres abeilles s'empresser près de vous
— Because that I see all the other bees hasten near of you

et vous servir ; aussi à la couronne d'or que vous avez sur la tête.
and you serve ; also by the crown of gold that you have on the head

— Enfant ! va, fit la dame, en riant cette fois franchement ; ce
— Child ! go made the lady while laughing this time frankly ; these
said

sont mes cheveux que tu prends pour une couronne ; quant aux
are my hairs that you take for a crown ; As to the
hair

abeilles que tu vois si empressées à me servir, elles ne sont,
bees that you see so eager to me serve they not are

apprends-le, ni esclaves, ni dames de la cour, ni servantes, ce
learn it neither slaves nor ladies of the court nor servants these

sont des filles dévouées qui ont soin de leur mère, qu'elles aiment. »
are of the girls dedicated who have care of their mother that they love

Nono, tout décontenancé, se rappela en effet que l'abeille qui l'avait
Nono all uncomfortable himself recalled in effect that the bee who him had

conduit, lui avait parlé de « notre mère », et comme il la voyait
led him had spoken of our mother and as he her saw

se tenir près de lui, avec un petit sourire railleur, il devint rouge
herself keep near of her with a little smile (of) scoffer he became red

comme une pivoine. Mais il retrouva la force de dire, pour
like a peony But he found again the force of to say for

s'excuser que c'était à l'école qu'on lui avait appris que les
himself to apologize that It was at the school that one him had learned that the

abeilles étaient gouvernées par une reine.
bees were governed by a queen

— Mon enfant, fit la dame, en reprenant sa gravité, tout en
— My child made the lady in taking again her seriousness all in

continuant à sourire avec bonté, ton professeur est un ignorant. Il
continuing to smile with goodness your professor is an ignorant He

parle de ce qu'il ne connaît pas. En étudiant la vie de nos ruches,
speaks of this that he not knows -not- In studying the life of our hives

les hommes ont jugé de nos mœurs d'après les leurs.
the men have judged -of- our mores of after -the- theirs
according to

Le premier qui a pu pénétrer les secrets de notre vie, voyant
The first who has been able to penetrate the secrets of our life seeing

les abeilles prendre des soins spéciaux pour une d'elles, s'évertuant à lui
the bees take of the cares special for one of them striving to her
care

épargner tout travail et toute fatigue, en a conclu que celle-là était
save all work and all exhaustion of it has concluded that that one was

un être privilégié, tout aussi inutile qu'un roi, que les autres lui devaient
a being privileged all as useless as a king that the others her owed

obéissance, que c'était sa volonté qui réglementait les travaux de la
obedience that It was her will which regulated the works of the

ruche. Il a fait imprimer cela. C'était bien trop semblable à ce qui
hive He has made publish that It was well too similar to this which

se passe chez vous, pour qu'on ne l'eût pas accepté comme vérité.
itself passes with you for that one not it had -not- accepted like truth

Les partisans de l'autorité en ont tiré un argument en sa faveur,
The supporters of the authority of it have drawn an argument in their favor

et l'on continue à enseigner dans les écoles que les abeilles sont
and it one continues to teach in the schools that the bees are

gouvernées par une reine.
governed by a queen

Chez nous, cependant, ce n'est pas cela. Chacune de nous remplit la
With us however this not is -not- that Each of us fills the

fonction inhérente à sa nature, mais il n'y a pas de reine,
function inherent to its nature but it not there has -not- -of- queen
                                         there is no

il n'y a pas de fonction imposée, les unes font le miel,
it not there has -not- -of- function compulsory the ones make the honey
there is no   some

d'autres soignent les jeunes ; si les besoins de la ruche l'exigent,
-of- others take care of the young ; if the needs of the hive it required

quelques-unes des habitantes peuvent même changer de fonction, mais
some of the inhabitants can even change of function but

sans que personne l'ordonne, seulement parce qu'elles sentent que c'est
without that anyone it orders only because that they feel that It is

le salut général qui l'exige.
the greeting (as well) general who it requires

Quant à moi, je ne suis pas une reine, mais simplement une mère,
As to me I not am -not- a queen but simply a mother

chargée de fournir les œufs qui donneront des travailleuses à notre
charged of to provide the eggs which will give of the workers to our
                                        will hatch

République, de futures mères pour les essaims nouveaux ; et si les
Republic -of- future mothers for the swarms new ; and if the

autres abeilles me choient, me soignent, me dorlotent, c'est tout
other bees me pamper me take care of me coddle It is all

simplement parce que j'accomplis un travail qu'elles ne peuvent faire
simply because that I accomplished a work that they not can do

n'ayant pas de sexe, et que son accomplissement m'empêche de
not having -not- -of- gender and that their accomplishment me prevents of

m'occuper de toute autre besogne. Admets que je sois une
(having) to occupy myself with all other task Granted that I am a

mère Gigogne, mais de reine, nous ne connaissons pas cela ici. »
mother Trundle but of queen we not know -not- that here
mother with lots of kids

Nono écoutait, ébahi, cette petite leçon d'histoire naturelle, qui
Nono listened dumbfounded this little lesson of history natural which

renversait toutes ses notions acquises. Mais au fond, comme il était
overturned all his notions acquired But at the back as he was

tant soit peu espiègle, et gardait un petit grain de rancune contre
so much (or) be it (a) bit playful and kept a little grain of rancor against

son professeur qui l'avait quelques fois réprimandé ou puni à tort,
his professor who him had some time reprimanded or punished to wrong
wrongly

il se formula intérieurement l'intention de le prendre, à son tour,
he himself formulated internally the intention of him to take at his turn

en flagrant délit d'ignorance, lorsqu'il viendrait lui parler de la royauté
in blatant offense of ignorance when he would come him to speak of the royalty

chez les abeilles. Et un sourire malicieux vint plisser le coin de ses
with the bees And a smile mischievous came crease the corner of his

lèvres.
lips

— Espiègle, va, fit la mère abeille. Et lui tapotant les joues : «
— Playful goes made the mother bee And him tapping the cheeks :
said

Souviens-toi du bien et du mal qu'on te fait, mais ne sois jamais
Remember of the well and of the bad that one you does but not be ever

injuste.
unfair

« Mais je te tiens, là, à te faire des discours qui te paraissent,
But I you hold there to yourself make of the speeches who you appear

sans doute, très ennuyeux, et ton amie me fait rappeler que tu as
without doubt very boring and your friend me made remember that you have

grand faim, et moi, je n'ai que très peu de temps à moi, il me
great hunger and me I not have than very little of time to me it me

faut retourner à ma besogne. Assieds-toi à cette table ; mes filles
is necessary to go back to my task Seat yourself at this table ; my girls

l'ont dressée à ton intention, et apaise ton appétit.
it have set at your intention and soothe your appetite

En effet, l'émotion éprouvée par Nono lui avait d'abord fait oublier sa
In fact the emotion experienced by Nono him had initially made forget his

faim, mais depuis quelques instants, ses yeux affamés ne pouvaient se
hunger but since some moments his eyes hungry not could himself

détacher d'une table qu'un groupe d'abeilles avait garnie de rayons de
detach from a table that a group of bees had furnished with combs of

miel posés sur des feuilles de figuier, excitant l'appétit de notre
honey posed on of the leaves of (a) fig tree exciting the appetite of our

jeune affamé par le doux parfum qu'ils dégageaient, lui chatouillant
young (boy) famished by the sweet perfume that they emanated him tickling

les narines.
the nostrils

Sans se le faire répéter, il se mit à table et goûta au
Without himself it to make repeat he himself put to table and tasted at the
                                                                           of the

miel. Dans une coupe de cire modelée à son intention, les abeilles
honey In a cup of wax modeled to his intention the bees

avaient distillé le doux nectar qu'elles recueillent dans le calice des
had distilled the sweet nectar that they gathered in the chalice of the

fleurs. Nono était extasié, et se régalait avec délices.
flowers Nono was ecstatic and himself regaled with delights

Il avait déjà largement entamé le miel, puisé à la coupe, sa faim
He had already widely started the honey drew at the cup his hunger
drank from

se calmait un peu, et il n'éprouvait plus autant de plaisir à
itself soothed a bit and he not felt (any)more as much of pleasure to

mordre dans le miel, à boire le nectar, commençant à les trouver
bite in the honey to drink the nectar starting to them find

trop sucrés.
too sweet

La ruche, les abeilles avaient disparu, sans qu'il s'en rendît
The hive the bees had disappeared without that he himself of it rendered

compte, son attention étant attirée en ce moment par un grouillement
account his attention being attracted in this moment by a swarming

qui sortait du bois en face de lui. Cela miroitait au soleil, avec
which left from the woods in face of him That shimmered at the sun with

des reflets d'or. Et cela s'avançait vers Nono qui était très
-of the- reflections of gold And that was advancing towards Nono who was very

intrigué, ne pouvant rien distinguer.
intrigued not being able nothing to distinguish

Comme cela s'avançait toujours, il finit par démêler un grouillement
Like that was advancing always he ended by to unravel a swarming
to discern

d'êtres. Hanté par ses lectures, il ne douta pas un seul instant que
of beings Haunted by his readings he not doubted -not- a single moment that

ce ne fut une armée de chevaliers en marche. Il voyait même déjà
this not was an army of knights in march He saw even already

distinctement des guerriers aux cuirasses dorées, aux casques
distinctly -of- the warriors to the breastplates golden -to the- helmets
with

surmontés de cornes, d'aigrettes, faisant miroiter au soleil les reflets
surmounted with horns with plumes making sparkle at the sun the reflections

verts de leurs boucliers d'émeraude. Ce n'était qu'à cause de leur
green of their shields of emerald This not was than to cause of their

éloignement qu'il les voyait si petits.
remoteness that he the saw so small

41

Mais quand cela fut plus près, Nono dut s'avouer qu'il avait été
But when that was more near Nono had to himself confess that he had been

là, encore, trompé par son imagination. Il n'avait devant lui que de
there still deceived by his imagination. He not had in front of him than -of-

vulgaires carabes dorés.
vulgar beetles golden

Et comme ils avançaient, il les voyait se dresser sur leurs
And like they advanced he them saw themselves raise up on their

pattes, n'apercevait plus que leur ventre tout noir. Adieu brillants
paws not could see more that their belly all black Farewell brilliant

guerriers, riches cuirasses, boucliers étincelants ! En se dressant sur
warriors rich breastplates shields gleaming ! In themselves raising on

leurs pattes, ils grandissaient, grandissaient, jusqu'à devenir grands comme
their paws they grew grew until to become large like

des poupées d'un sou, mais, ô déception cruelle, il semblait à
-of-the- dolls of a nickel but oh disappointment cruel it seemed to

Nono n'avoir devant lui qu'une troupe de croque-morts lilliputiens.
Nono not to have in front of him than a band of undertakers lilliputian

Une douzaine d'entre eux marchaient deux à deux, portant sur chaque
A dozen of between them moved two by two carrying on each

épaule une brindille, coupée aux buissons d'alentour, formant une civière
shoulder a twig cut to the bushes of around forming a litter
                                      from the surrounding

sur laquelle reposait une large feuille de Paulownia dont ils avaient
on which rested a wide leaf of Paulownia of which they had

froncé les bords en les attachant avec des épines de façon à en
frowned the edges in them attaching with of the thorns of way to of it

former un semblant de corbeille : de ces corbeilles, les unes étaient
to form a semblant of basket : of these baskets the ones were

remplies de ces succulentes fraises des bois si parfumées, d'autres
filled of these delicious strawberries of the woods so fragrant -of- others

contenaient des framboises au parfum plus acide.
contained -of-the- raspberries at the perfume more acid
                              with the   tart

Derrière chaque civière marchait un groupe de carabes d'où se
Behind each litter marched a group of beetles from where itself

détachaient de temps à autre ceux qui relayaient les porteurs fatigués.
detached from time to other those who relieved the carriers weary
time

Tout cela se dirigeait processionnellement vers Nono, assis sur le
All that itself headed in procession towards Nono seated on the

tronc d'arbre en quoi sa chaise s'était transformée, la table disparue.
trunk of (the) tree in what his chair itself was transformed the table missing
itself had

Lorsque le cortège fut arrivé devant lui, les carabes se
When the procession was arrived in front of him the beetles themselves
had

rangèrent en demi-cercle, les porteurs de brancards un peu en avant.
lined up in semi circle the carriers of stretchers a bit in front

Un d'eux s'en détacha et grimpa sur le genou de Nono. Arrivé
One of them himself of them detached and climbed on the knee of Nono Arrived

là, il fit un salut, se dressa sur ses deux pattes de devant, le
there he made a greeting himself raised on his two paws of (the) front the

derrière en l'air, et, de ses pattes postérieures, se frotta
behind in the air and of his paws front himself rubbed

vigoureusement les élytres, en tirant un son fort peu harmonieux, mais
vigorously the elytra in pulling one tone strong little harmonious but
sheath not very

que goûta fort Nono, car voici ce qu'il crut comprendre :
that pleased strong Nono because see-here this that he believed to understand :
much

— Jeune enfant, je suis celui que tu as secouru pendant que j'étais
— Young child I am the one that you have rescued during that I was

en danger. Sans t'en rendre compte, tu as mis en pratique la
in danger Without you for it render account you have put in practice the

grande loi de solidarité universelle qui veut que tous les êtres
great law of solidarity universal which wants that all the beings

s'entr'aident les uns les autres. Nous ne pouvons, comme les abeilles,
help each other the ones the others We not can like the bees

t'offrir un régal, fruit de notre travail ; mais voici des fraises
offer you a treat fruit of our work ; but see-here -of the- strawberries

et des framboises excellentes, cueillies à ton intention. Elles te
and -of the- raspberries excellent picked to your intention They you

plairont, j'espère, et compléteront le champêtre repas offert par nos
will appeal I hope and complement the rural meal given by our

sœurs. »
sisters

Et ayant fait un signe, les porteurs vinrent déposer leurs fardeaux aux
And having made a sign the carriers came to deposit their burdens at the
                                                        put

pieds de celui auquel ils étaient destinés.
feet of the one to which they were destined (for)

Mais avant d'aller plus loin, je vois un sourire d'incrédulité se glisser
But before of to go more far I see a smile of incredulity itself slip

sur les lèvres de mes jeunes lecteurs ; je les entends se
on the lips of my young readers ; I them hear themselves

chuchoter que mon orateur a pris une drôle de position pour
whisper that my speaker has taken a funny -of- position for

prononcer son discours. Vous ne voyez pas très bien votre maître
to pronounce his speech You not see -not- very well your master

d'école faisant sa leçon en marchant sur les mains, ou votre
of (the) school making his lesson in moving on the hands or your

proviseur, à la distribution des prix, prononçant sa harangue la tête
principal at the distribution of the prizes pronouncing his harangue the head

en bas, les pieds en l'air.
in low the feet in the air

Mais, mes chers enfants, la mère abeille nous l'a appris, il ne
But my dear children the mother bee us it has learned it not

faut jamais juger des choses d'après soi-même, et croire que
is necessary ever to judge -of- the things of after oneself and believe that
                                    according to

ce que nous faisons doit servir de règle à l'univers. Et si nombre de
this that we make must serve of rule to the universe And if (a) number of

nos orateurs, politiques ou autres, étaient forcés de faire ainsi leurs
our speakers political or others were forced of to make thus their

harangues, cela leur ferait peut-être descendre quelques idées dans la
harangues that them would make maybe go down some ideas in the

tête, que leur lourdeur empêche sans doute d'y monter pendant la
head that their heaviness prevents without doubt of there climb during the

station debout, tant leurs discours sont vides et creux.
station upright so much their speeches are empty and hollow
standing

À la vue des fruits appétissants, Nono sentit l'eau lui venir à la
At the sight of the fruits appetizing Nono felt the water him come to the

bouche. Mais il commençait à se former, il comprit qu'il devait,
mouth But he began to himself form he understood that he must

avant de s'attabler comme un goulu, remercier les carabes de leur don
before of sitting down like a glutton thank the beetles of their gift
for

généreux.
generous

— Monsieur le carabe, vous et vos camarades, êtes vraiment trop
— Mr. the beetle you and your comrades are really too

aimables, et je suis ravi de votre présent ; c'est de grand cœur
friendly and I am delighted with your present ; It is of great heart

que je vais manger ces fraises qui me font l'effet d'être
that I go eat these strawberries which me make the effect of to be

excellentes. Mais, en vérité, je ne mérite pas tant, vous exagérez le
excellent But in truth I not deserve -not- so much you exaggerate the

service que je vous ai rendu. Vous étiez pris dans un lacis de
service that I you have rendered You were taken in a maze of

branches, vous voyant dans l'embarras, je vous en ai tiré
branches you seeing in the embarrassment I you of it have pulled out

sans aucune peine pour moi. Vous voyez que l'action n'a rien de
without any pain for me You see that the action not has nothing of

bien méritoire, et je suis confus de mériter si peu vos louanges.
well meritorious and I am confused of to deserve so little your praises

— Oh ! fit le carabe, si on mesure le service à la peine qu'il
— Oh ! made the beetle if one measures the service to the pain that it
said trouble

coûte, le tien est de minime importance. Mais comme c'est la vie que
costs the yours is of minimal importance But like It is the life that

je te dois, ça mérite considération pour moi. Mais un service ne se
I you owe that deserves consideration for me But a service not itself

mesure pas ainsi. Ce que l'on prise, c'est la façon dont il est
measures -not- thus This that it one takes it is the way of which it is

rendu, la spontanéité et la bonne grâce qui l'accompagnent.
rendered the spontaneity and the good grace which it accompany

Prends donc ces fruits d'aussi bon cœur que nous te les offrons.
Take then these fruits with as much good heart as we you them offer

Tu nous feras plaisir. »
You us will do (a) pleasure

Et le carabe ayant agité ses antennes en guise de salut, se
And the beetle having agitated his antennas in way of greeting (as well) himself
fancy

prépara à redescendre de la tribune qu'il avait choisie.
prepared to down from the tribune that he had chosen

— En ce cas, merci, fit Nono, vous le voyez, j'use de la permission.
— In this case thank you made Nono you it see I use of the permission
said

»

Et le carabe ayant quitté son genou, Nono se baissa, prit une des
And the beetle having left his knee Nono himself lowered took one of the

corbeilles, et l'eut bientôt dévorée en deux bouchées, passant à une
baskets and it had soon devoured in two mouthfuls passing to a

deuxième.
second

Les carabes, le voyant attablé, reprirent leur forme d'insectes et
The beetles him seeing at the table resumed their shape of insects and
at dinner

s'envolèrent vers le bois.
themselves flew towards the woods

Et Nono qui les regardait s'envoler, en eut un petit serrement de
And Nono who them watched fly away of it had a little tightening of

cœur, en pensant qu'il allait encore se trouver seul. Il les vit
(the) heart in thinking that he went still himself to find alone He them saw

se perdre sous le feuillage. Il lui semblait que c'étaient des
themselves lose under the foliage It him seemed that they were -of the-

amis de vieille date qui le quittaient.
friends of old -date- who him left

Au pays d'Autonomie
At the country of Autonomy

Le soleil continuait sa course. S'il ne voulait pas de laisser
The sun continued its course. If he not wanted -not- of to let

surprendre par la nuit dans sa solitude, il ne fallait pas que
(himself) surprise by the night in his loneliness it not was necessary -not- that
it would not help if

notre égaré se laissât abattre par le chagrin. Il lui fallait,
our lost (one) himself let beat down by the sorrow It him was necessary

au contraire, rappeler à lui toute son énergie et se
at the contrary to call back to him(self) all his energy and himself

remettre en route.
put back again on (the) road

Secouant donc la tête, en signe de résolution et comme pour
Shaking then the head in sign of decision and like for
as if

chasser les idées importunes, il se mit debout, pour reprendre
to chase (away) the ideas unwelcome he himself put upright for to take up again

sa marche, non sans avoir noué dans son mouchoir deux des
his march not without to have knotted in his tissue two of the
wrapped

corbeilles de fruits, qui lui restaient, et les avoir attachées à son
baskets of fruits which him remained and them to have attached to his

poignet.
wrist

Mais, sans qu'aucun bruit lui eût révélé sa venue ni sa présence,
But without that any noise him had revealed her coming nor her presence

une grande et belle femme se tenait devant lui. Son visage et
a tall and beautiful woman herself kept in front of him. Her face and
stood

son regard étaient aussi doux que celui de la mère des abeilles, mais
her look were so sweet as the one of the mother of the bees but

on sentait, sous le charme du sourire, une volonté forte, une énergie
one felt under the charm of the smile a will strong an energy

puissante.
strong

Nono s'arrêta intimidé, regardant curieusement la dame.
Nono himself halted intimidated watching with curiosity the lady

— Tu es brave, mon enfant, et c'est ce que j'aime chez les petits
— You are brave my child and it is this that I love with the small

garçons ; mais je ne veux pas te laisser plus longtemps dans
boys ; but I not want -not- you let more long in

l'inquiétude. C'est moi qui, t'ayant remarqué depuis longtemps, et
the worry It is me who you having noticed since (a) long time and

t'ayant entendu exprimer le désir d'avoir un livre de contes, ai
you having heard express the desire of to have a book of (fairy)tales have

voulu te donner le plaisir de le vivre toi-même.
wanted you to give the pleasure of it to live yourself

J'ai commencé par t'enlever de chez tes parents, sans que tu
I have started by you to take away from with your parents without that you

t'en aperçusse. Sois sans inquiétude à leur égard. Ils savent
yourself of it noticed Be without worry at their respect They know

où je t'ai emmené, et seront tenus au courant de ce que tu
where I you have taken and will be kept at the running of this what you
news

feras, et de ce que tu verras. Quant à ce qui t'arrivera, à ce
will do and of this that you will see As to this which you will happen to this

que tu verras, cela dépendra de toi. Je te mettrai aux prises avec les
that you will see that depends of you I you will put at the grips with the
height
of

circonstances. Comme tu agiras, elles seront bonnes ou néfastes pour toi.
circumstances As you will act they will be good or adverse for you

C'est donc toi qui, en définitive, feras tes aventures, et les
It is then you who in definitive will make your adventures and them

ornementeras par ta façon de te comporter.
will decorate by your way of yourself behave
how you behave yourself

49

— Madame la fée, je vous promets d'être bien sage, fit Nono, intimidé
— Madam the fairy I you promise of to be well wise made Nono nervous
said

par ce long discours, où il n'avait guère compris que ceci, c'est
by this long speech where he not had hardly understood (other) than this It is

qu'il faudrait être sage et obéissant.
that it would be necessary to be wise and obedient

— Sage ! obéissant ! c'est, en effet, ce qu'on demande aux habitants
— Wise ! obedient ! It is in fact this that one requests to the inhabitants

du monde d'où tu viens. Ici, que l'on te demandera, c'est
of the world from where you come Here what it one you will ask it is

d'être d'abord toi-même, d'être franc, loyal, de dire toujours ce que tu
of to be initially yourself of to be honest loyal of to say always this that you

penses, d'agir en conformité avec ta pensée, de ne jamais faire à
think of to act in conformity with your thought of not ever to make to

tes camarades ce que tu ne voudrais pas qu'ils te fissent, d'être à
your comrades this that you not would like -not- that they you did of to be at

leur égard ce que tu voudrais qu'ils fussent envers toi, le reste
their respect this that you would like that they were towards you the rest

ira de soi.
will go by itself

Je te parle peut-être un langage un peu incompréhensible pour ton
I you speak maybe (in) a language a bit incomprehensible for your

âge. Mais lorsque, par ignorance et non par mauvais cœur, tu
age But when by ignorance and not by bad heart you

te seras trompé, je serai là pour te venir en aide.
yourself will be mistaken I will be there for you to come in aide
did something wrong

N'aie donc pas peur, viens, je vais te mener près de camarades de
Not have then -not- fear come I go you lead near of comrades of

ton âge qui t'apprendront, mieux que moi, à être ce qu'il faut.
your age who you will teach better that me to be this that -it- is necessary

»

Et Nono vit près de lui un beau char attelé de six belles
And Nono saw near of him a beautiful chariot hitched with six beautiful

cigognes.
storks

Sur un signe de la dame, muet d'admiration, il prit place près d'elle
On a sign of the lady mute of admiration he took place near -of- her

sur le char, et les cigognes, prenant leur vol, s'élevèrent dans les
on the chariot and the storks taking their flight themselves lifted in the
rose

airs. Le jeune voyageur vit peu à peu disparaître les détails de la
skies The young traveller saw bit by bit disappear the details of the

campagne qui semblait défiler sous lui, les bois devenant de plus en
countryside which seemed to parade under him the woods becoming -of- more in
and

plus petits, jusqu'à ce que le vert de leur feuillage ressembla au
more small until to this that the green of their foliage resembled at the

tapis d'une prairie.
carpet of a meadow

Après avoir plané un certain temps, les cigognes abaissèrent leur vol,
After to have soared a certain time the storks lowered their flight

se rapprochant de terre, Nono vit se dessiner d'abord les collines.
themselves moving closer of earth Nono saw itself draw initially the hills

les rivières au-dessous de lui, puis il distingua les arbres, puis un
the rivers at the under of him then he distinguished the trees then a
below

bâtiment qui lui sembla grand d'abord comme un jouet, au milieu
building which him seemed large initially like a toy at the middle
the size

d'un jardin immense que l'on devinait à ses pelouses, à ses
of a garden immense that it one guessed to (be) these lawns at its
with

corbeilles aux couleurs variées. Dans ce jardin se promenaient une
baskets at the colors varied In this garden themselves walked a

foule de personnes qui semblaient se divertir.
crowd of people who appeared themselves to entertain

C'est vers ce jardin que se dirigèrent les cigognes, venant
It is towards this garden that themselves directed the storks coming

déposer les voyageurs au pied du perron de la construction
to deposit the travelers at the foot of the stone porch of the construction
set down

entrevue qui était un palais magnifique.
between-seen which was a palace magnificent
seen vaguely (before) appeared to be

À l'arrivée du char, ceux que Nono avait aperçus dans le jardin et
At the arrival of the chariot, those that Nono had perceived in the garden and

qui étaient des petites filles et des petits garçons dont le plus
who were -of the- small girls and -of the- small boys of which the most

vieux ne dépassait pas une douzaine d'années, étaient accourus, et
old not passed by -not- a dozen of years were run up and
came running up

lorsque la compagne de Nono en descendit, tous se précipitèrent
when the companion of Nono there descended, all themselves rushed

vers elle avec des acclamations de joie :
towards her with -of the- cheers of joy :

— C'est Solidaria, notre amie Solidaria, s'écriaient-ils. Nous vous cherchions
— It is Solidaria, our friend Solidaria, they cried. We you searched

sans pouvoir deviner où vous étiez passée ? Vous nous aviez quittés
without to be able to guess where you were gone ? You us had left

sans nous avertir.
without us to inform

— Là là, fit la dame, qui avait du mal à satisfaire toute
— There there, made the lady, who had of the trouble to satisfy all
said

cette cohue se cramponnant à elle dans l'espoir d'attraper une
this crowd themselves clutching to her in the hope of to catch a

caresse, un baiser, ou une bonne parole, si vous vous jetez ainsi sur
caress, a kiss, or a good word, if you yourself throw thus on

moi, vous allez me faire tomber.
me, you go me make fall

C'est une surprise que je vous réservais : Voyez, je suis allée vous
It is a surprise that I you reserved : See, I am gone you
had for you

chercher un nouveau camarade. Je compte sur vous pour le
to seek a new comrade I count on you for him

mettre au courant de notre genre de vie, et la lui rendre assez
to put at the running of our genre of life and it him render enough
inform way

agréable pour qu'il s'y plaise.
pleasant for that it himself there pleases

Mais, une dernière recommandation, ajouta-t-elle, en se tournant vers
But a last recommendation added she in herself turning towards

Nono, ne t'éloigne jamais trop de tes camarades. Notre ennemi,
Nono not yourself distance ever too (much) of your comrades Our enemy

Monnaïus, roi d'Argyrocratie, envoie ses émissaires rôder dans les bois
Monnaïus king of argyrocratie sends his emissaries to prowl in the woods

qui entourent notre petit domaine ; ses janissaires s'emparent, pour
which surround our little domain ; his janissaires -themselves- seize for
soldiers

les mener en esclavage, des imprudents qui se mettent hors de
them to lead in slavery of the unwary (ones) who themselves put out of
those uncareful ones

portée d'être secourus. »
range of to be helped

Puis, ayant adressé un dernier sourire d'encouragement aux enfants, elle
Then having addressed a last smile of encouragement to the children she

disparut dans un nuage qui la déroba à leurs yeux.
disappeared in a cloud which her concealed to their eyes

Les enfants s'étaient dispersés ; quelques-uns pourtant étaient restés
The children themselves were scattered ; some however were remained
had had

à examiner le nouvel arrivant.
to examine the new arrival

— Comment t'appelles-tu ? fit, en s'adressant à Nono, une petite fille
— How yourself call you ? made in addressing -to- Nono a little girl
What's your name said

à l'air futé, jeune personne paraissant avoir au plus huit ans.
to the air smart young person appearing to have at the most eight years
with

53

— Nono, fit notre héros tout intimidé de voir tous les yeux braqués
— Nono made our hero all nervous of to see all the eyes leveled
    said

sur lui.
on him

— Moi, je m'appelle Mab, reprit l'espiègle, si tu veux nous serons
— Me I myself call Mab continued the playful (girl) if you want we will be
    my name is

camarades, tu as une figure qui me plaît. Je te montrerai à quoi
friends you have a face which me pleases I you will show at what

nous jouons. Tu verras, on s'amuse ici. Pas de maîtres pour vous
we play You will see one himself amuses here Not of masters for you
    No

mettre en pénitence, ou vous ennuyer tout le temps pour vous faire
to put in penitence or you bother all the time for you to make

tenir tranquille. Et puis, je te ferai faire connaissance avec mes amis
keep quiet And then I you will make make acquaintance with my friends

Hans et Biquette. Ce sont mes meilleurs camarades, mais
Hans and Biquette This are my best friends but

il y en a d'autres, tu feras connaissance avec tous.
it there in has -of- other you will make acquaintance with all
    there are more of them

N'est-ce pas, Hans, tu veux bien être camarade avec le nouveau ? fit
Not is this -not- Hans you want well to be comrade with the new (boy) ? made
Isn't it   said

la fillette.
the little girl

— Moi, certainement, je veux bien, fit le personnage, qui pouvait bien
— Me certainly I want well made the character who could well

avoir dix ans, à condition que ce soit un bon zigue. Quel âge as-tu
to have ten years to condition that this be it a good bloke What age have you

? fit-il en s'adressant à Nono.
? made he in addressing himself at Nono
  he said

— Neuf ans !
— Nine years !

- D'où viens-tu ? fit une autre petite fille, une blondinette de
- From where come you ? made an other little girl, a blonde of
     do you come said

sept ans.
seven years

— Oh, cette Sacha, ce quelle est curieuse ! fit Mab.
— Oh this Sacha this that one is curious ! made Mab
    how   said

— Demande-lui donc ce que ça peut lui faire ? fit un autre.
— Ask him then this what that can him do ? made a other
    said

» Ici on ne s'occupe pas d'où l'on vient. Pourvu que l'on
Here one not himself occupies -not- from where it one comes Provided that it one

soit de bons camarades, c'est suffisant.
is -of- good friends It is sufficient

Allons nous amuser, plutôt. »
Go us amuse rather
Let's go have fun

Et prenant Nono par la main.
And taking Nono by the hand

— Nous allons visiter le jardin, veux-tu !
— We go visit the garden want you !
    do you want to

— Oui, je veux bien.
— Yes I want well
    sure

— Tu oublies qu'il va être l'heure d'aller faire la cueillette pour
— You forget that it goes to be the hour of to go to make the picking for

notre souper », fit une autre demoiselle de neuf ans ; c'était la
our supper made an other dragonfly of nine years ; It was the
    said

Biquette dont avait parlé Mab.
Biquette of which had spoken Mab

— Ah ! oui, j'oubliais. Du reste, tu auras le temps de le voir
— Ah ! Yes I forgot Of the rest, you will have -the- time of it to see
    Anyway

demain. Allons chercher nos corbeilles. »
tomorrow Go to seek our baskets

Et la bande se dirigea vers une pelouse où se tenait un
And the band itself directed towards a lawn where himself kept a

homme de haute taille à l'aspect vigoureux. Ses bras musculeux
man of high size at the appearance vigorous. His arm brawny

étaient à nu ; son visage aux traits énergiques, encadré d'une barbe
were -to- bare ; his face at the traits energetic framed by a beard
with

noire soyeuse, respirait la force et l'énergie ; des yeux très doux
black silky breathing the force and the energy ; -of the- eyes very sweet

corrigeaient ce que l'expression du visage aurait pu avoir de
corrected this that the expression of the face would have been able to have of

trop sévère.
too severe

Entouré par les enfants, il leur distribuait de petites corbeilles et de
Surrounded by the children he them distributed -of- small baskets and of

petits sécateurs appropriés à leurs forces. Tous tendaient les mains,
small secateurs appropriate to their forces All extended the hands
cutters stretched out

criant : Moi ! moi, Labor !
calling out : Me ! me Labor !

— Et ma sœur Liberta n'aura donc personne pour l'aider
— And my sister Liberta not will have then anyone for her to help

aujourd'hui ? fit Labor en souriant et montrant une jeune femme en
today ? made Labor in smiling and showing a young woman in
said

grande robe flottante, couleur vert d'eau, la chevelure dénouée
large dress floating color green of water the hair undone

retombant sur les épaules.
falling on the shoulders

— Moi j'y suis allé ce matin, firent plusieurs garçons et filles.
— Me I there am gone this morning made several boys and girls
have said

— Oh ! moi, je veux bien y aller, fit Biquette.
— Oh ! me I want well there to go made Biquette
said

— Moi aussi, moi aussi, firent plusieurs autres, et s'emparant de petits
— Me also me also made several others and seizing -of- small
said

seaux que la jeune femme leur tendait, ils la suivirent vers un
buckets that the young woman them extended they her followed towards a
held out to

bâtiment situé à l'extrémité de la pelouse.
building situated at the end of the lawn

Nono regardait sans rien dire, se tenant près de Mab et de
Nono watched without nothing to say himself holding near of Mab and of

Hans, qui étaient restés près de Labor.
Hans who were remained near of Labor
had

— Prends donc une corbeille, fit Hans, en poussant Nono du coude,
— Take then a basket made Hans in pushing Nono by the elbow

Labor ! une corbeille pour le nouveau.
Labor ! one basket for the new (arrival)

— Ah ! c'est toi que Solidaria a pris sous sa protection, fit Labor.
— Ah ! It is you that Solidaria has taken under her protection made Labor

Approche, mon garçon. Je vois que tu t'es déjà fait des amis.
Approach my boy I see that you yourself is already made of the friends
have

Crois-tu que tu te plairas ici ?
Believe you that you yourself will please here ?
will like it

— Je crois que oui, fit Nono en prenant la corbeille et le sécateur
— I believe that yes made Nono in taking the basket and the secateur
I will cutter

que lui tendait Labor.
that him extended Labor

— Moi, j'en suis certain. Va avec tes camarades qui t'attendent. Ils
— Me I of it am certain Go with your comrades who you await They

t'apprendront ce qu'il faut faire. »
will teach you this that it is necessary to do

La distribution des corbeilles terminée, les jeunes espiègles s'étaient
The distribution of the baskets ended the young rascals themselves were
had

57

divisés par groupes, se répandant dans le verger qui attenait à
divided by groups themselves spreading in the orchard which adjoined to

la pelouse dont il était séparé par des murs soutenant des
the lawn of which it was separated by -of the- walls supporting of the

treilles aux fruits dorés, et toutes sortes d'arbres à fruits.
trellises to the fruits golden and all kinds of trees to fruits
wooden frames with the with

— Viens, fit Sacha, les autres sont partis avec Liberta, ils vont traire
— Come made Sacha the others are left with Liberta they go milk
said

les vaches. Moi j'aime bien le lait, mais ça ne m'amuse pas d'être
the cows Me I love well the milk but that not amuses me -not- of to be
it

derrière les vaches, j'ai toujours peur qu'elles m'envoient quelque coup
behind the cows I have always fear that they send me some blow

de pied. C'est plus amusant de grimper sur les arbres. – Oh ! moi,
of foot It is more fun of to climb on the trees – Oh ! me

reprit Hans, j'aime bien travailler aux étables. Il n'y a pas de
continued Hans I love well to work at the cowsheds It not there has -not- -of-
There is no

danger que les vaches vous fassent de mal, ce sont de bonnes bêtes,
danger that the cows you do -of- harm these are -of- good animals

bien tranquilles, mais j'y suis allé ce matin, et je n'aime pas à
well quiet But I there am gone this morning and I do not like -not- to
have

faire deux fois de suite la même chose.
do two times of following the same thing
in

Quelques autres enfants s'étaient joints au groupe Nono, Hans et
Some other children themselves were joined to the group (of) Nono Hans and
had

Sacha.
Sacha

— Qu'est-ce que vous allez cueillir ! fit l'un d'eux.
— What is it that you go pick ! made -the- one of them
said

— Je ne sais pas. Qu'est-ce que tu aimes, toi ? fit Hans en
— I not know -not- What is it that you love you ? made Hans in
do not said

s'adressant à Nono. Tu vois, il y a des raisins, des pêches,
-himself- addressing -to- Nono You see it there has of the grapes of the peaches
there are

des poires, des prunes, des bananes, des ananas, des
-of the- pears -of the- plums -of the- bananas -of the- pineapples -of the-

groseilles, des fraises. Tu n'as que l'embarras du
gooseberries -of the- strawberries You not have (other) than the embarrassment of -the-
have a mass

choix. »
choice

Et du geste, il montrait à Nono, le vaste verger où se
And with the gesture he showed to Nono the vast orchard where itself

trouvaient réunis, non seulement les fruits de toutes les latitudes, mais
found united not only the fruits of all the latitudes but

où murissaient en même temps les fruits de toutes les saisons ;
where ripened in (the) same time the fruits of all the seasons ;

où les arbres de la même espèce se montraient à tous les
where the trees of the same kind themselves showed at all the

degrés de maturité, depuis la fleur en bouton, jusqu'au fruit mûr et
degrees of maturity from the flower in bud up to the fruit ripe and

succulent prêt à être cueilli.
succulent ready to be plucked

Ils étaient en ce moment au pied d'un superbe cerisier portant de
They were in this moment at the foot of a superb cherry tree carrying -of-

belles « guignes » noires et dodues.
beautiful wild cherries black and plump

— Oh ! des cerises, il y a longtemps que je n'en ai pas
— Oh ! -of the- cherries it there has (a) long time that I not of it have -not-
it has been

mangé, fit Nono, alléché par les fruits qui pendaient au-dessus de sa
eaten made Nono allured by the fruits which hung above of his

tête.
head

— Eh bien, grimpe, je vais te faire la courte échelle. »
— Eh well climb I go you make the short ladder

Et s'étant adossé à l'arbre, il entrelaça ses deux mains, faisant signe à
And having backed to the tree he twined his two hands making sign to
back

Nono d'y mettre le pied, puis de grimper sur ses épaules.
Nono of there to put the foot then of to climb on his shoulders

Mais, hélas ! Il n'était pas encore assez haut pour atteindre les
But alas ! He not was -not- still enough high for to reach the

branches les plus basses, et, élevé à la ville, il n'avait jamais appris
branches the most low and raised at the city he did not have ever learned
in

à grimper à un arbre.
to climb (in)to a tree

— Tiens, regarde, fit un des enfants, gros garçon roux et trapu,
— Hold look made one of the children (a) big boy red and thickset
said

qui était resté avec le groupe, voilà comment on fait. »
who was remained with the group see there how one does
had

Et, ayant embrassé l'arbre, il grimpa comme un singe, et fut bientôt
And having embraced the tree he climbed like a monkey and was soon

installé entre deux branches d'où il ne tarda pas à faire
installed between two branches from where he not delayed -not- to make

pleuvoir une avalanche de fruits dans le tablier d'une camarade, jeune
rain an avalanche of fruits in the apron of a comrade young

personne de six ans, que l'on nommait Pépé, à cause du jouet
person of six years that -it- one named Pepe at cause of the toy

qu'elle avait toujours en ses bras.
that she had always on her arm

Nono regardait d'un œil d'envie le garçon dans l'arbre.
Nono watched with an eye of envy the boy in the tree

— Attends, fit Hans, je reviens à l'instant. Et il courut vers une
— Wait made Hans I come back at the instant And he ran towards a
said in a moment

sorte de hangar d'où il ne tarda pas à rapporter une échelle
kind of shed from where he not delayed -not- to bring back a ladder

légère qu'il appliqua contre le cerisier.
light that he applied against the cherry tree
                 supported

— Maintenant tu peux aller rejoindre Sandy.
—   Now   you can go   rejoin   Sandy

Mais tu n'aimes pas que les cerises ? As-tu goûté aux
But you do not love -not- (other) than the cherries ? Have you tasted -to the-

bananes, aux ananas ?
bananas -to the- pineapples ?

— Non, je n'en ai jamais vu, fit Nono déjà installé dans l'arbre,
— No I not of it have ever seen made Nono already installed in the tree
                                  said

la bouche pleine de cerises.
the mouth full of cherries

— Eh bien, je vais en cueillir pour notre dîner. »
— Eh well I go of them pick for our dinner

Mab, elle, s'était attachée à de superbes groseillers à grappes, qui
Mab she herself was attached to -of- great gooseberries by bunches which
      herself had

croissaient en buissons touffus près du cerisier.
grew in bushes thick near of the cherry tree

— Hein ! fit Sandy, c'est amusant de cueillir soi-même son dîner.
— Huh ! made Sandy this is fun of to pick oneself his dinner
       said

— Oui, c'est très agréable » fit Nono, en engouffrant une poignée de
— Yes this is very pleasant made Nono in engulfing a fist of
                          said

guignes qu'il venait de cueillir, sa main prenant plus souvent le
wild cherries that he came of to pick his hand taking more often the

chemin de sa bouche que celui de son panier. Mais comme les
way of his mouth than the one of his basket But like the

branches pliaient sous les fruits, il put amplement satisfaire sa
branches bent under the fruits he could amply satisfy his

gourmandise, et, malgré cela, emplir sa corbeille et celle de Sandy qui
gluttony and in spite of that to fill his basket and that of Sandy who

était descendu, il y avait déjà longtemps, s'étant rappelé que
was descended it there had already (a) long time himself having recalled that
had

personne n'avait parlé d'aller cueillir des feuilles. Il en fallait
no one did not have spoken of to go pick of the leaves It of it was necessary

pour décorer les fruits à table. Il avait laissé sa corbeille à Nono
for decorate the fruits at (the) table He had left his basket to Nono

pour aller vers les treilles où il choisit les plus belles feuilles.
for to go towards the trellises where he chose the most beautiful leaves

Comme Nono s'attardait à picorer de ci, de là, quelques groseilles,
As Nono himself delayed to peck of this of there some gooseberries

Mab qui avait fini sa récolte depuis longtemps, le prit par la main,
Mab who had finished her harvest since (a) long time him took by the hand

l'entraînant vers la place où Nono avait aperçu Labor et où
him dragging towards the place where Nono had perceived Labor and where

chacun des enfants rapportait sa moisson, qu'il versait sur la pelouse
each of the children reported their harvest that he shed on the lawn

pour la ranger ensuite en pyramide dans les corbeilles.
for it to arrange subsequently in pyramid in the baskets

Personne, en effet, n'avait pensé à faire provision de feuilles, aussi
No one in fact did not have thought to make (a) provision of leaves also
had thus

Sandy fut-il acclamé de tous lorsqu'il arriva avec une ample provision.
Sandy he was acclaimed of all when he arrived with an ample provision

Quand les corbeilles furent garnies, et bien parées, les enfants se
When the baskets were garnished and well decked the children themselves

dirigèrent vers le château que Nono n'avait fait qu'entrevoir à sa
headed towards the castle that Nono did not have did than glimpse at his

descente du char.
descend of the chariot

Toto, Mab, Biquette et Sacha qui, décidément, l'avaient pris sous leur
Toto Mab Biquette and Sacha who definitely him had taken under their

protection, marchaient avec lui.
protection moved with him

Nono s'étonnait qu'ils fussent abandonnés à eux-mêmes, Solidaria,
Nono was astonished that they were abandoned to themselves Solidaria

Liberta, Labor, à part les courtes apparitions où il n'avait fait que
Liberta Labor at a- side the short appearances where it did not have made than

les entrevoir, avaient disparu sans plus donner signe d'existence.
them glimpse had disappeared without (any)more to give sign of existence

— Cela t'étonne, répondit Hans, c'est tous les jours comme cela. Nous
— That you surprises answered Hans this is all the days like that We

ne les apercevons que lorsque nous avons besoin d'eux. Alors, pas
not them perceive than when we have need of them Then no

besoin de les chercher. Nous les voyons à côté de nous, comme s'ils
need of them to seek We them see at side of us like if they

devinaient que nous avons besoin de leur aide.
divined that we have need of their aide

— Et lorsqu'on n'est pas sage, comment vous punit-on ? Qui est-ce
— And when one not is -not- wise how you punishes one ? Who Is this

qui vous punit?
who you punishes

— Personne, fit Mab. Comment veux-tu que l'on ne soit pas sage,
— No one said Mab How want you that -it- one not be -not- wise

quand on n'a personne sur le dos pour vous empêcher de vous
when one not has anyone on the back for you to prevent of you

amuser, ou pour vous forcer à faire ce qui ne vous plaît pas.
to amuse or for you to force to do this which not you pleases -not-

— Oui, mais qu'est-ce qui prend soin du jardin et des arbres, et
— Yes but what is it who takes care of the garden and of the trees and

des vaches qui donnent le lait que vous buvez ?
of the cows which give the milk that you drink ?

— Nous, donc ! c'est très agréable, tu verras, de bêcher, d'arroser, de
— We then ! This is very pleasant you will see of to dig of to water of

semer, surtout que, s'il est nécessaire, Labor est là pour nous aider
to sow especially that if it is necessary Labor is there for us to help

avec sa troupe de petits lutins qui n'ont qu'à mettre la main au
with his band of small sprites who not have than to put the hand at the

travail le plus dur pour qu'il se fasse sans effort.
work the most hard for that it itself does without effort

Mais tu auras tout le temps de voir cela puisque tu vas rester avec
But you will have all the time of to see that since you go to stay with

nous. Nous voici arrivés.
us We see-here arrived

La gourmandise punie
The gluttony punished

Le	château	vers	lequel	s'étaient	dirigés	les	enfants	s'élevait	sur
The	castle	towards	which	themselves were / themselves had	directed	the	children	itself arose	on

une	large	esplanade	bien	sablée,	coupée	de	vastes	pelouses,	dont
a	wide	esplanade	well	sanded / covered with sand	cut / traversed	by	large	lawns	of which

quelques-unes	étaient	plantées	d'arbres.
some	were	planted	with trees

Sous	ces	arbres,	ceux	des	enfants	qui	n'avaient	pas	été	employés	à
Under	these	trees	those	of the	children	who	not had	-not-	been	employed	at

la	récolte	des	fruits,	ou	à	la	traite	des	vaches,	avaient	dressé	de
the	harvest	of the	fruits	or	at	the	milking	of the	cows	had	set up	-of-

grandes	tables	carrées,	que,	ce	soir	là,	en	l'honneur	du	nouveau
large	tables	square	that	this	evening	there	in	-the- honor	of the	newly

venu,	on	avait	ajoutées	bout	à	bout,	mais	que,	ordinairement,	on	dressait
come / arrived	one	had	added	end	to	end	but	that	usually	one	drew up

séparées	les	unes	des	autres,	couvertes	de	belles	nappes,	supportant
separated	the	ones	from the	others	covered	with	beautiful	sheets	supporting

des	plats	et	des	assiettes	enjolivés	de	dessins	naïfs	aux
-of the-	dishes	and	with -the-	plates	embellished	of	drawings	naive	to the / with

couleurs	crues.
colors	raw / primal

Des	chaises	indiquaient	la	place	de	chaque	convive.
-Of the-	chairs	indicated	the	place	of	each	guest

Les	arrivants	rangèrent	leurs	fruits	sur	des	coupes	de	la	même
The	arrivals	lined up	their	fruits	on	-of the-	bowls	of	the	same

faïence	que	les	assiettes.	Il	y	avait	un	échantillon	de	presque	tous
earthenware	as	the	plates	It	there	had / There was	a	sample	of	almost	all

les fruits, non seulement pommes, pêches, raisins, abricots, dattes, oranges,
the fruits not only apples peaches grapes apricots dates oranges

bananes, mais une foule d'autres que Nono n'avait jamais vus. Des
bananas but a mass of others that Nono did not have ever seen -Of the_

pâtisseries de toutes formes, dues à l'ingéniosité de Labor, étagées dans
pastries of all forms due to the ingenuity of Labor layered in

de jolies coupes, alternaient avec les fruits. Des fleurs dans des
-of- pretty cups alternated with the fruits -Of the- flowers in -of the-

vases aux formes graciles et variées ajoutaient l'éclat de leurs
vases to the forms gracile and varied added the sparkle of their
with

couleurs plus vives à la teinte plus effacée des fruits.
colors more keen at the shade more effaced of the fruits

D'autres enfants transvasaient le lait crémeux en de jolis petits pots
-Of- other children decanted the milk creamy in -of- pretty small jars

de grès aux formes élégantes, aux tons chauds et harmonieux.
of earthenware at the forms elegant to the tones warm and harmonious
with with

Cela flattait l'œil, en même temps qu'un parfum discret chatouillait les
That flattered the eye in (the) same time as a perfume discreet tickled the

narines, amenant l'eau à la bouche des moins gourmands.
nostrils causing the water to the mouth (even) of the least gluttonous

Quand tout le petit monde fut arrivé que la récolte fut rangée sur les
When all the little world was arrived that the harvest was ordered on the
had as

tables, chacun prit place selon ses goûts et préférences, se
tables each one took place according to their likes and preferences themselves

plaçant à côté du camarade qui, provisoirement, l'attirait le plus.
placing at (the) side of the comrade who tentatively them attracted the most

Nono était entre ses nouveaux amis qui lui nommèrent ceux qui
Nono was between his new friends who him named those who

étaient le plus près. En face d'eux, il y avait Gretchen, Fritz, Lola,
were the more near In face of them it there had Gretchen Fritz Lola
front there were

Wynnie, Beppo, Pat, Stella. Il semblait que tous les noms de la terre
Wynnie Beppo Pat Stella It seemed that all the names of the earth

y   étaient   représentés.
there   were   represented

Du   reste,   non   loin   de   lui,   Nono   put   voir   de   petites   frimousses
Of the   rest   not   far   from   him   Nono   could   see   -of-   small   sweet faces
For the

noires   et   jaunes,   aux   yeux   bridés.
black   and   yellow   to the   eyes   bridled
                      with   narrow

Tous   riaient,   babillaient,   comme   l'avait   dit   la   petite   Mab,   sans
All   laughed   babbled   like   him had   said   the   little   Mab   without

    s'occuper   de   quel   coin   de   la   terre   ils   étaient   venus.
themselves to occupy   from   what   corner   of   the   earth   they   were   come
                                                had

On   fit   circuler   les   coupes   autour   de   la   table,   chacun   choisissait   à
One   made   circulate   the   cups   around   of   the   table   each   chose   to

sa   convenance   ;   les   uns   prenaient   de   tout,   pendant   que   d'autres
their   convenience   ;   the   ones   taking   of   all   while   that   -of- others

   se   bourraient   de   l'espèce   qui,   pour   l'instant,   était   l'objet   de
themselves   stuffed   of   the species   which   for   the instant   was   the subject   of

leur   préférence.   Mais   la   distribution   se   fit   très   cordialement,
their   preference   But   the   distribution   itself   made   very   cordially
                                         was done

l'appétit   le   plus   vorace   sachant   qu'il   aurait   toujours   de   quoi
the appetite   the   most   voracious   knowing   that it   would have   always   of   what
                                      always would have   something

se   satisfaire   amplement.
itself   satisfy   amply
  to satisfy itself

—   Tiens   !   c'est   moi   qui   vais   te   servir,   fit   Mab   en   prenant   une   coupe,
—   Hold   !   it is   me   who   go   you   serve   made   Mab   in   taking   a   cup
                       will   said

qu'est-ce   que   tu   préfères   :   pêches,   raisins   ?
what is it   that   you   prefer   :   peaches   grapes   ?

—   Non,   fit   Hans,   voici   des   bananes   que   j'ai   cueillies
—   No   made   Hans   see-here   of the   bananas   that   I have   picked
        said

à   son   intention.   »
at   his   intention
      for him

Et chacun mettait sur l'assiette de Nono ses fruits préférés.
And each put on the plate of Nono their fruits favorite

— Je veux bien goûter de tout, fit Nono. Et il se mit à peler
— I want well to taste of all made Nono. And he himself put to peel
said

une banane, Hans lui ayant fait voir qu'il fallait enlever la
a banana, Hans him having made to see that it was necessary to take away the

pelure. »
peel

Mais, dès la première bouchée, il dut s'arrêter.
But from the first bite he had to himself halt
stop

— Tu n'aimes donc pas cela demanda Hans un peu déçu ;
— You do not love then -not- that asked Hans a bit disappointed ;

car il s'attendait à des exclamations de plaisir.
because he himself awaited -to- -of the- exclamations of pleasure

— Si, fit Nono, ce n'est pas mauvais ; pourtant il me semble que je
— Yes made Nono this not is -not- bad ; however it me appears that I
said

préfère le raisin ; et il mordit à même la grappe que
prefer the grapes ; and he bit to (the) same (time) the bunch (of grapes) that

Mab avait mise sur son assiette. Mais après en avoir avalé quelques
Mab had put on his plate. But after of it to have swallowed some

grains, il dut s'avouer vaincu. Reposant la grappe sur son
pieces he had to himself confess conquered Putting back the bunch (of grapes) on his

assiette, il repoussa doucement celle-ci, regardant d'un œil navré
plate he pushed softly this one there watching with an eye heartbroken

les coupes aux fruits si divers et si appétissants dont il lui semblait,
the cups to the fruits so diverse and so appetizing of which it him seemed
with

avant de se mettre à table, ne pas pouvoir se rassasier,
before of himself to put at (the) table not -not- to be able himself to sate (the hunger)

et que, maintenant, son estomac bourré, se refusait à avaler.
and that now his stomach stuffed himself (he) refused to swallow

— Eh bien ! qu'as-tu donc ? firent à la fois Mab et Hans,
— Eh well ! what have you then ? made at the (same) time Mab and Hans,
said

ses voisins de droite et de gauche, en le voyant s'arrêter de manger
his neighbors of right and of left in him seeing himself halt stop of to eat

et repousser son assiette.
and to push back his plate

— Je n'ai pas faim ! fit-il, d'un ton qui n'aurait pas
— I not have am not hungry -not- hunger ! made he said he to himself with a tone who would not have -not-

été plus triste s'il avait eu à annoncer la perte d'une moitié de sa
been more sad if he had had to announce the loss of a half of his

famille.
family

— Comment, t'as pas faim ! fit Mab, de si beaux fruits ! »
— How you have you're not hungry no hunger ! made said Mab, of so beautiful fruits !

Nono, secoua la tête.
Nono shook the head

— Tu es malade, alors? fit Hans.
— You are sick then made said Hans

— Tu as du chagrin ? » ajouta Mab.
— You have of the sorrow ? added Mab

Biquette, Sacha, s'étaient levées et maintenant, autour de Nono,
Biquette Sacha themselves were raised and now around of Nono

s'enquéraient, elles aussi, de ce qu'il avait.
they questioned they also of this that he had

Honteux et confus, Nono finit par se laisser arracher que, déjà
Shameful and confused Nono ended by himself to let tear out that already

gavé du miel des abeilles, et des framboises et des fraises,
stuffed of the honey of the bees and of the raspberries and of the strawberries

dons des carabes, sa gourmandise l'avait poussé à se bourrer encore
gifts of the beetles his gluttony him had pushed to himself stuff still

de cerises pendant qu'il les cueillait. Son estomac distendu se refusait
of cherries during that he them picked His stomach distended itself refused

à avaler quoi que ce soit.
to swallow what that this be

— Bois un peu de lait, fit Sacha, cela les fera descendre, tu
— Drink a bit of milk made Sacha that them will make go down you
said

mangeras cette belle pêche ensuite. »
will eat this beautiful peach subsequently

Nono essaya d'en avaler quelques gouttes, mais le lait ne voulait
Nono tried of of it to swallow some drops but the milk not wanted

pas descendre lui non plus.
-not- to go down him not more
either

Et jetant un dernier regard de convoitise sur les fruits succulents qui
And throwing a last look of lust on the fruits delicious which

attiraient ses regrets, le jeune gourmand dut se contenter de
attracted his regrets the young glutton had to himself content of

regarder manger ses camarades qui, rassurés, s'étaient remis à
to watch eat his comrades who reassured themselves were set back to

becqueter les fruits de leurs préférences, se promettant, lui, d'être
peck the fruits of their preferences themselves promising him of to be

plus sage à l'avenir, et de modérer sa gourmandise.
more wise at the future and of to moderate his gluttony

Il dut leur raconter ses aventures avec les abeilles et les carabes, la
He had to them tell his adventures with the bees and the beetles the

mention qu'il avait faite de son repas dans le bois ayant éveillé leur
mention that he had made of his meal in the woods having awoken their

curiosité.
curiosity

Quand tout le monde fut rassasié, l'on se mit à desservir les
When all the world was satiated it one himself put to serve the

tables, rapportant les nappes à la lingerie, la vaisselle à la cuisine,
tables brought back the sheets to the linen room the dishes to the kitchen

où des machines inventées par Labor, lavaient et essuyaient plats
where -of the- engines invented by Labor washed and wiped dishes

et assiettes, que l'on n'avait plus ensuite qu'à
and plates (so) that them they did not have (any)more subsequently (other) than to

ranger dans les buffets qui ornaient la cuisine, située en un bâtiment
arrange in the cupboards which decorated the kitchen located in a building

un peu éloigné du château, caché par un rideau d'arbres, d'arbustes
a bit removed from the castle hidden by a curtain of trees of shrubs

et de fleurs ; les tables et les sièges furent rangés sous des
and of flowers ; the tables and the seats were stored under -of the-

hangars y attenant.
sheds there adjoining

Lorsque tout fut en ordre, les enfants se répandirent dans le
When all was in order the children themselves spread in the

jardin, discutant des jeux auxquels ils allaient se divertir. La
garden, discussing -of-the games at the which they went themselves to entertain The
with which

plupart des filles voulaient jouer à la maman ou à la maîtresse
largest part of the girls wanted to play to the Mama or to the mistress
teacher

d'école, vagues réminiscences de leurs jeux avant l'arrivée à
of (the) school vague reminiscences of their games before the arrival to

Autonomie, les garçons à saute-mouton, à chat perché ; et après
Autonomy (land) the boys at leapfrog at cat perched ; and after
cat and mouse tag

avoir bien discuté, tous finirent par s'organiser en groupes
to have well discussed all finally by themselves to organize in groups

d'après leurs préférences.
of after their preferences
according to

Mais, peu à peu, quelques-une se détachaient du groupe dont
But bit by bit some of them themselves detached of the group of which

ils faisaient partie, attirés qu'ils étaient par d'autres à côté, qui
they made part attracted that they were by -of- others to (the) side which

semblaient mieux leur convenir ; quelques garçons se laissèrent
appeared better them to convene ; some boys themselves let

attirer par les douceurs du jeu de la poupée ; quelques filles, parmi
draw by the sweets of the game of the doll ; some girls among
to the

les plus « diables », avaient mis leurs jupons en culotte, et jouaient
the most devils had put their petticoats in cheeky and played
tomboy their panties

bravement à saute-mouton.
bravely at leapfrog

Insensiblement les groupes s'étaient mêlés, il en était sorti
Imperceptibly the groups themselves were mixed he of it was gone out

d'autres pour jouer à colin-maillard, à cache-cache, à pigeon-vole, et
-of- others for to play at blind man's buff at hide and seek at pigeon flies and

autres divers jeux.
other diverse games

Nono, qui avait débuté en jouant à chat perché avec Hans, Mab,
Nono who had started in playing at cat perched with Hans Mab

Biquette et Sacha, se trouvait à la fin engagé dans une partie de
Biquette and Sacha himself found at the end committed in a game of

colin-maillard, avec une vingtaine d'autres garçons ou filles, et y
blind man's buff with a twenty-some of other boys or girls and there

comptait déjà une demi-douzaine d'amis des deux sexes qui avaient
counted already a half-dozen -of- friends of the two genders who had

nom Gretchen, May, Pat, Beppo, Coralie, jolie petite mulâtresse de la
name Gretchen May Pat Beppo Coralie pretty little mulatto of the

Guadeloupe, et Doudou, un solide noir Congolais.
Guadeloupe and Doudou a solid black Congolese

Mab, Hans, faisaient partie d'un groupe très occupé à résoudre des
Mab Hans made part d'un group very busy at to resolve of the
were

devinettes que chacun posait à son tour. Biquette et Sacha sautaient à
guesses that each set at their turn Biquette and Sacha jumping at
skipping

la corde.
the rope

Ceux qui étaient fatigués de jouer, venaient s'asseoir sur le perron,
Those who were weary of to play came -themselves- sit on the stone porch

où, étendus sur les marches, ils suivaient du regard les jeux
where stretched out on the steps they followed with the look the games

de leurs camarades.
of their comrades

Le soleil était couché depuis un moment déjà, l'obscurité tombait
The sun was laid down since a moment already the dark fell
had set

lentement, mais la soirée était douce, les étoiles s'allumaient une à une
slowly but the evening was sweet the stars themselves lit a by a

dans le ciel, les éclats de voix des joueurs s'éteignaient eux
in the sky the bursts of voices of the players themselves extinguished them

aussi, peu à peu.
also bit by bit

Solidaria parut sur le haut des marches du perron:
Solidaria appeared on the height of the steps of the stone porch

— Mes enfants, dit-elle, une surprise aujourd'hui. Une troupe de
— My children said she a surprise today A band of

gymnasiarques est venue nous offrir de vous donner ce soir une
gymnasiarchs is come us to offer of you give this evening a

représentation de leurs exercices. Il s'agit de tout préparer pour
representation of their exercices. It itself deals of everything to prepare for
show tricks

bien les recevoir. Où voulez-vous qu'ait lieu le spectacle ? dans la
well them receive Where want you that has place the spectacle ? in the

salle de théâtre ou dehors ?
room of theater or outside ?

— Dehors, dehors, firent les enfants qui étaient accourus, et qui
— Outside outside made the children who were run up and who
said had rushed up

se sentaient sous le charme de cette soirée.
themselves felt under the charm of this evening

— Eh bien, alors, à l'œuvre. Voici Labor qui vous aidera. »
— Oh well then to the work See-here Labor who you will help

Et les enfants, enthousiasmés, se mirent à battre des mains,
And the children excited themselves put to beat with the hands
clap

sautant de joie.
jumping of joy

Fin de soirée
End of (the) evening

Les	enfants	avaient	couru	à	la	remise	où	l'on	conservait	les	outils
The	children	had	run	to	the	shed	where	-it- one	retained	the	tools

et	les	accessoires,	et	là,	aidés	de	Labor,	et	de	quelques-uns	de	ses
and	the	accessories	and	there	helped	by	Labor	and	by	some	of	his

petits	génies,	ils	en	tirèrent	des	poteaux,	des	bâches,	qu'ils
little	genies, sprites	they	of it	pulled	-of the-	posts	-of the-	tarpaulins	that they

apporteront	sur	l'esplanade.
will bring	on	the esplanade

Là	ils	dressèrent	une	immense	tente	carrée	faisant	face	aux	marches
There	they	pitched	an	immense	tent	square	making	face	to the	steps

du	perron	qui	devaient	servir	de	gradins	pour	les	spectateurs.
of the	stone porch	which	must	serve	of	stands	for	the	spectators

Nono	était	émerveillé	de	voir	courir	les	lutins	de	Labor ;	avec	leur	aide,
Nono	was	marveled marveling	of	to see	run	the	sprites	of	Labor ;	with	their	aide

les	mâts	les	plus	lourds	étaient	soulevés	par	une	demi-douzaine	d'enfants
the	masts	the	most	heavy	were	raised	by	a	half-dozen	of children

sans	plus	d'efforts	qu'une	baguette	d'osier,	les	bâches	qui	formaient
without	more	-of- effort	than a	stick	of wicker	the	tarpaulins	which	formed

la	tente,	malgré	leur	poids,	étaient	soulevées	et	tendues	sans	le
the	tent	in spite of	their	weight	were	raised	and	extended	without	the

moindre	effort	apparent.
least	effort	apparent

Ces	lutins	étaient	de	petits	hommes	tout	contrefaits,	pas	très	beaux	à
These	sprites	were	of	small	men	all	imitated	-not-	very	beautiful	to

voir,	couverts	de	capes	rouges,	comme	Nono	en	avait	vu	dans	les
see	covered	with	capes	red	like	Nono	of it	had	seen	in	the

livres de contes qu'il avait lus ; mais lestes comme des singes,
books of (fairy)tales that he had read ; but fleet like -of the- monkeys

forts comme des bœufs et, malgré leur aspect peu aimable, de
strong like -of the- oxen and in spite of their appearance bit pleasant -of-
not very

très joyeux compagnons au fond, aimant parfois, à faire quelques
very happy companions at the bottom desiring sometimes to make some

farces. Là, entre autres, Dick occupé au dressage d'un mât, ayant
jokes There between others Dick occupied at the dressage of a mast having

déjà taquiné l'un d'eux, qui se trouvait près de lui, s'amusa
already teased -the- one of them who himself found near of him himself amused

de nouveau à le tirer par sa cape. Le lutin parut ne rien
of new to him pull by his cape The leprechaun appeared not nothing
again on

sentir mais s'arrangea de façon à agrafer la culotte de Dick au
to feel but himself contrived of way to hook the underwear of Dick to the

mât qu'on levait en ce moment. Et Dick suspendu en l'air, agitait
mast that they raised in that moment And Dick suspended in the air moved

bras et jambes comme une araignée au bout d'une ligne. On se
arms and legs like a spider at the end of a line One himself

dépêcha de le sortir de cette position périlleuse. À part cet incident,
despatched of him to get out of this position perilous At side this incident
A-

tout alla bien, et, en très peu de temps, la salle de spectacle fut
all went well and in very bit of time the room of spectacle was

improvisée, avec trapèzes, anneaux, barres fixes. C'était la fée Électricia,
improvised with trapezoids rings bars fixed It was the fairy Electricia

autre compagne de Labor, qui s'était chargée de l'éclairage de la salle.
other companion of Labor who herself was charged of the lighting of the room
herself had

Et elle avait fait magnifiquement les choses. D'énormes lampes, du
And she had done beautifully the things -Of- enormous lamps of the

haut des pylônes auxquelles elles étaient suspendues, versaient une
height of the pylons at the which they were suspended shed a
by which

lumière d'un blanc légèrement bleuté comme un rayon lunaire. On y
light with a white slightly bluish like a ray lunar One there

voyait clair comme en plein jour.
saw clear like in full day

— Bon ; voilà qui va bien, fit Labor, après s'être assuré de
— Good ; see there which goes well made Labor after herself to be assured of
said herself to have

la solidité des amarres des trapèzes et des barres. Nos artistes
the solidity of the moorings of the trapezoids and of the bars Our artists
strength

peuvent venir, nous sommes prêts à les recevoir.
can come we are ready to them receive

— Et voici une collation qu'on leur a préparée, » fit Solidaria, en
— And see-here a collation that one them has prepared made Solidaria in

soulevant la portière qui cachait l'entrée d'une autre tente formant un
making rise the door which hid the entry of an other tent forming an

élégant salon où pouvaient se tenir les artistes. Petit réduit arrangé
elegant salon where could itself keep the artists Little nook arranged

avec goût, qu'ornaient toutes sortes de fleurs fournies par les
with taste that decorated all kinds of flowers provided by the
that was decorated by

parterres d'Autonomie.
(flower) beds of Autonomy

— Alors, tout est en ordre, commençons à prendre nos places, fit
— Then all is in order (we) start to take our seats made
let's start said

Labor.
Labor

— Électricia peut avertir les artistes que leur salle est prête, ajouta
— Electricia can warn the artists that their room is ready added

Solidaria.
Solidaria

Et, suivis des enfants, ils se dirigèrent vers le perron,
And followed by the children they themselves headed towards the stone porch

où chacun prit la place qui lui convenait.
where each one took the place which her (or him) suited

Lorsque chacun fut assis et que le silence se fut établi, un
When each one was seated and that the silence itself was established an
                   when   had

orchestre invisible se fit entendre, préparant ainsi la venue des
orchestra invisible itself made hear preparing thus the come of the
                                        coming

artistes.
artists

À peine eut-il égrené ses dernières notes que les artistes parurent.
At pain had it dished out its last notes that the artists appeared
Barely

Ils étaient cinq. Quatre d'entre eux ressemblaient à d'énormes
They were five Four of between them resembled to -of- enormous

grenouilles aux tons verts et jaunes ; le cinquième, plus petit, s'était
frogs at the tones green and yellow ; the fifth more little itself was
     with   itself had

affublé de la peau d'une rainette verte.
decked with the skin of a tree frog green

Se plaçant en ligne, face au perron, ils firent un salut à
Themselves placing in (a) line face at the stone porch they made a greeting to
                      facing the

l'assemblée, ouvrant une grande gueule et des grands yeux bêtes
the assembly opening a large mouth and -of the- great eyes (of) animals

qui firent rire aux éclats tout ce petit monde.
which made laugh at -the- bursts all this little world

Puis ils commencèrent, aux anneaux, ensuite aux trapèzes, une série de
Then they began at the rings then at the trapezoids a series of

tours qui faisaient ressortir la grâce et la hardiesse des artistes. La
turns which made come out the grace and the breadth of the artists The

petite rainette qui, certainement, était le clown de la troupe, reprenait
little tree frog who certainly was the clown of the band retook
                                         continued

les mêmes tours en les chargeant d'une façon si comique, que ce fut
the same turns in them charging of a way so comical that this was

elle qui eut la plus grande part des applaudissements.
she who had the most large part of the applause

Lorsqu'ils eurent ainsi fait une série de contorsions et de cabrioles
When they had thus made a series of contortions and of capers

inénarrables, de renversements insensés, de rétablissements, de suspensions
unutterable of reversals foolish of recoveries of suspensions

et de chutes hardies ou comiques, les artistes revinrent se mettre
and of falls bold or comical the artists came back themselves to put

en ligne, saluant l'assemblée qui applaudissait enthousiasmée.
in line saluting the assembly which applauded excited

Mais, instantanément, disparut leur défroque de grenouilles, ils
But instantly disappeared their castoff of frogs they

apparurent habillés de maillots bleu-ciel dont les broderies et les
appeared dressed of jerseys sky blue of which the embroidery and the

paillettes d'argent les faisaient ressembler à de jolis papillons.
flakes of silver them made ressemble to -of- pretty butterflies

Et les jeunes spectateurs reconnurent cinq de leurs camarades qui, en
And the young spectators recognized five of their comrades who in

cachette, leur avaient préparé cette surprise.
hiding-place them had prepared this surprise
hiding

Les applaudissements redoublèrent lorsqu'on les eût reconnus.
The applause redoubled when one them had recognized

Eux, impassibles, saluèrent, et commencèrent aux barres parallèles,
They impassively saluted and began at the bars parallel

composées de quatre rangs, une série de tours d'équilibre et de sauts,
composed of four ranks a series of turns of balance and of jumps

qui soulevèrent à nouveau les applaudissements enthousiastes de la
which raised to new the applause enthusiastic of the
again

jeune assistance, qui frappait encore énergiquement des mains après
young public who clapped still vigorously with the hands after

que les petits artistes se furent retirés dans le salon qui leur
that the small artists themselves were withdrawn in the salon which them
had

avait été préparé, et le spectacle finit.
had been prepared and the spectacle ended

Pendant la durée des exercices, la musique n'avait cessé de se
During the duration of the drills the music not had ceased of itself

faire entendre, mais en sourdine, mêlant son rythme aux mouvements
to make hear But in mute mixing its rhythm to the movements
softer

des gymnasiarques.
of the gymnasiarchs

Nono ouvrait des yeux grands comme des portes cochères. « As-tu
Nono opened -of-the eyes large like of the doors (for) coaches Have you
garage doors

vu, dit-il à son voisin Hans, le petit comme il était rigolo ?
seen said he to his neighbour Hans the little (one) like he was fun ?

Comment qu'il s'appelle ?
How that he himself calls ?
What's his name

— C'est Ahmed, fit Hans qui était non moins enthousiasmé. As-tu
— That is Ahmed made Hans who was not less enthused Have you
said

vu le grand ? comme il se tenait par ses talons à l'échelle, la
seen the tall one ? how he himself kept by his heels at the ladder the

tête en bas.
head in low
down

Et tous échangeaient leurs réflexions, ne tarissant pas d'enthousiasme sur
And all exchanged their reflections not drying up -not- of enthusiasm on

les tours qui les avaient le plus frappées.
the turns which them had the most struck
excited

— Là, là, c'est bien, fit Amorata, autre sœur de Solidaria, en
— There there this is well made Amorata other sister of Solidaria in

paraissant, maintenant, il va falloir penser à aller se coucher ; vos
appearing now it goes to need to think to go oneself lay down ; your

yeux commencent à se gonfler de sommeil, mais auparavant je vous
eyes begin to themselves inflate of sleep but before I you

apporte des nouvelles de vos parents, comme je vous ai promis d'en
bring of the news of your parents like I you have promised of it

donner chaque soir. »
to give each evening

Et sur un signe qu'elle fit, une bande des gnomes de Labor apporta,
And on a sign that she made a band of the gnomes of Labor brought

derrière le groupe des enfants, un appareil, pendant qu'une grande toile
behind the group of the children an apparatus during that a large canvas

blanche était tendue au fond de la tente, l'obscurité se fit
white was stretched out at the back of the tent the darkness itself made
it became dark

tout à coup, et un jet lumineux partant de l'appareil, vint tracer un
all at strike and a beam luminous leaving from the device came to draw a
suddenly

énorme cercle sur la toile blanche.
huge circle on the canvas white

Nono se demandait ce que cela voulait dire, étant anxieux de savoir
Nono himself asked this what that wanted to say being anxious of to know

si, lui, nouveau venu, allait avoir aussi des nouvelles de sa famille ?
if he new come(r) went to have also -of the- news of his family ?

Les yeux fixés sur le cercle lumineux, il ne vit d'abord qu'un
The eyes fixed on the circle luminous he not saw initially (more) than a

brouillard léger qui s'agitait, se divisait, pour se rassembler
fog light which itself moved itself divided for itself to reassemble

ensuite en points qui finirent par former une image distincte, que
subsequently in points which finished by to form an image separate that

Nono reconnut de suite.
Nono recognized of following
immediately

C'était la chambre où sa famille prenait ses repas. Une porte
It was the room where his family took their meal A door

entr'ouverte laissait voir une autre pièce, où le grand frère se
ajar let see an other room where the large brother himself

préparait à se coucher.
prepared to himself lay down

Assis à table, dans la première pièce, le père lisait son journal ;
Seated at (the) table in the first room the father read his newspaper ;

sa sœur Cendrine, près du père, écrivait ses devoirs ; la mère, à un
his sister Cendrine near of the father wrote her duties ; the mother at an
homework

autre coin de la table, reprisait un vêtement.
other corner of the table mended a clothing

À un bruit qui venait de la porte, elle dressa la tête, puis se
At a noise which came from the door she raised the head then herself

levant, alla ouvrir. C'était la concierge qui apportait une lettre.
raising went to open It was the concierge who brought a letter

La concierge avait bien l'air de vouloir tailler sa petite bavette, mais
The concierge had well the air of to want to sharpen his little bib but

les parents qui paraissaient animés du plus vif désir de connaître le
the parents who appeared moved of the most lively desire of to know the

contenu de la lettre, ne firent rien pour la retenir. Aussitôt partie,
contents of the letter not made nothing for him to retain Immediately left

la mère ayant ouvert la lettre, la lut à haute voix. C'était Solidaria
the mother having opened the letter it read at high voice It was Solidaria
loud

qui envoyait des nouvelles de son protégé.
who sent -of the- news of her protegee

Cendrine qui avait écouté attentivement exprima le désir d'avoir de
Cendrine who had listened closely expressed the desire of to have -of-

belles aventures comme son frère. Mais on lui répondit que ce n'était
beautiful adventures like her brother But they her answered that this not was

pas fait pour les petites filles.
-not- made for the small girls

En quoi se trompaient ses parents, opina en lui-même Nono qui
In what themselves deceived his parents opined in him self Nono who
thought

voyait, parmi ses camarades, les filles aussi nombreuses que les garçons.
saw among his comrades the girls as much as the boys

Titi, lui, exprima le désir de trouver un pays où l'on pourrait
Titi him expressed the desire of to find a country where -it- one could

aussi bien vivre sans être forcé d'aller s'enfermer douze heures dans un
so well live without to be forced of to go be locked twelve hours in a

atelier.
workshop

Puis, l'image s'effaça, le cercle lumineux se resserra, et finalement,
Then the image faded the circle luminous itself tightened and finally

disparut, la lumière inonda la salle à nouveau.
disappeared the light flooded the room to new
again

— Hein ! fit Nono, s'adressant à Mab, tu as vu papa et
— Huh ! made Nono -himself- addressing to Mab you have seen Papa and

maman ?
Mama ?

— Oui, et aussi ma sœur May qui jouait avec Pussy notre petit chat
— Yes and also my sister May who played with Pussy our little cat

noir et blanc qui est si joli.
black and white who is so pretty

— Mais non, je te parle de mon père et de ma mère à moi.
— But no I you speak of my father and of my mother to me

— Ah, j'oubliais, fît Mab en riant, je ne sais pas comment cela se
— Ah I forgot made Mab in laughing I not know -not- how that itself
said

fait, il n'y a qu'une image sur la toile, mais chacun de nous y
does it not there has than one image on the canvas but each of us there

voit ceux qu'il aime, et rien autre.
sees those that he loves and nothing else

— Oui, c'est une drôle de lanterne magique, fit Hans. Toi, tu
— Yes this is a funny (thing) of (a) lantern magic made Hans You yourself
said

as vu tes parents, moi j'y ai vu les miens, Mab, les siens,
have seen your parents me I there have seen the mine Mab the hers

chacun de nous tous ici, de même, sans rien voir de ce que les
each of us all here of same without nothing to see of this that the
the

autres y voyaient. »
others there saw

Nono n'en revenait pas, mais habitué, en cette journée, à voir des
Nono not of it returned -not- but used in this day to see of the
didn't understand

choses plus extraordinaires les unes que les autres, s'il n'avait pas
things more extraordinary the ones than the others if he not had -not-

encore perdu la faculté de s'étonner, il se faisait peu à peu
yet lost the faculty of himself to surprise he himself made bit by bit
ability got used

aux choses les plus extraordinaires.
to the things the most extraordinary

La petite population d'Autonomie gravit les marches du perron. Nono
The little population of Autonomy climbed the steps of the stone porch Nono

suivant ses camarades, ils se trouvèrent sous le
followed his comrades they themselves found under the

péristyle où s'ouvrait une grande baie donnant
peristyle where itself opened a large picture window giving
{porch surrounded by columns}

accès à un vestibule où s'ouvraient plusieurs autres portes, ainsi que
access to a vestibule where itself opened several other doors like that
as well as

différents escaliers conduisant aux étages supérieurs.
different stairs leading to the floors higher

— Viens, fit Hans, nos chambres sont au premier. Il y en a
— Come made Hans our rooms are at the first (floor) It there of it has
said There of them is

une de vide à côté de la mienne, tu la prendras. »
one -of- empty at (the) side of the mine you it take

La foule des enfants s'était dispersée par les escaliers. Hans, Nono,
The crowd of the children itself was dispersed by the stairs Hans Nono
itself had

Mab, Biquette montèrent les marches de celui qui se trouvait à leur
Mab Biquette climbed the steps of the one which itself found at their

droite.
right

— Tu vois, fit Hans en entrant dans une pièce et en tournant un
— You see made Hans in entering in a room and in turning a
said

bouton qui fit jaillir la lumière, voilà où tu peux te
button which made gush forth the light see there where you can yourself

mettre ; ma chambre est à côté, celle de Mab en face, celles de
put ; my room is at (the) side that of Mab in front those of

Biquette et de Sacha sont plus loin, mais dans le même couloir. »
Biquette and of Sacha are more far but in the same corridor

Et Nono vit que cette pièce, assez spacieuse, éclairée pendant le jour
And Nono saw that this room enough spacious lit during the day
quite

par une grande fenêtre donnant sur les jardins, était coquettement
by a large window giving on the gardens was coquettishly
opening

meublée d'une petite couchette aux draps fins et d'une blancheur
furnished by a little sleeping berth to the sheets fine and with a whiteness
with

éclatante. En un coin, la table de toilette : une armoire, deux chaises,
bright In a corner the table of dress : a cupboard two chairs

complétaient l'ameublement.
completed the furnishings

— Tiens, fit Mab arrivant avec trois ou quatre livres qu'elle était allée
— Hold made Mab arriving with three or four books that she was gone

chercher dans sa chambre, nous avons oublié de passer à la
to search in her room we have forgotten of to pass at the

bibliothèque ; mais si tu veux lire avant de t'endormir, voilà
library ; but if you want to read before of yourself fall asleep see there

des volumes où tu pourras choisir en attendant. »
of the volumes where you can choose in awaiting

Et Hans, lui montrant une petite cruche de lait sur la table, près
And Hans him showing a little jug of milk on the table near

du lit : voici de quoi boire, si tu as soif la nuit.
of the bed : see-here of what to drink if you have thirst the night
are thirsty

— Si la lumière te gêne, ajouta Dick qui était entré, tu n'auras
— If the light you bothers added Dick who was entered you not have
had

qu'à tourner ce bouton. »
than to turn this button

Et,	joignant	le	geste	à	la	parole,	il	fit	l'obscurité	dans	la
And	joining	the	gesture	to	the	word	he	made	the darkness	in	the

chambrette.
small bedroom

Ayant	tourné	à	nouveau	le	bouton,	la	lumière	reparut.
Having	turned	to	new	the	button	the	light	reappeared

Nono,	un	peu	fatigué	de	tant	d'émotions,	remercia	de	tout	cœur
Nono	a	bit	tired	of	so much	of emotions	thanked	with	all	(his) heart

ses	camarades,	leur	souhaita	le	bonsoir	en	les	embrassant	;	chacun
his	comrades	them	wished	the	good evening	in	them	embracing kissing	;	each

regagna	sa	chambre,	et	le	silence	se	fit	dans	le	palais.
returned to	their	room	and	the	silence	itself	made descended	in on	the	palace

Le travail à Autonomie
The work at Autonomy

Il faisait grand jour, le lendemain, quand Nono fut éveillé par une
It made large day the following day when Nono was awakened by a
was broad daylight

bande de ses camarades qui avaient envahi sa chambrette.
band of his comrades who had invaded his small bedroom

— Hou ! le paresseux, fit Mab, en lui faisant les cornes, le
— Boo ! the lazy (one) made Mab while him making the horns the
said

paresseux qui dort encore et le soleil qui l'aveugle. Hou ! hou !
lazy (one) who sleeps still and the sun which him blinds Boo ! boo !

— Allons ! lève-toi, fit Hans, nous venons te chercher pour aller
— Go ! rise yourself made Hans we came you to seek for to go
get up said

jardiner.
gardening

— Non, fit Mab, il m'a promis hier soir de venir voir traire
— No made Mab he me has promised yesterday evening of to come to see milk
said

les vaches avec moi, je l'emmène.
the cows with me I him take
will take him

Nono s'était lestement levé, avait passé sa culotte, s'habillant en
Nono himself was nimbly raised had passed his underwear himself dressing in
had put on

un clin d'œil. — Les garçons avaient mis bas couvertures et draps,
a wink of eye — The boys had put down blankets and sheets
flash

remué les matelas et fait le lit, pendant que les petites filles
shaken the mattress and made the bed during that the small girls

époussetaient, balayaient et rangeaient partout.
dusted swept and arranged everywhere
ordered

Quand ce fut fini, les enfants l'entraînèrent à une des pièces du
When this was finished the children him took along to one of the rooms of the

sous-sol, organisée en salle de bains. Deux grandes piscines tenaient la
under-ground organized in room of baths Two large pools held the
basement set up as bathroom

plus grande partie de la pièce. Dans l'une de l'eau fraîche, dans
most large part of the room In the one of the water fresh in
cold

l'autre de l'eau tiède pour les frileux. Autour de la salle,
the other of the water lukewarm for the chilly (ones) Around -of- the room
warm

des appareils pour toutes sortes de douches. Se déshabiller, et
-of the- appliances for all kinds of showers Themselves to undress and

se jeter à l'eau fut l'affaire d'un instant pour toute la
themselves to throw (in)to the water was the case of a moment for all the

bande espiègle.
band playful

Puis lorsqu'on se fut séché, l'on passa dans une autre grande
Then when they themselves was dried -it- they passed in an other large
had

pièce qui servait de salle à manger où les enfants étaient en train
room which served of room to eat where the children were in process
as dining room

de déjeuner : avalant qui du lait chaud, d'autres du chocolat,
of to lunch : swallowing who -of the- milk warm -of- others -of the- chocolate
this one

d'autres du café. Biquette, qui avait filé à la cuisine, en
-of- others -of the- coffee Biquette who had moved to the kitchen from there
gone

revint avec un pot plein de chocolat dont elle versa une grande tasse
returned with a pot full of chocolate of which she poured a large cup

à Nono.
for Nono

— Tiens, fit-elle, nous l'avons préparé à ton intention.
— Hold she asked we it have prepared to your intention
for you

— Et voici de la bonne galette bien beurrée » fit Sacha qui,
— And see-here -of- the good wafer well buttered made Sacha who
a said

depuis un instant, était actionnée à étendre le beurre sur la galette
since a moment was actioned to spread the butter on the wafer
was busy

bien chaude.
well hot

Nono remercia ses amis et se mit à déjeuner avec appétit,
Nono thanked his friends and himself set to have breakfast with appetite

pendant que les autres faisaient de même.
during that the others did of same
while the

Quand tous furent restaurés, la bande se dispersa. Mab, prenant Nono
When all were restored the band itself scattered Mab taking Nono

par la main, l'entraîna du côté des étables. Mais déjà les vaches
by the hand him led of the side of the cowsheds But already the cows
to the

étaient parties aux pâturages.
were left to the pastures

En traversant les étables, Mab fit remarquer à son compagnon comme
In traversing the cowsheds Mab made notice to her companion how

elles étaient propres, bien tenues, et différentes de celles qu'ils avaient
they were clean well kept and different from those that they had

vues à la campagne, celles-ci toujours sombres, sales, sentant mauvais, la
seen at the countryside these always dark dirty feeling bad the
in

litière ressemblant plus à du fumier qu'à de la paille.
litter resembling more -to- -of the- manure than -to- -of- the straw

Ici rien de semblable. C'était de grandes salles spacieuses, parfaitement
Here nothing -of- similar It was of large rooms spacious perfectly
There were

éclairées, dallées de larges pierres, bien unies et cimentées entre elles,
lit paved with wide stones well united and cemented between them

allant légèrement en pente de façon à conduire le liquide vers de
going lightly in slope of way to lead the liquid towards -of-

petits canaux qui l'entraînaient au dehors.
small canals which it took away to the outside

89

De solides cloisons, en planches façonnées d'une manière élégante,
Of solid partitions, in boards shaped of a way elegant
(stable) walls of

séparaient chaque bête lui formant une case où elle pouvait se
separated each animal him forming a box where she could herself

mouvoir à l'aise. Les râteliers étaient pleins de foin, une litière de paille
move at the ease The racks were full of hay a litter of straw
comfortably

bien fraîche était répandue à terre. Une jolie plaque de marbre à
well fresh was spread on earth A pretty plate of marble at
the ground

chaque box donnait le nom de sa locataire.
each box gave the name of its tenant

— Tu vois comme nos bêtes sont bien ici, remarqua Mab. Tiens,
— You see how our animals are well here, noted Mab. Hold
Look

voilà la loge de ma préférée ; c'est celle que j'aime à soigner.
see there the box of my favorite ; this is that one that i love to take care of

(Indiquant la plaque :) tu vois, c'est Blanchette qu'elle s'appelle. Viens,
Showing the plate :) you see this is Blanchette that she herself calls Come

maintenant, nous allons les retrouver dans le pré. »
now we go them find back in the meadow

Et traversant l'étable, ils ouvrirent une porte donnant sur un grand
And traversing the stable, they opened a door giving on a large
opening

pré où les vaches paissaient et s'ébattaient à l'air.
meadow where the cows pastured and -themselves- were frolicking to the (open) air
in

Quelques-uns des Autonomiens étaient en train d'en traire.
Some of the (boys and girls of) Autonomia were in process of them to milk

— Voilà ma Blanche », fit Mab, en courant à une des vaches, qui
— See there my White made Mab in running to one of the cows who
said

poussa un meuglement joyeux en voyant accourir sa jeune maîtresse, qui,
emitted a moo happy in seeing hastening her young mistress who

passant ses deux bras autour de son cou, l'embrassa sur le mufle.
passing her two arm around of her neck her kissed on the muzzle

— Regarde comme elle est propre. Nous sommes camarades,
— Look how she is clean. We are friends

toutes les deux. Elle sait aussi que je lui porte des friandises.
all the two / us two She knows also that I her carry -of the- treats

Et ce disant, elle tira de sa poche une poignée de sel que la
And this saying, she pulled from her pocket a fist(ful) of salt that the

bête sembla savourer avec délices.
animal seemed to enjoy with delight

Puis, s'emparant d'un petit banc et d'un seau, Mab se mit en devoir
Then seizing -of a little bench and -of a bucket Mab herself put in duty

de traire la vache.
of to milk the cow

Au bout d'un instant de cet exercice, elle proposa à Nono d'essayer à
At the end of a moment of this exercise, she proposed to Nono of to try at

son tour. Nono prit sa place, mais ses doigts inexpérimentés servant mal
his turn. Nono took her place, But his fingers inexperienced served badly

sa bonne volonté, il ne parvint pas à extraire une seule goutte de
his good will, he not succeeded -not- to extract a single drop of

lait ; à son grand déplaisir, car à voir la facilité avec laquelle Mab
milk ; to his great displeasure, because to see the ease with which Mab

le faisait couler dans le seau, rien ne lui avait semblé aussi facile.
it did flow in the bucket nothing -not- him had appeared so easy

Cependant, à force d'essais et d'explications de la part de son amie,
However, at force of tries and of explanations from the side of his friend,

il parvint à en faire jaillir quelques gouttes. Ce fut alors un
he succeeded to of it make gush forth some drops. This was then a

transport de joie de la part des deux enfants comme s'ils avaient
movement carrying away of joy from the side of the two children as if they had

accompli une merveille, et Nono, qui commençait à se
accomplished a wonder(ful thing), and Nono, who began / had begun to himself

décourager, reprit du cœur à la besogne. Mais Mab, toujours
discourage, continued of the heart / with renewed courage at the task. But Mab always

remuante, reprit sa place et ne s'arrêta que lorsque le seau fut
restless took back her place and not herself halted than when the bucket was
stopped

plein.
full

Nono, que le rôle de spectateur n'amusait plus, s'était mis à
Nono that the role of spectator not amused (any)more himself was put to
himself had

cueillir des fleurs dont était émaillée la prairie. En ayant fait une
pick -of the- flowers of which was enamelled the meadow In having made an
decorated

ample moisson, et voulant faire une surprise à ses amies Mab et
ample harvest and wanting to make a surprise to his friends Mab and

Sacha, qui avaient été si prévenantes pour lui, il alla s'installer à
Sacha who had been so considerate for him he went himself install at
to in

l'ombre d'un énorme noyer, et là, se mit à tresser, avec les
the shadow of a huge walnut (tree) and there himself put to plait with the

fleurs qu'il avait cueillies, de belles guirlandes, mariant les couleurs
flowers that he had picked -of= beautiful garlands marrying the colors

selon la disposition qui lui semblait le plus harmonique.
according to the disposition which him seemed the most harmonic

Il avait terminé sa deuxième guirlande et commencé une troisième,
He had finished his second garland and started a third

lorsque, levant les yeux, il vit Mab qui le contemplait.
when raising the eyes he saw Mab who him contemplated

— Mâtin ! tu es joliment occupé, fit-elle. Pour qui donc ces belles
— Cur ! you are nicely occupied she asked For who then these beautiful
Rascal

guirlandes ?
garlands ?

— Il y en a une pour toi, fit Nono, en la lui arrangeant sur
— It there of them has one for you made Nono in it her arranging on
There is of them said

les cheveux.
the hairs
hair

— Pour moi, cette belle guirlande ? fit Mab, enthousiasmée, en
— For me this beautiful garland ? made Mab excited in
said

courant se mirer à un ruisseau qui coulait au bord du pré.
running herself to watch at a stream which flowed at the edge of the meadow
in

Puis, revenant : il faut que je t'embrasse. Et ce disant, elle lui
Then coming back : it is necessary that I you kiss And this saying she him

appliqua deux bons gros baisers sur les joues.
applied two good big kisses on the cheeks

— Celle-ci, fit Nono, qui venait de terminer, est pour Sacha, l'autre
— This one here made Nono who came of to end is for Sacha the other
said

pour Biquette. Et les plaçant autour de son cou, pour ne pas les
for Biquette And them placing around of his neck for not -not- them

froisser, il alla chercher le seau de Mab, pour le porter à la
crumple he went to seek the bucket of Mab for it to carry to the

laiterie. Puis ils se mirent à la recherche de leurs deux amies.
dairy place Then they themselves set at the search of their two friends

Ils allèrent au jardin, et y trouvèrent Hans qui, avec quelques
They went to the garden and there found Hans who with some

autres camarades, bêchait un coin de terrain où ils se
other comrades dug a corner of ground where they themselves

proposaient de faire quelques expériences.
offered of to make some experiences

Ils avaient lu dans un livre de jardinage, qu'en greffant des arbres
They had read in a book of gardening that in grafting from the trees

de même espèce, on pouvait faire porter différentes sortes de fruits
of (the) same kind one could make carry different sorts of fruits

sur le même tronc, des roses de différentes couleurs, sur le même
on the same trunk of the pink of different colors on the same

rosier. Désireux de s'assurer du fait, ils voulaient faire
rosebush Desirous of themselves to ascertain of the fact they wanted to make

des plantations de sujets qu'ils se proposaient de greffer. Nono
of the plantations of subjects that they themselves offered of to graft Nono

admira l'ardeur avec laquelle ils remuaient la terre, bêchant, creusant,
admired the ardor with which they moved about the earth digging digging

préparant les engrais qu'on leur avait indiqués comme les plus
preparing the fertilizer that one them had indicated as the most

convenables aux essences qu'ils se proposaient d'expérimenter.
suitable to the species that they themselves proposed of to experiment (with)

Hans ignorait où se trouvaient Biquette et Sacha.
Hans did not know where himself found Biquette and Sacha

Nono et Mab allèrent plus loin. Ils trouvèrent Biquette dans une des
Nono and Mab went more far They found Biquette in one of the

serres, y faisant la toilette aux plantes que l'on y cultivait.
greenhouses there making the dress to the plants that it one there cultivated

À la vue de la belle guirlande, elle claqua des mains, sautant de
At the sight of the beautiful garland she clapped with the hands jumping of

joie. Toutes ses compagnes lâchèrent leur travail pour venir l'admirer
joy All her companions let go their work for to come admire

aussi, et Nono dut leur promettre de leur apprendre comment en
also and Nono had to them promise of them to teach how of them

fabriquer de semblables.
to make -of- similar

Interrogée sur l'endroit où devait se trouver Sacha, Biquette assura
Questioned on the place where must herself find Sacha Biquette assured

qu'on la trouverait dans la partie du jardin affectée à la culture
that one her would find in the part of the garden affected to the culture
destinée

des graines.
of the seeds

Mab et Nono se dépêchèrent d'y courir ; ils y
Mab and Nono themselves despatched of to there run ; they there
said goodbye so they could run there

trouvèrent Sacha, un petit pinceau à la main, prenant, avec ce pinceau,
found Sacha a little brush at the hand taking with this brush

une petite poussière jaune que plus d'un de vous a sans doute
a little dust yellow that more of one of you has without doubt
than one

remarquée dans les fleurs lorsqu'elles sont complètement épanouies.
noticed in the flowers when (they) are completely blooming

Avec ce même pinceau, Sacha barbouillait de cette poudre jaune le
With this same brush Sacha daubed with this powder yellow the

calice d'autres fleurs différentes.
chalice of other flowers different

— À quoi donc t'amuses-tu là ? firent Mab et Nono intrigués.
— At what then you amuse yourself there ? made Mab and Nono intrigued
said

Sacha raconta que leur professeur Botanicus leur avait expliqué qu'en
Sacha told that their professor Botanicus them had explained that in

mariant certaines plantes entre elles, on en obtenait des graines d'une
marrying certain plants between them one of it obtained of the seeds of a
joining

espèce différente de formes et de couleurs. C'est ce qu'on appelait les
kind different of forms and of colors This is this that one called the

hybrides.
hybrids

Et comme Nono ne comprenait pas, n'ayant jamais ouvert un livre
And as Nono not understood -not- not having ever opened a book

d'histoire naturelle, elle lui expliqua comment se formait la graine dans
of history natural she him explained how itself formed the seed in
of natural history

les fleurs.
the flowers

Cette poussière jaune qu'elle recueillait sortait d'une petite poche nommée
This dust yellow that she collected came out of an little pocket named

anthère, cette poussière était recueillie par une autre partie de la fleur
anther this dust was gathered up by an other part of the flower

que l'on nomme le stigmate ; car le plus souvent, les deux
that -it- one names the stigma ; because the most often the two

organes sont dans la même fleur ; mais il y a certaines espèces
organs are in the same flower ; but it there has certain species
there are

où ces organes sont sur des pieds séparés.
where these organs are on of the feet separated
stems

Dans le premier cas, la plante est dite hermaphrodite, dans le second
In the first case the base is called hermaphrodite in the second

cas, les pieds qui portent les anthères sont dit mâles, ceux qui
case the stems which carry the anthers are said males those which
to be male

recueillent cette poussière sont les femelles. Et ce sont ceux-là
gather this dust are the females And these are those ones

seulement qui produisent la graine.
only who produce the seed

Le stigmate conduit les grains de poussière jaune qu'il a recueillis dans
The stigma led the grains of dust yellow that it has collected in

une glande que l'on appelle ovaire, là ils grossissent, pendant que
a gland that -it- one calls (the) ovary there they grow during that

grossit aussi l'organe qui les a recueillis. C'est ce qui forme les
grows also the organ which them has collected It is this which shapes the

fruits, comme les pommes, les poires ; les pépins à l'intérieur sont la
fruits like the apples the pears ; the pips at the interior are the

graine produite par les grains de poussière jaune.
seed produced by the grains of dust yellow

À l'état libre ce sont les insectes qui, en venant chercher leur
At the state free these are the insects who in coming to seek their

nourriture dans les fleurs, transportent cette poussière jaune d'une fleur
food in the flowers carry this dust yellow from one flower

à l'autre. Ici, Sacha remplissait, avec son pinceau, le rôle des insectes,
to the other Here Sacha filled with her brush the role of the insects

seulement au lieu de porter la poussière jaune, appelée pollen, dans
only at the place of to carry the dust yellow called pollen in

des fleurs identiques, c'était sur des fleurs de genres différents, afin
-of the- flowers identical it was on of the flowers of kinds different so

de créer une nouvelle variété.
of to create a new variety

Mais tout en donnant ces explications et en montrant à Nono, dans
But all in giving these explanations and while showing to Nono in
while

une fleur qu'elle avait cueillie, les organes qu'elle nommait, Sacha jetait
a flower that she had plucked the organs that she named Sacha threw

des regards d'admiration sur la guirlande que portait Mab et sur
-of the- looks admiration on the garland that carried Mab and on

celle que Nono avait à son bras.
the one that Nono had on his arm

— C'est pour toi, fit Nono en la lui posant sur la tête.
— This is for you made Nono in it her setting on the head
said

Sacha fut non moins enthousiasmée que Mab et Biquette. À ses amies
Sacha was not less excited than Mab and Biquette To her friends

qui étaient accourues, Nono dut également promettre de leur en
who were running up Nono had to equally promise of them of it
came

apprendre la fabrication.
to learn the manufacturing

Ce fut un véritable succès ; pendant huit jours, à Autonomie, on ne
This was a true success ; during eight days at Autonomy (land) one not

pensa plus qu'à fabriquer des guirlandes. Les prés, à la fin,
thought (any)more than at to make -of the- garlands The meadows at the end
than of

ne fournissant plus assez de fleurs, les jardins furent quelque peu
not providing (any)more enough -of- flowers the gardens were some bit

pillés, et je ne sais pas si les serres auraient été épargnées, si
looted and I not know -not- if the greenhouses would have been saved if

un jeu nouveau n'était venu opérer une diversion, faisant abandonner
a game new not was come to operate a diversion making abandon
not had to create

les guirlandes.
the garlands

Mais avec tout cela, l'heure du déjeuner était venue. Les tables furent
But with all that the time of the lunch was come The tables were
had

servies encore au dehors, sur l'esplanade, car il faisait un temps
served still at the outside on the esplanade because it made a weather
was

superbe.
superb

Nono qui, cette fois, avait faim, put goûter non seulement aux fruits
Nono who this time had hunger could taste not only -to- the fruits

qu'il aimait, mais à une foule d'autres qu'il ne connaissait pas. Et,
that he loved but to a mass of others that he not knew -not- And

ne pouvant plus manger, comme s'il avait eu peur d'en manquer il
not being able more to eat as if he had had fear of of them miss he

fourra dans sa poche une demi douzaine de fruits presque semblables à
stuffed in his pocket a half dozen of fruits almost similar to

des pommes, dont il ne connaissait pas le nom, mais qui lui
-of the- apples of which he not knew -not- the name but which him

semblaient excellents, et que, lorsqu'on se fut levé de table, il
seemed excellent and that when one oneself was raised from (the) table he

courut porter à sa chambre.
ran to carry to his room

L'école
The school

En se levant de table, les enfants s'étaient répandus sur
In themselves raising from (the) table the children themselves were spread out over
had

les pelouses, où ils avaient organisé toutes sortes de jeux. Nono,
the lawns where they had organized all kinds of games. Nono,

redescendu de sa chambre, était venu se mêler à eux. Mais un
redescended from his room was come (of) himself to mix to them But a
having come back had with

groupe de jeunes demoiselles de cinq à sept ans voulut qu'il
group of young ladies of five to seven years wanted that he

commençât de suite ses leçons sur l'art de tresser les fleurs, et il
should begin of following his lessons on the art of to plait the flowers, and he

avait accédé à leur désir.
had acceded to their desire.

C'est au milieu de ce groupe qu'une heure plus tard vinrent le
It is at the middle of this group than one hour more late came them
later

chercher Hans, Mab et compagnie.
to seek Hans Mab and company

— Nous allons à l'école, lui dirent-ils, tu viens avec nous ?
— We go to the school him they said you come with us ?

— Tu verras comme on s'y amuse, ajouta Dick qui s'était
— You will see how one oneself there amuses added Dick who himself was
had

joint à eux.
joined to them.

Nono, qui ne demandait pas mieux que de voir du nouveau, promit
Nono who not asked -not- better than of to see of the new promised
new things

à ses élèves de reprendre sa leçon le lendemain et suivit le
to his students of to take up again his lesson the following day and followed the

groupe des étudiants.
group of the students

Ils entrèrent en une salle spacieuse, au rez-de-chaussée du palais,
They entered in a room spacious at the level-of-road of the palace
ground floor

où étaient rangés des tables, des bancs et des chaises ; mais
where were stored -of the- tables -of the- benches and -of the- chairs ; but

non de ces grandes tables, longues comme des jours sans pain, qui
none of these large tables long like of the days without bread which

encombrent toute la salle et que l'on ne peut changer de place.
encumber all the room and that -it- one not can change of place

C'était de petites tables carrées que l'on pouvait transporter à la
It was -of- small tables square that -it- one could transport to the
They were

place que l'on désirait, et disposer comme on voulait ; car les
place that -it- one desired and to dispose like one wanted ; because the

écoliers avaient la faculté de se réunir par groupes.
schoolchildren had the faculty of themselves to gather by groups

Nono et ses amis allèrent se placer à une de ces tables où
Nono and his friends went themselves place at one of these tables where

ils s'installèrent à leur aise. Nombre de leurs camarades avaient
they themselves installed at their ease. (A) number of their comrades had

déjà pris place en différents endroits de la salle.
already taken place in different locations of the room

C'était Liberta qui présidait aux leçons, mais cherchant plutôt à s'attirer
It was Liberta who presided to the lessons but searching rather to attract
trying

les questions des enfants que de leur farcir la tête d'idées que, la
the questions of the children than of them stuff the head with ideas that the

plupart du temps, ils ne comprennent pas.
largest part of the time they not understood -not-

Lorsque tout le monde fut assis, Liberta demanda aux écoliers ce
When all the world was seated Liberta asked -to- the schoolchildren this

qu'il fallait mettre à l'étude ?
that it was necessary to put to the study ?

— Racontez-nous l'histoire de l'imprimerie, crièrent quelques voix.
— Tell us   the story   of   the printing   shouted   some   voices

— Non, faites-nous de l'astronomie, firent quelques autres.
— No   make us   of   the astronomy   made   some   others
      give us   said

— Oh ! non, expliquez-nous la formation de la terre.
— Oh ! no   explain us   the   formation   of   the   earth

— La géographie, c'est plus amusant.
— The geography   this is   more   fun

— On en a fait hier, protestèrent quelques autres voix.
— One of it has done yesterday   protested   some   other   voices
   We did so

— Eh bien ! des problèmes, fit tout un groupe de garçons de dix
— Eh well ! -of the- problems made all a group of boys of ten
            sums   said

à douze ans.
to twelve years

— Tout ce que vous voudrez, fit Liberta en souriant, mais il
— All this that you want made Liberta in smiling but it
               said

faudrait pourtant vous entendre. Par quoi commençons-nous ?
would be necessary however you to hear By what begin we ?

— Que l'on commence par les problèmes si l'on veut, fit un autre
— That -it- one begins by the problems if it one wants made an other
    we   begin with   sums   said

groupe, mais que l'on continue ensuite par la géographie.
group but that it one continues subsequently by the geography
            we continue   with

— Oui, et ensuite on n'aura pas le temps de faire de
— Yes and subsequently one not will have -not- the time of to do -of-
             we

l'astronomie, grognèrent quelques mécontents.
-the- astronomy groaned some unsatisfied ones

— Ni de parler de la formation de la terre, ajoutèrent d'autres.
— Nor of to speak of the formation of the earth added -of- others

— Ni de nous raconter quelque jolie histoire, renchérit un groupe de
— Nor of us to tell some pretty story added a group of

plus petits.
most small
the smallest kids

— Eh ! bien, si vous voulez, fit Liberta, il y a moyen de tout
— Eh ! well if you want made Liberta it there has means of all
said there is a

arranger. Voulez-vous que la première partie de notre journée soit
to arrange Want you that the first part of our day is

consacrée à résoudre des problèmes, ensuite nous passerons à la
devoted to resolve of the problems subsequently we pass to the
sums

géographie. Et demain, sans faute, nous raconterons des histoires,
geography And tomorrow without fault we will tell -of the- stories

nous étudierons ensuite la formation de la terre. Quant à
we study subsequently the formation of the earth As to

l'astronomie, ce soir, après dîner, cela me semble tout indiqué de
the astronomy this evening after dinner that me appears all indicated of

l'étudier en plein ciel, alors que brillent les étoiles.
it to study in full sky then that shine the stars
as

— Oui ! oui ! crièrent la plupart des élèves.
— Yes ! yes ! shouted the largest part of the students

Mais en un coin, le groupe des jeunes qui voulait des histoires,
But in a corner the group of the young ones who wanted -of the- stories

protestait, ne voulant pas attendre au lendemain, voulant partir si
protested not wanting -not- to await -at- the following day wanting to leave if

on ne leur donnait pas satisfaction.
one not them gave -not- satisfaction

Liberta prit un livre sur la table devant elle et le leur donna.
Liberta took a book on the table in front of her and it them gave

— Puisque vous voulez absolument des histoires, dit-elle, voici de quoi
— Since you want absolutely of the stories said she see-here of what

choisir. Vous y trouverez celle de Gutenberg et de l'imprimerie. Vous
to choose You there will find that of Gutenberg and of the printing You

pouvez vous mettre dans un coin, ou aller au jardin, comme il vous
can yourself set in a corner or go to the garden like it you

plaira, et lire tout ce que vous voudrez. »
will please and read all this that you want

Les choses ainsi arrangées, on put commencer, le silence s'était
The things thus arranged one could begin the silence itself was
itself had

rétabli.
reestablished

On se mit donc à l'étude des problèmes. Liberta commença par
One himself put then to the study of the problems Liberta started by
sums

en dicter quelques-uns qu'un des élèves venait résoudre au
of them to dictate some that one of the students came to solve at the
. came

tableau. Puis ce fut le tour aux élèves d'en dicter, que leurs
(black)board Then this was the turn to the students of from them dictate that their

camarades devaient résoudre.
comrades must to resolve

Nono remarqua un des élèves qui voulait toujours parler avant son
Nono noted one of the students who wanted always speak before his

tour, haussait les épaules lorsqu'un de ceux interrogé semblait embarrassé,
turn shrugged the shoulders when one of those interrogated seemed embarrassed

et qui voulait toujours trouver des solutions meilleures.
and who wanted always to find of the solutions best

— Jacquot, — c'était le nom de l'élève — Jacquot, fit Liberta, à
— Jacquot — it was the name of the students — Jacquot made Liberta at
said

votre tour, dictez un problème.
your turn dictate a problem
sum

Jacquot énonça un problème où il était question d'heures, de
Jacquot enunciated a problem where it was question of hours of
uttered sum question

secondes, de litres, et de mètres. Un problème très compliqué et qu'il
seconds of liters and of meters A problem very complicated and that he

était fier d'avoir trouvé.
was proud of to have found

C'était si compliqué que personne ne put le résoudre, et que l'auteur
It was so complicated that no one -not- could it solve and that the author

lui-même invité à l'expliquer, s'embarrassa si bien dans ses opérations
him self invited to it explain himself embarrassed so well in its operations

qu'il ne put en sortir.
that he not could of it go out

Comme il était pas mal vaniteux, les autres enfants se moquèrent
Like he was not bad conceited the other children themselves mocked
little

de lui, et Liberta lui fit remarquer qu'il valait mieux prendre
of him and Liberta him made notice that it was worth better to take
was

des problèmes plus simples et bien les raisonner que d'en prendre
-of the- problems more simple and well them to reason than of them to take
sums explain

de si compliqués et ne pas les comprendre. Puis elle lui fit voir
of so complicated and not -not- them to understand Then she him made see

en quoi péchait son problème, et pourquoi il était impossible de lui
in what sinned his problem and why it was impossible of for it
went wrong sum

trouver une solution.
to find a solution

Jacquot, très mortifié, alla à sa place. Mais il profita d'un moment
Jacquot very mortified went to his place But he took advantage of a moment

où l'on ne faisait plus attention à lui, pour s'esquiver.
where -it- one not made more attention to him for himself to slip (out)

À un moment, ce fut au tour de Nono de dicter. Et il en
At a moment it was -at- the turn of Nono -of- to dictate And he of it

dicta un qu'il se rappelait avoir fait à l'école où il s'agissait
dictated one that he himself reminded to have made at the school where it itself dealt

d'un marchand qui ayant acheté tant de pièces de drap, de tant
of a merchant who having bought so many -of- pieces of sheet of so many

de mètres, pour la somme de tant, on demandait ce qu'il
-of- meters for the sum of so much one asked this that it

fallait qu'il le vendît le mètre pour faire un bénéfice de tant.
was necessary that he it sold the metre for to make a profit of so much

— Ton problème est bien posé, fit Solidaria qui venait de paraître
— Your problem is well perched made Solidaria who came of to appear
said

parmi les enfants, mais il est posé selon les règles égoïstes que
among the children But it is posed according to the rules egoists that
capitalist

l'on vous enseigne aux écoles d'un monde où l'on ne travaille
-it- one you teaches at the schools of a world where -it- one not works

qu'en vue de spéculer sur ses semblables.
(other) than in sight of to speculate on ones similars
to earn money the backs of ones fellow humans

Ici, le problème se pose tout autrement ; à ta place, je dirais :
Here the problem itself poses all otherwise ; at your place I would say :

« Étant donné qu'un homme a tant de pièces de drap, qu'il peut,
Being given that a man has so many -of- pieces of sheet that he can

dans chaque pièce, tirer tant d'habits, à combien d'amis pourra-t-il
in each piece pull so many of clothes to how many -of- friends will he
from

faire plaisir, en en donnant un à chacun ? »
make pleasure in of them giving one to each one ?

Va, mon enfant, ajouta-t-elle, en embrassant Nono, tu es peut-être
Go my child added she in kissing Nono you are maybe

encore un peu jeune pour bien en saisir la différence, mais lorsque
still a bit young for well of it to grasp the difference but when

tu seras en âge de comparer, tu comprendras. »
you will be in age of to compare you will understand

Cela termina la leçon d'arithmétique, et l'on passa, comme il était
That ended the lesson of math and -it- one passed like it was

convenu, à celle de géographie.
agreed to that of geography

Liberta expliqua aux enfants ce que c'était qu'un continent, un cap, une
Liberta explained to the children this that it was that a continent a cape an
what a continent was

île, une presqu'île, un archipel. Et, au moyen d'un appareil semblable
island a peninsula an archipelago And at the means of an apparatus similar
by

à une lanterne magique, elle faisait passer sous leurs yeux, la
to a lantern magic she made pass under their eyes the

représentation de ce qu'elle leur expliquait.
representation of this that she them explained

Pour que sa leçon fût moins aride, elle l'entrecoupait de récits se
For that her lesson was less dry she it interspersed with stories themselves

rapportant à ses explications, et pendant qu'elle racontait, l'appareil faisait
reporting to her explanations and while that she told the device made
relating

défiler sur le mur, les scènes animées de l'anecdote racontée.
parade on the wall the scenes animated of the anecdote narrated

Les partisans de l'histoire avaient eux-mêmes fini par déserter leur
The supporters of the story had themselves finished by to desert their

coin, venant écouter les récits de Liberta.
corner coming to hear the stories of Liberta

D'autres, au contraire, que cela ennuyait ou qui éprouvaient le besoin
-Of- others on the contrary that that bored or who experienced the need

de se dégourdir les jambes, s'étaient levés sans bruit ; filant
of themselves to stretch the legs themselves were raised without noise ; moving
themselves had

du côté des jardins.
of the side of the gardens
to the

Aussi Liberta, qui savait qu'il ne faut pas abuser de l'attention
Also Liberta who knew that it not is necessary -not- to abuse -of- the attention

des enfants, même lorsqu'ils sont intéressés, le jeune âge éprouvant le
of the children even when they are interested the young age experiencing the

besoin de se remuer, de s'agiter, courir, faire du bruit, leva la
need of itself to stir of itself to move run to make -of the- noise lifted the
ended

séance. Et les enfants, libres, coururent au jardin où Labor, avec
meeting And the children free ran to the garden where Labor with

quelques-uns ceux qui avaient préféré le grand air, présidait aux travaux
some (of) those who had prefered the large air presided to the works
open

de culture.
of culture

Nono fut attiré en un groupe qui, près d'une forge portative, travaillait
Nono was attracted in a group who near of a forge portable worked
to

à réparer les bêches, fourches et autres instruments aratoires.
to repair the spades hayforks and others instruments (of) plowing

Il voyait les étincelles bleues et rouges, pareilles à des
He saw the sparks blue and red similar to -of the-

feux d'artifices, jaillir du fer incandescent sous les coups de
fires of artificials spout from the iron incandescent under the blows of
fireworks

marteau. Et lui aussi, voulant en faire jaillir de semblables, se
(the) hammer And him also wanting of it to make spout of similar himself
like that

mit à marteler le fer, se faisant expliquer comment il fallait le
put to hammer the iron himself making explain how it was necessary it

façonner pour que son travail fût utilisable.
to fashion for that his work was usable
to do

Le soir arriva, que Nono, qui s'était mêlé à tout, croyait
The evening arrived that Nono who himself was mixed to everyone believed
himself had with

n'être encore qu'au milieu de la journée, tant elle lui avait
not to be still than at the middle of the day so much she him had
it

semblé courte.
appeared short

Après la leçon d'astronomie, qui eut lieu après le dîner, dans un
After the lesson of astronomy which had place after -the- dinner in an
took

observatoire arrangé sur une tour du château, Amorata leur donna
observatory arranged on a tower of the castle Amorata them gave

des nouvelles de leurs parents, puis tout le monde alla se
-of the- news of their parents then all the world went themselves

coucher.
to lay down

Mais, auparavant, les amis de Nono l'emmenèrent à la bibliothèque où
But before the friends of Nono him took along to the library where

il fit choix de deux volumes dont les titres et les images
he made (a) choice of two volumes of which the titles and the images

semblaient lui promettre des merveilles.
appeared him to promise -of the- wonders

Monté dans sa chambre, Nono, qui avait encore, au dîner, fourré dans
Mounted in his room Nono who had still at the dinner shoved in
Climbed up to

sa poche quelques fruits de la table, voulut les joindre à ceux qu'il
his pocket some fruits from the table wanted them join to those that he

avait pris à midi ; mais, en ouvrant le tiroir de l'armoire où il
had taken at noon ; but in opening the drawer of the wardrobe where he

les avait mis, il ne fut pas peu surpris de voir à leur place
them had put he not was -not- little surprised of to see at their place

d`affreux petits lutins qui lui faisaient des grimaces, pendant que ceux
of horrible little sprites which him made of the funny faces during that those

qu'il apportait se changeaient, dans sa main en d'aussi horribles
that he brought themselves changed in his hand in of likewise horrible

gnomes qui se cramponnaient après lui, essayant de l'entraîner.
gnomes which themselves clung after him trying of him to drag along
to

Nono, effrayé, jeta un cri perçant.
Nono frightened threw a cry piercing
uttered

Solidaria, près de lui, n'eut qu'à faire un signe pour faire disparaître
Solidaria near -of- him not had than to make a sign for to make disappear

ces effrayantes petites apparitions.
these frightening small apparitions

Nono était tout tremblant.
Nono was all trembling
trembling all over

— Ce qui t'arrive est de ma faute, fit Solidaria, j`aurais
— This which happens to you is -of- my fault made Solidaria I should have
said

dû te prévenir qu'en ce pays, ce n'est plus comme en le monde
had to you warn that in this country this not is more like in the world
　　warned you

d'où tu viens. Il n'y a pas à craindre de jamais manquer de
from where you come It not there has -not- to fear of ever lack of
　　There is nothing

rien. Ces fruits que tu mets de côté, tu n'aurais jamais pu les
nothing These fruits that you put of side you not would ever been able them
anything　　　　　　a-

manger, puisque tu as, à table, toujours plus qu'il ne te
to eat since you have at (the) table always more than -it- -not- (to) you

faut. Ce seraient des ordinaires, ils se gâteraient pour
is necessary This would be of the ordinary they themselves would spoil for

rien.
nothing

Mais ici, comme c'est un défaut sans excuse de mettre à part des
But here like it is a fault without excuse of to put to side of the
　　　　　　　　　　　　　　　　　　　　　　　a-

choses dont on ne peut tirer aucun parti soi-même, alors qu'elles
things of which one not can draw any action oneself then that they
　　　　　　　　　　　　　advantage　　since

peuvent être utiles à d'autres ; pour punir les avares, elles se
can be useful to -of- others ; for to punish the scrooges they themselves

changent en lutins qui, s'ils avaient été plus nombreux, t'auraient
change in sprites which if they had been more numerous would have you

entraîné chez notre ennemi Monnaïus avant que je puisse te venir en
dragged along with our enemy Monnaïus before that I could you come in
　　　to

aide.
aide

Pour cette fois-ci, sois-en quitte pour la peur, mais ne recommence
For this time there be-in quits for the fear but not start again
　　　　　　　　　by　　　　　　do it again

pas. »
-not-

Et, ayant embrassé Nono, elle disparut comme elle était venue, tandis
And having embraced Nono she disappeared like she was come while
　　　　　　　　　　　　　　　　　had

que ce dernier, tout penaud, se glissait tout frissonnant dans le lit,
that this last (one) all sheepish himself slipped all shivering in the bed

craignant de voir reparaître les horribles monstres qui l'avaient tant
fearing of to see reappear the horrible monsters who him had so much

effrayé.
frightened

La promenade
The walk

Nono	se	trouvait	à	Autonomie,	depuis	un	certain	temps,	et	ce
Nono	himself	found	at	Autonomy (land)	since	a	certain	time	and	this

temps	semblait	avoir	passé	comme	un	rêve.
time	seemed	to have	passed	like	a	dreams

Le	temps	s'était	écoulé	calme	;	chaque	jour	amenant	des	travaux	et
The	time	itself was / itself had	passed	calm	;	each	day	bringing	-of the-	works	and

des	plaisirs	variés,	qui	empêchaient	les	enfants	de	s'ennuyer	un	seul
-of the-	pleasures	varied	which	prevented	the	children	of	to be bored	a	single

instant.
moment

Nono	connaissait	maintenant	tous	ses	camarades	par	leur	nom,	savait	qui
Nono	knew	now	all	his	comrades	by	their	name	knew	who

étaient	leurs	parents,	ce	qu'ils	étaient,	de	quel	pays	ils	venaient.
were	their	parents	this	that they	were / what profession these had	of	what	country	they	came

La	plupart	du	temps,	les	heures	d'école	se	dépensaient	dans
The	largest part	of the	time	the	hours	of school	themselves	dispensed	in

les	jardins,	sur	les	pelouses	;	mais,	pour	varier,	on	avait	projeté,	depuis
the	gardens	on	the	lawns	;	but	for	to vary	one	had	projected planned	since

longtemps	déjà,	une	longue	promenade	à	travers	les	bois	qui
(a) long time	already	a	long	walk	-at-	through	the	woods	which

avoisinaient	le	pays	d'Autonomie.	Et	ce	jour	était	venu.
were around	the	country	of Autonomy	And	this	day	was	come had

La	veille,	on	avait	préparé	tout	l'attirail	nécessaire	à	cette
The	evening before	they	had	prepared	all	the paraphernalia	necessary	for	this

excursion	qui	devait	être,	en	même	temps,	une	leçon	d'histoire
excursion	which	must	be	in	(the) same	time	a	lesson	of history

naturelle.
natural

On devait emporter de petites cannes, munies de marteaux, pour
they must carry -of- small sticks provided with hammers for

détacher les morceaux de rochers, de petits fers de bêche, pour
to detach -the- pieces of rocks -of- small irons of spade for
spades

sortir de terre, avec leurs racines, les plantes que l'on désirerait
to get out of (the) earth with their roots the plants that -it- they would desire

étudier, ou ramener à Autonomie... Des filets pour attraper au vol
to study or to bring to Autonomy -Of the- nets for to catch at the flight

les insectes complétaient cet attirail de naturalistes.
the insects completed this equipment of naturalists

Les vivres étaient entassés dans de petits sacs ajustés aux épaules des
The rations were piled up in -of- small bags adjusted to the shoulders of the
attached

petits garçons qui, étant plus forts, avaient charge de porter
small boys who being more strong had charge of to carry

l'approvisionnement de la troupe. Chacun avait, de plus, une musette, son
the provisioning of the band Each had of more a flute their
on top

bidon, et un gobelet pendu à son côté.
water bottle and a cup hung at their side

Lorsque tout le monde fut prêt, on se mit en route, dès le
When all the world was ready one oneself put in road from the
everybody

matin, avant que le soleil, trop chaud, ne rendît la marche trop
morning before that the sun too warm not rendered the march too
made

fatigante.
tiring

Initiativa, autre bon génie de Autonomie, sœur de Liberta et de
Initiativa other good genius of Autonomy (land) sister of Liberta and of

Solidaria, conduisait la colonne.
Solidaria led the column

Les enfants marchaient en babillant entre eux, ou en chantant des
The children moved while babbling/chatting between them or while singing -of- the

ballades que Harmomia, fille de Solidaria, avait composées
ballads that Harmomia daughter of Solidaria had composed

à leur intention.
at their intention
for them

Ce ne fut que lorsqu'on eut atteint les sentiers moins connus, que
It not was than when they had reached the trails least known that

l'on commença à s'occuper de découvrir quelques espèces moins
-it- they started to themselves occupy of to discover some species less

communes devant servir de base à la leçon de la halte. Chacun partit
common before serve of base to the lesson of the stop Each one left

à la découverte, le long du sentier, sous les taillis, ayant soin
to the discovery the long of the path under the thickets having care
along

seulement de marcher dans la direction de la halte.
only of to walk in the direction of the stop

Pour sa part Nono découvrit de superbes fleurs en forme de vase
For his side Nono discovered -of- great flowers in shape of (a) vase

au col allongé. Il courut, tout essoufflé, montrer sa trouvaille à
at the collar elongated He ran all out of breath to show his find to
with a

Botanicus, un de leurs professeurs, en lui disant :
Botanicus one of their professors in him saying :

— Regardez donc, monsieur Botanicus, la belle cage à mouches que
— Look then Mr. Botanicus the beautiful cage for flies that

je viens de trouver ! et il entr'ouvrit tout doucement une des fleurs
I come of to find ! and he half opened all softly one of the flowers

qui était déchirée, mais, malgré ses précautions, il s'en envola deux
which was torn but in spite of his precautions it itself of it flew two

ou trois petites mouches aux reflets vert-dorés.
or three small flies to the reflections green gold
with the

Botanicus prit les fleurs, puis assujetissant ses lunettes d'or sur son nez,
Botanicus took the flowers then putting on his glasses of gold on his nose

déclama :
declaimed :

— Ceci est l'Aristolochia clematitis ; une plante de la famille des
— This is the Aristolochia Clematitis ; a plant of the family of the

aristolochiées, et non une vulgaire cage à mouches. Ce qui a
Aristolochies, and not a vulgar cage for flies This which has

pu vous faire croire cela, c'est que, en effet, lorsque cette plante
been able you to make believe that this is that in effect when this plant

est en fleur, celle-ci est conformée de façon à laisser pénétrer les
is in flower this one here is shaped of way to let enter the

petits insectes semblables à ceux que vous voyez prisonniers. Mais, vous
small insects similar to those that you see captives But you

voyez ces poils qui sont plantés en biais le long du col à
see these hairs which are planted in angle the long of the collar at

l'intérieur de la fleur et dont la pointe se dirige vers le fond
the interior of the flower and of which the point itself directs towards the back

?
?

Et il leur montrait l'intérieur de la fleur ouverte.
And he them showed the interior of the flower opened

— Eh bien, tant que la fleur n'est pas fécondée, ces poils qui
— Eh well in as much as the flower not is -not- fertilized these hairs which

laissent bien entrer les mouches, les empêchent de sortir. Les mouches
let well enter the flies them prevent of to go out The flies

en se débattant, laissent tomber sur les stigmates de la fleur, le
in themselves thrashing let fall on the stigmata of the flower the

pollen qu'elles ont apporté du dehors. Aussitôt que la fleur est
pollen that they have brought from the outside Immediately that the flower is

fécondée, les poils tombent et laissent échapper les prisonnières ; mais,
fertilized the hairs fall and let escape the prisoners ; But

auparavant, les anthères se sont ouvertes, ont laissé échapper le
before the anthers themselves are opened have left escape the

pollen qu'elles contiennent, et les mouches vont le porter sur d'autres
pollen that they contain and the flies go it carry on -of- other

plantes.
plants

Et il leur montra une autre fleur plus avancée, où en effet, les
And he them showed an other flower more advanced where in fact the

poils de l'intérieur étaient tombés.
hairs of the interior were fallen
had

Ce Botanicus était un être original qui, depuis peu, habitait
This Botanicus was a being original who since little lived in
unique a short while

Autonomie. Il connaissait toute l'histoire naturelle par cœur ; à
Autonomy (land) He knew all the history natural by heart ; at

première vue, il pouvait dire le nom, la famille, le genre, l'espèce,
first sight he could say the name the family the sort the species

l'habitat, l'époque de la floraison, si c'était une plante ; de la
the habitat the time of the flowering if it was a plant ; of the
bloom

ponte, si c'était un insecte. C'était un vrai dictionnaire ambulant.
laying season if it was an insect It was a true dictionary traveling

Mais, en dehors de son histoire naturelle, il était d'une naïveté
But in outside of his history natural he was of a naivete

phénoménale. Maladroit de ses doigts, il était incapable de tout travail
phenomenal Clumsy with his fingers he was incapable of all work

manuel. Lorsqu'il voulait aider les autres habitants de la colonie, c'était
manual When he wanted to help the other inhabitants of the colony it was

rare qu'il ne lui arrivât pas quelque accident. S'il voulait, par
rare that -it- not him arrived -not- some accident If he wanted for
happened

exemple, aider à mettre le couvert, on était sûr de le voir mettre
example help to set the covered one was sure of him to see set
table break

en pièces une pile d'assiettes, ou renverser sur la nappe un ou deux
in pieces a pile of plates or overthrow on the sheet one or two

pots de lait.
jars of milk

Dans les débuts, les enfants avaient essayé de lui faire comprendre
In the beginnings the children had tried of him to make understand

qu'ils auraient plus vite fait sans lui ; mais Botanicus, qui voulait
that they would have more quickly done without him ; but Botanicus who wanted

absolument se rendre utile, persistait à vouloir venir en aide chaque
absolutely himself render useful persisted to want to come in aide each

fois qu'un travail se présentait ; de sorte que les Autonomiens
time that a work itself presented ; of kind that the (boys and girls of) Autonomia

en avaient pris leur parti, s'ingéniant seulement à prévenir les
of it had taken their left themselves striving only to prevent the

accidents lorsqu'ils les voyaient près de se produire.
accidents when they them saw near of themselves to produce

Avant de venir à Autonomie, il occupait une place de professeur de
Before of to come to Autonomy (land) he occupied a place of professor of

physiologie végétale dans un laboratoire de Paris. S'il avait eu la
physiology vegetable in a laboratory of Paris. If he had had the

moindre parcelle d'ambition, un peu de souplesse d'échine, su flatter
least parcel of ambition a bit of flexibility of spine known to flatter

les hommes au pouvoir, et possédé un peu plus d'aptitude pour
the men at the in power, and possessed a bit more of aptitude for

donner des entorses aux vérités et aux rapprochements qui
to give of the violations/twistings to the of the truths and to the reconciliations which

se dégageaient de ses leçons, nul doute qu'il n'eût obtenu une
itself emanated from his lessons, no doubt that he would have obtained a

haute place, de grands honneurs et de gros appointements.
high place, with great honors and with big pay

Mais, absorbé par sa passion favorite, l'étude, il s'occupait fort peu
But, absorbed by his passion favorite the study he himself occupied very little

de ces mesquineries. Il était ravi lorsqu'il avait pu classer
with these pettinesses He was delighted when he had been able to rank

quelque espèce nouvelle, ou lorsqu'il venait de découvrir de quelque
some species new or when he came of to discover of some

insecte un trait de mœurs ignoré.
insect a feature of mores unknown

Plus d'une fois, au cours de ses leçons, il lui arrivait d'émettre des
More than one time at the course of his lessons it him arrived of to issue of the

aperçus nouveaux qu'il tirait de ses études pour les appliquer à la
perceptions new that he drew from his studies for them to apply to the
opinions

vie sociale, ce qui, le plus souvent, allait à l'encontre des théories
life social this which -the- most often went to the opposite of the theories

que faisaient enseigner les hommes au pouvoir.
that made teach the men at the power
in

Botanicus était loin de faire cela par esprit d'opposition. À vrai dire,
Botanicus was far from to make that by mind of opposition At true to say

le plus souvent, il émettait ses idées, les plus subversives, sans se
the most often he issued his ideas the more subversive without himself

douter qu'il formulât une critique contre la société dans laquelle il
to doubt that he should formulate a critique against the society in which he
to think

vivait ; mais elles n'en étaient que plus terribles par leur vérité
lived ; but they not of it were than more terrible by their truth

scientifique. Aussi, places, honneurs et gros émoluments allaient à des
scientist So seats honors and big emoluments went to -of the-

collègues moins savants, dont la science était plutôt faite de leçons
colleagues less savant of which the science was more made of lessons

apprises que d'études personnelles, mais qui savaient ingénieusement
learned that of study personal but who knew ingeniously

habiller et déguiser les vérités, lorsqu'il s'en trouvait par hasard dans
to dress and disguise the truths when it itself of it found by chance in

leurs leçons.
their lessons

Et un beau jour, sous prétexte d'économies à réaliser, on supprima
And one beautiful day under pretext of savings to realize one abolished

la chaire de Botanicus, pour se débarrasser du professeur gênant.
the pulpit of Botanicus, for himself to get rid of the professor embarrassing

Botanicus entra dans un lycée où l'on apprenait la science
Botanicus entered in a high school where -it- one taught the science

officielle aux petits rejetons de ceux qui s'intitulent les « classes
official to the little rejects of those who themselves entitle the classes

dirigeantes » ; mais, là encore, il ne sut pas retenir sa langue, et
ruling ; but there still he not knew -not- to retain his tongue and

comme il était d'un caractère très indulgent, ne savait prononcer aucune
like he was of a character very indulgent not knew to pronounce any

parole de sévérité, encore moins punir, les horribles petits morveux qui
word of severity, still least punish the horrible small snotty noses who

tremblaient sous leur précédent professeur qui les accablait de
shook under their previous professor which them overwhelmed of

pensums, de mauvaises notes, et les privait de sortie, ne tardèrent
impositions of bad grades and them deprived of to exit (so) not (they) delayed

pas à se moquer du nouveau, à lui jouer les tours les plus
-not- to themselves mock of the new (teacher) to him play the turns the most
tricks

terribles ce qui servit de prétexte à la direction pour le
terrible this which served of pretext to the direction for him
school leadership

remercier et le mettre sur le pavé.
to thank and him to put on the pavement

Solidaria, qui le connaissait, l'avait fait venir à Autonomie, mettant à
Solidaria who him knew him had made come to Autonomy (land) putting at

sa disposition plantes, insectes, instruments et tout ce dont il
his disposition plants insects instruments and all this of which he

aurait besoin pour ses études, à la seule condition d'enseigner aux
would have need for his studies, at the sole condition of to teach to the

autres ce qu'il savait. Botanicus avait accepté avec joie ; car
others this that he knew. Botanicus had accepted with joy ; because

il n'y avait pas pour lui de plus grand plaisir, lorsqu'il avait fait
it not there had -not- for him of more great pleasure when he had made
there was not

une découverte, que d'en faire part à tous.
a discovery, than of it to make share to all

Après avoir vécu un peu de temps à Autonomie, il n'avait pas
After to have lived a bit of time at Autonomy (land) he did not have -not-
in

tardé à se rendre compte combien ses facultés avaient été faussées
delayed to himself render account how much his faculties had been distorted

en s'enfermant exclusivement en une seule étude ; c'est pourquoi il
in locking himself exclusively in a single study ; this is why he

essayait de se refaire aux choses ordinaires de la vie ; mais, à
tried of himself to redo at the things ordinary of the life ; but at

chaque maladresse, il comprenait que c'était trop tard. Aussi, avec un
each clumsiness he understood that it was too late So with a

bon sourire résigné il disait aux enfants :
good smile resigned he said to the children :

— Je suis trop vieux pour changer maintenant. Il faut, mes enfants,
— I am too old for change now It is necessary my children

me prendre comme je suis. Mais que mon exemple vous serve de leçon.
me to take as I am But that my example you serve as lesson

Que vos préférences ne vous empêchent pas de vous rendre compte,
That your preferences not you prevent -not- of you to render account

même de ce qui vous semble le moins important.
even of this which (to) you appears the least important

Tel était l'homme. Mais revenons à notre promenade. Justement, je vois
Such was the man But (let's) return to our walk Exactly I see
Right now

Pat qui s'avance avec une plante qu'il vient de déraciner et qu'il
Pat who himself advances with a plant that he comes of uproot and that he
comes up just uprooted

semble considérer avec grand intérêt.
appears to consider with large interest

— Monsieur Botanicus, voyez donc la drôle de plante. Je crois que c'est
— Mr. Botanicus see then the funny of plant I believe that this is
this funny plant

un piège à mouches !
a trap for flies !

— Çà, fit Botanicus, assurant ses lunettes, et en élevant la plante à
— That made Botanicus, ensuring his glasses, and in raising the plant to
said adjusting

hauteur de ses yeux, c'est la Dionée attrape-mouches, genre de plante
(the) height of his eyes, that is the Dionee traps-flies (a) sort of plant
Venus flytrap

de la famille des Droséracées aux feuilles radicales, coupées sur les
from the family of the Sundews with the leaves radical cut on the
upwards

bords de profondes dentelures dont les deux moitiés — comme vous
edges with deep serrations of which the two halves — like you

pouvez le voir — et il leur fit admirer la plante — sont teintes
can it see — and he them made admire the plant — are colored

d'un beau rose de chair et se reploient brusquement, à la
with a beautiful pink of flesh and themselves refold abruptly at the

façon d'un piège à loup, sur l'insecte qui, attiré par l'éclat de
way of a trap for (a) wolf over the insect which attracted by the sparkle of

cette couleur, est assez imprudent pour venir s'y poser.
its color, is enough careless for to come itself there pose

Non seulement, cette plante les fait prisonniers, mais elle les mange !
Not only this plant them makes captives but she them eats !

»

Et comme les enfants ouvraient des yeux interrogateurs.
And how the children opened -of- the eyes interrogators
questioning

— Mais oui, elles les mange ! non pas comme vous mangez une
— But yes they them eat ! not -not- like you eat an

pomme avec une bouche et des dents. Mais laissez-la quelque temps
apple with a mouth and -of the- teeth But leave it some time

avec cette mouche qu'elle vient de prendre, la feuille qui s'est fermée
with this fly that she comes of to take the leaf which itself is closed

se rouvrira, mais il n'y aura plus de mouche. Elle l'aura
itself will reopen but it not there will have more -of- fly She her will have
there will be no

digérée !
digested !

— Monsieur Botanicus ! monsieur Botanicus, fit Mab en accourant. Venez
— Mr. Botanicus ! Mr. Botanicus made Mab in running up Come
said

donc voir un insecte noir, qui roule une boule dix fois grosse comme
then see an insect black which rolls a ball ten times (as) big as

lui.
him

— Ça, fit Botanicus, lorsqu'il fut arrivé, toujours armé de ses lunettes,
— That made Botanicus when he was arrived always armed with his glasses
said had

près des insectes, c'est le Scerabeus sacer, coléoptère qui se
near of the insects that is the Beetle sacred beetle which itself
dung beetle

distingue par un front râpeux, dont le prothorax est sur les côtés,
distinguishes by a face grated of which the prothorax is on the sides

garni de petits points élevés, aux élytres marqués de six sillons
decorated with small points raised to the elytra marked by six furrows
sheath

longitudinaux peu prononcés. Les cuisses postérieures sont sans dent à
longitudinal (a) bit pronounced The thighs front are without tooth at

leur bord postérieur ; il a des franges noires à la tête, au corselet
their side posterior ; it has of the fringes black at the head at the bodice
waist

et aux pattes. Les femelles les ont rouge brun aux jambes
and at the paws The females them have red brown at the legs

postérieures. Une coloration noire faiblement luisante achève de caractériser
front A coloring black feebly shining achieves of to characterize

le scarabée sacré. Les Égyptiens l'avaient en grande vénération. Ils en
the beetle sacred The Egyptian him had in large veneration They of it

avaient fait le symbole de la vie.
had made the symbol of the life

Cette boule que vous le voyez rouler, il va l'enterrer ; à l'intérieur,
This ball that you him see roll he goes to bury it ; at the interior

un œuf y est déposé. Lorsque le petit sera éclos, il n'aura
an egg there is deposited When the little (one) will be blooming he not will have

qu'à manger son berceau, fait des parties les plus délicates de cette
than to eat his cradle made of the parts the most delicate of this

boule que vous voyez triturer par cette bande de scarabées de toutes
ball that you see triturate by this band of beetles of all

sortes qui méritent ainsi le nom de bousiers qu'on leur donne. »
kinds who deserve thus the name of dung beetles that one them gives

Botanicus s'arrêta pour respirer, pendant que les enfants examinaient
Botanicus himself halted for to breathe during that the children examined
stopped

les insectes fort affairés.
the insects (which were) very busy

On les voyait, en effet, se remuer au milieu de la pâte
One them saw in fact themselves move at the middle of the dough

gluante. On pouvait assister à la confection de la boule qui avait
gluey One could assist to the confection of the ball which had

tant intrigué les enfants.
so much intrigued the children

Un Scarabée sacré ramenait sous son ventre, les parties qu'il avait
A Beetle sacred reapplied under his belly the parts that he had

choisies, et leur donnait une première façon puis faisant rouler la
selected and them gave a first form then making roll the

bonde avec ses pattes, il finissait de l'arrondir en y ajoutant
bung with his paws he ended of rounding it in there adding

graduellement de la matière.
gradually of the material
more

— Si nous avions le temps, fit Botanicus qui avait repris haleine,
— If we had the time made Botanicus who had resumed breath
said

nous pourrions suivre cet insecte dans sa besogne. On en a vu
we could to follow this insect in his task One of it has seen

qui faisaient des boules grosses comme une pomme. Il y en a
which made of the balls big like an apple It there of them has
There are of them

qui	en	font	de	la	grosseur	du	poing.	Puis	vous	pourriez	admirer
which	of it	make	of	the	size	of the	fist	Then	you	might	admire

leur	ingéniosité	à	les	rouler	jusqu'au	lieu	où	ils	ont	résolu	de
their	ingenuity	to	them	roll	up to the	place	where	they	have	decided	of

l'enfouir,	puis	aussi,	comment,	parfois,	il	se	trouve	de	leurs	congénères
to bury it	then	also	how	sometimes	it	itself	finds	of	their	congeners
							there are some of			

qui,	sous	prétexte	de	les	aider	s'emparent	du	fruit	de	leur	travail,
who	under	pretext	of	him	help	themselves empower	of the	fruit	of	their	work

tout	comme	cela	se	passe	chez	les	hommes.	—	Mais	cela	nous
all	like	that	itself	passes	with	the	men	—	But	that	us
							people				

prendrait	trop	de	temps.	Il	nous	faut	nous	remettre	en
would take	too (much)	of	time	It	(to) us	is necessary	ourselves	to set again	on

route.	»
(the) road	

Et,	peu	à	peu,	la	bande	se	répandait	par	les	chemins,	à	travers	les
And	bit	by	bit	the	band	itself	spread	by	the	paths	-at-	through	the

taillis,	à	la	recherche	de	quelque	curiosité.	On	faisait	halte	de	temps
thickets	-at-	the	search	of	some	curiosity	One	made	halt	from	time

en	temps	pour	rallier	les	retardataires.
in	time	for	to rally	the	latecomers
to					

En	marche	depuis	quelques	heures	déjà,	les	enfants	commençaient	à
In	march	since	some	hours	already	the	children	began	to

sentir	l'appétit	s'éveiller,	lorsqu'ils	arrivèrent	à	une	large	clairière,
feel	the appetite	itself awake	when they	arrived	on	a	wide	clearing
		awaken						

tapissée	d'un	beau	gazon	court	et	serré.	Au	centre	s'élevait	un
carpeted	with a	beautiful	lawn	short	and	closed	At the	center	itself arose	a
						dense				

cèdre	magnifique	sous	lequel	on	installa	le	couvert.
cedar	splendid	under	which	one	settled	the	covered
							eating utensils

Non	loin	de	là,	ombragée	d'un	énorme	saule,	sourdait	une	source
Not	far	from	there	shaded	by a	huge	willow	welled	a	source

fraîche, où l'on alla s'approvisionner, pour la mélanger aux
fresh where -it- one went oneself provision for it mix to the
stock up

excellentes liqueurs fabriquées avec les fruits que l'on récoltait à
excellent liqueurs fabricated with the fruits that -it- one harvested at

Autonomie.
Autonomy (land)

Les provisions déballées, on leur fit honneur, car les promeneurs
The supplies unpacked one them made honor because the walkers
ate them with pleasure

avaient amassé de l'appétit. Puis, lorsqu'il fut un peu calmé, les
had amassed -of- -the- appetite Then when it was a bit calmed the
gotten when the appetite

enfants heureux et exubérants accablèrent Solidaria, Botanicus, Initiativa,
children happy and exuberant overwhelmed Solidaria Botanicus Initiativa

de questions et de demandes sur toutes sortes de choses.
with questions and with requests about all kinds of things

Botanicus, pour sa part, avait fort à faire de répondre à tous, sur le
Botanicus for his side had strong to make of to answer to all on the
was very busy with

nom d'une plante, sa classification, l'utilité de tel ou tel organe, ses
name of a plant its classification the usefulness of such or such organ its
this or that

propriétés, ses particularités.
properties its particularities

Pour les insectes, lorsqu'on les avait bien examinés, on leur rendait la
For the insects when one them had well examined one them gave back the

liberté, dont les papillons, surtout, n'étaient guère à même de profiter
freedom which the butterflies especially not were hardly to even of to enjoy
capable

après tant de manipulations, leurs ailes légères ayant subi trop
after so much of manipulations their wings light having undergone too (much)
handling

d'avaries pour pouvoir leur être de quelque utilité.
of damages for to be able (to) them to be of some utility
damage

C'était la grande recommandation de Solidaria de ne prendre que
It was the large recommandation of Solidaria of not to take (other) than

ceux dont on avait absolument besoin, et de déployer pour les
those of which one had absolutely need and of to deploy for them

attraper, la plus grande adresse, afin de ne pas leur froisser les ailes.
catch the most large address so of not -not- them to crumple the wings
                care

Enfin quand tout le monde fut reposé, on se remit en route.
Finally when all the world was rested one oneself handed over on road
      everybody had

Mais on avait assez d'herborisation, Botanicus conduisit la petite troupe
But one had enough of botanizing Botanicus led the little band

à une carrière où il devait leur donner quelques notions de géologie.
to a quarry where he must them give some notions of geology

C'était une carrière de sable à ciel ouvert, au fond de laquelle on
It was a quarry of sand to sky opened to the bottom of which one
              open

pouvait descendre. Botanicus leur fit remarquer que la masse de terre
could go down Botanicus them made notice that the mass of earth

était formée de plusieurs couches de teintes et de matériaux différents,
was formed of several layers of colors and of materials different

leur expliquant que cette différenciation des couches était due à ce
them explaining that this differentiation of the layers was due to this

que des causes variées y avaient coopéré ; que c'étaient des
that of the causes varied there had cooperated ; that there were of the

dépôts amenés par les eaux et qui étaient lentement accumulés,
deposits brought by the waters and which were slowly accumulated

chaque couche exigeant des milliers et des dizaines de milliers
each bed demanding of the thousands and of the tens of thousands

d'années.
of years

Puis, ayant fouillé dans le sable, ils eurent la chance de découvrir
Then having rummaged in the sand they had the fortune of to discover

quelques-uns de ces silex taillés par les hommes primitifs pour leur
some of these flints cut by the men primitive for them

servir d'instruments, d'outils et d'armes, et dont Botanicus leur avait
to serve of instruments of tools and of weapons and of which Botanicus them had

déjà — already
parlé — spoken
lors — then / at other
d'autres — of others
excursions. — excursions

Cette — This
fois-ci, — time
il — he
leur — them
montra — showed
comment — how
on — one
reconnaissait — recognized
un — a
silex — flint
taillé — cut

intentionnellement, — intentionally
leur — them
dessinant — drawing
les — the
différentes — different
formes — forms
de — of
ceux — those
que — that
l'on — it one

connaissait. — knew

Ayant — Having
déterré — unearthed
un — a
rognon — kidney / rounded mineral
de — of
silex, — flint
et — and
s'armant — himself arming
d'une — with an
autre — other

grosse — big
pierre — stone
ronde, — round
il — he
essaya — tried
de — of
leur — them
donner — to give
quelques — some
notions — notions
de — of
la — the

façon — way
dont — of which
on — one
supposait — supposed
que — that
s'y — themselves there / it handled
prenaient — (they) took
nos — our
ancêtres — ancestors
pour — for

obtenir — to obtain
ces — these
lames — blades
longues, — long
minces — thin
et — and
coupantes — cutting
sur — on
les — the
bords, — edges
que — that

l'on — -it- one
suppose — assumed
avoir — to have
été — been
des — of the
couteaux — knives
; — ;
ces — these
autres — others
larges, — wide
presque — almost

quadrangulaires, — quadrangular
que — that
l'on — -it- one
désigne — designed / classified
sous — under
le — the
nom — name
de — of
haches. — axes
Mais, — But

malgré — in spite of
toutes — all
ses — his
tentatives, — attempts
il — he
ne — not
réussit — succeeded
qu'à — than to
obtenir — to obtain
des — of the

spécimens — specimens
bien — well
imparfaits — imperfect
et — and
bien — well
informes — shapeless
comparés — compared
à — to
ceux — those
qu'ils — that they

avaient — had
découverts. — uncovered / found

Pourtant — However
tels — such
quels, — those as is
cela — that
suffit — sufficed
à — to
donner — give
aux — to the
enfants — children
une — an
idée — idea
du — of the

mécanisme — mechanism
de — of
l'opération. — the operation
L'imperfection — The imperfection
des — of the
essais, — trials
leur — them
expliqua — explained

Botanicus, provenait du manque d'habitude. Les facilités de la vie
Botanicus came of the lacks of habit The facilities of the life

actuelle nous ont tellement gâtés, que s'il nous fallait revenir aux
current us have so much spoiled that if it (to) us was necessary to return to the

conditions d'existence de l'homme préhistorique, il nous faudrait
conditions of existence of the man prehistoric it (to) us would be necessary
prehistoric humans

déployer, pour faire ce qu'il faisait avec un cerveau rudimentaire, une
to deploy for to do this that he did with a brain rudimentary a

somme énorme d'efforts et d'intelligence.
sum huge of efforts and of intelligence
mass

Plus loin, se dressait un dolmen. Botanicus y conduisit ses auditeurs.
More far itself drew up a dolmen Botanicus there led his audience

Il leur fit remarquer le poids énorme des larges pierres dont il
He them made notice the weight huge of the wide stones of which it

était formé. En France ajouta-t-il, on a longtemps attribué leur
was formed In France added he one has long attributed their

construction aux Gaulois, prétendant y reconnaître les autels où ils
construction to the Gauls pretending there to recognize the altars where they

accomplissaient leurs sacrifices ; mais si les Gaulois ont pu
accomplished their sacrifices ; but if the Gauls have been able

s'en servir pour cet objet, on sait maintenant qu'ils existaient
themselves of it serve for this object one knows now that they existed

bien avant eux.
well before them

C'étaient les monuments funéraires d'une population inconnue qui a
They were the monuments funeral of a population unknown which has

laissé ainsi sa trace à travers l'Europe et l'Afrique. Des fouilles
left thus its trace -at- through -the- Europe and -the- Africa -Of the- digs

opérées à l'intérieur ont permis d'y découvrir des poteries et
operated at the interior have permitted to there discover -of the- pottery • and

des instruments contemporains des hommes qui taillaient la pierre.
-of the- instruments contemporary of the men who hewed the stone

Mais comme il se faisait l'heure de rentrer, on refit à la hâte une
But   as   it   itself   made   the time   of   to return   one   remade   at   the   haste   a
   they   ate

légère collation des restes du déjeuner, et on reprit gaiement la
light   collation   of the   remains   of the   lunch   and   they   continued   merrily   the

route de Autonomie en se tenant par groupes.
road   of   Autonomy (land)   while   each other   keeping   by   groups
    in

La rencontre
The encounter

La	troupe	revenait	donc	tout	doucement,	sans	se	presser,	lorsque
The	band	returned	then	all	softly calmly	without	itself	to hasten	when

Nono	vit	un	superbe	sphinx	tête de mort.	Il	eut	tout de	suite	l'idée
Nono	saw	a	superb	sphinx	death's head hawkmoth	He	had	all of	following immediately	the idea

de s'en emparer. Mais, lorsqu'il croyait s'en saisir, l'insecte, d'un
of himself of it to possess But when he believed himself of it to seize the insect with a

coup d'aile imprévu, échappait au filet et venait voltiger, comme pour
strike of wing unexpected escaped at the net and came to flutter like for

le narguer, tout près du chasseur qui, emporté par l'ardeur de la
him to taunt all near of the hunter who taken along by the ardor of the

chasse, se trouva bientôt entraîné loin de ses camarades.
hunt himself found soon dragged along far from his comrades

Enfin, arrivé près d'un gros chêne, le papillon semblant à portée, Nono
Finally arrived near -of- a big oak the butterfly seeming at bearing in reach Nono

crut le moment propice pour en faire la capture. Il calcula la
believed the moment propitious for of it to make the capture He calculated the

distance qui le séparait de l'insecte, assujettit le manche du filet
distance which him separated from the insect grabbed the handle of the net

et le lança... en plein sur le nez d'un gros monsieur, ventru, richement
and it launched in full on the nose of a large gentleman paunchy richly

habillé, à la figure vulgaire, au nez plat ; une énorme chaîne d'or
dressed at the with face vulgar at the with a nose flat ; a huge chain of gold

se balançant sur sa bedaine. Des diamants ornaient le plastron de
himself swinging on his belly -Of the- diamonds decorated the breast front of

sa chemise, une grosse escarboucle brillait au nœud de sa cravate ;
his shirt a big carbuncle gleamed at the knot of his tie ;

ses doigts étaient garnis de bagues. Il s'appuyait sur une canne
his fingers were garnished of rings He himself supported on a cane
leaned

d'or.
of gold

— Eh bien, mon petit, fais donc attention. Un peu plus tu
— Eh well my little (one) make then attention A bit more you

m'aplatissais le nez. — Nono remarqua intérieurement que ça aurait
me flatten the nose — Nono noted internally that that would have

été difficile de le rendre plus plat. — Tu n'as pas l'intention, que
been difficult of it to render more flat — You not have -not- the intention that
to make didn't mean to do it

je sache, de me prendre en ton filet ? Il me semble un peu petit, du
I know of me to take in your net ? It me appears a bit small of the
for the

reste.
rest

Et, content de ce qu'il prenait pour une fine plaisanterie, le gros
And satisfied of this that he took for a fine joke the fat

monsieur rit bruyamment aux éclats. Seulement son rire sonnait faux,
gentleman laughd loud at the bursts Only his laugh sounded false
with

et sa figure était loin d'inspirer la sympathie, lorsqu'on l'étudiait de
and his figure was far of to inspire the sympathy when one him studied from

près.
near

Mais Nono était un peu jeune pour être physionomiste. Et s'il fut
But Nono was a bit young for to be physiognomist And if he was

effrayé, ce fut de l'apparition subite du gros monsieur, et de se
frightened this was of the appearance sudden of the fat gentleman and of himself

voir éloigné de ses camarades, se rappelant les recommandations de
to see removed from his comrades himself recalling the recommendations of
far away remembering

Solidaria.
Solidaria

Cependant, comme il entendait, par intervalles, les chants et les éclats
However as he heard by intervals the chants and the bursts

de rire de la petite troupe, il comprit qu'ils ne devaient pas
of laughter of the little band he understood that they not must -not-

être fort éloignés, ce qui le rassura un peu.
be very far this which him reassured a bit

Cependant, il ne s'expliquait pas très bien comment il se trouvait
However he not himself explained -not- very well how he himself found
it was not very clear

un gros monsieur sous son filet alors que c'était un sphinx qu'il
a fat gentleman under his net then that it was a sphinx that he
where before

chassait.
chased

— Monsieur, je vous demande pardon ; je ne vous avais pas vu. Je
— Sir I you ask forgiveness ; I not you had -not- seen I

poursuivais un papillon que je croyais prendre lorsque je vous ai frappé
pursued a butterfly that I believed to take when I you have struck

de mon filet. Vous ai-je fait du mal ?
with my net You have I done of the harm ?

— Non, ce n'est rien, tu ne m'as attrapé que le bout du nez,
— No this not is nothing you not me have caught than the end of the nose

fit le gros monsieur en se le frottant. Mais comment se fait-il
made the fat gentleman in himself it rubbing But how itself does it
said can it be

que tu sois là tout seul à courir après les papillons ?
that you are there all alone to run after the butterflies ?

— Oh ! je ne suis pas seul, répliqua vivement Nono, toujours dominé
— Oh ! I not am -not- alone replied strongly Nono always dominated
still

par une vague crainte. Mes camarades sont en train de jouer dans le
by a vague fear My comrades are in process of to play in the

bois... Vous les entendez ! Et il prêta l'oreille.
woods You them hear ! And he lent the ear

— Ah ! Et vous êtes venus vous promener ici, avec vos maîtres ?
— Ah ! And you are come you walk here with your masters ?

— Nous n'avons pas de maîtres, dit fièrement Nono. Ce sont des
— We not have -not- -of- masters said proudly Nono These are -of the-
    don't have

amis ! Ils travaillent avec nous, jouent avec nous, nous enseignent ce
friends ! They work with us play with us us teach this

qu'ils savent, mais ne nous forcent jamais à faire ce que nous ne
that they know but not us force ever to do this that we not

savons pas, ou ne voulons pas faire.
know -not- or not want -not- to do

— Oh ! mon petit coq, comme tu te gendarmes », ricana le gros
— Oh ! my little rooster how you yourself police sneered the fat

monsieur. « C'est ce que je voulais dire. Tu es d'Autonomie à ce que
gentleman It is this that I wanted to say You are from Autonomy at this that

je vois. Et ça te plaît de ne jamais être qu'avec des enfants
I see And that you pleases of not ever to be (other) than with -of the- children

de ton âge, de toujours faire et voir la même chose ?
of your age of always to make and to see the same thing ?

— Nous ne faisons pas toujours la même chose. Nous changeons de
— We not do -not- always the same thing We change -of-

travaux et de jeux comme nous voulons, quand ça nous plaît.
works and -of- games like we want when that us pleases

— Oui, mais ça n'empêche pas que c'est toujours la même existence.
— Yes but that not hinders -not- that this is always the same existence

Vous voyez toujours le même pays, les mêmes personnes. Ça ne te
You see always the same country the same people That not you

plairait pas de voyager, de voir des pays nouveaux ?
would please -not- of to travel of to see of the countries new ?

Dans le pays que j'habite, moi, continua le gros monsieur, on voyage
In the country that I live me continued the fat gentleman one journeys

tout le temps. On va à la mer, on va dans les montagnes. Ainsi,
all the time One goes to the sea one goes in the mountains Thus

moi, je n'ai à m'occuper de rien, que de me promener. Il
me I not have to myself take care of nothing (other) than of myself to walk It

suffit d'avoir une baguette magique comme j'en ai une — et il
is enough of to have a stick magic like I of it have one — and he

montra sa canne — pour avoir tout ce que l'on désire.
showed his cane — for to have all this that -it- one wishes

Ainsi, te voilà en nage d'avoir couru après un insecte que tu
Thus you see there in swim of having run after an insect that you
all sweaty

voulais, et que tu n'as pas pu attraper. Moi, sans me
wanted and that you not have -not- been able to catch Me without myself

déranger, je vais te donner ce Bombyx qui voltige là, au-dessus de
to bother I go you give this Moth which vaults there above of
flutters

ce buisson que tu vois, près de toi. »
this bush that you see near of you

Et le personnage, levant sa baguette dans la direction qu'il indiquait,
And the character raising his stick in the direction that he stated

fit un signe, et le Bombyx se trouva dans les doigts de Nono.
made a sign and the Moth himself found in the fingers of Nono

L'enfant prit craintivement l'insecte et le considéra attentivement.
The child took fearfully the insect and it considered/studied closely

C'était une femelle du genre des Lépidoptères. Il lui sembla que
It was a female of the sort of the Lepidoptera It him seemed that

l'insecte le considérait d'un air suppliant pendant que ses pattes étaient
the insect him considered with an air supplicant during that its paws were
looked at

agitées d'un tremblement convulsif.
agitated by a tremor convulsive

— Tiens ! voici une épingle pour le piquer dans ta collection, fit
— Hold ! see-here a hairpin for it to stick in your collection made
pin said

le monsieur en tendant une fine épingle d'or à Nono. »
the gentleman in extending a fine hairpin of gold to Nono

Mais celui-ci ouvrit les doigts, donnant la volée à l'insecte qui s'envola
But that one opened the fingers giving the flight to the insect which itself flew

en bourdonnant.
while buzzing

— Tu as eu tort, fit le gros monsieur, c'est une espèce très rare,
— You have had wrong made the fat gentleman It is a species very rare
You were wrong (to let it go) said

Tu aurais pu en tirer un bon prix, si tu n'en fais pas
You would have been able of it to draw a good price if you not of it make -not-
for it to get

collection. As-tu faim ? as-tu soif ? Assieds-toi, bois et mange, le
collection Have you hunger ? Have you thirst ? Seat yourself drink and eat the
Are you hungry Are you thirsty

couvert est mis. »
covered is set
dinner table

Il avait de nouveau étendu sa baguette dans la direction du gros
He had of new stretched out his stick in the direction of the big
again

chêne. Nono ébahi vit se dresser des tables portant une variété
oak Nono dumbfounded saw itself raise up -of the- tables carrying a variety

de plats garnis de viandes, de sauces, de pâtisseries. Des fioles
of dishes garnished of meat of sauces of pastries -Of the- vials

contenant des boissons de toutes les couleurs rafraîchissaient dans des
containing -of the- drinks of all the colors refreshed in of the

seaux d'argent remplis de glace.
buckets of silver full of ice

— Non, je n'ai pas faim, fit Nono que le gros homme
— No I not have -not- hunger made Nono that the fat man
I'm not hungry said

commençait à intéresser et qui lui semblait moins vilain.
began to interest and who him seemed less ugly

— Tu m'as l'air tout plein gentil, et tu me plais, reprit le gros
— You me have the air all full nice and you me please continued the fat
very

homme. J'aimerais avoir un fils comme toi. Veux-tu me suivre ? je te
man I would like to have a son like you Want you me to follow ? I you

montrerai tout plein de jolies choses que tu ignores.
will show all full of pretty things that you don't know
lots

— Je vous remercie, mais je ne vous connais pas. Je ne veux pas
— I you thank but I not you know -not- I not want -not-

quitter mes amis d'Autonomie. Ils seraient trop inquiets s'ils ne me
to leave my friends of Autonomy They would be too worried if they not me

voyaient pas revenir.
saw -not- return

— Tu vois que je peux tout ce que je veux, J'ai un moyen de les
— You see that I can all this that I want I have a means of them

prévenir.
warn

— Non, répliqua l'enfant, revenu à ses appréhensions. Je veux retourner
— No replied the child come back to his apprehensions I want to go back

vers Solidaria.
to Solidaria

— Tu crois que je mens ? que je ne suis pas capable de te faire
— You believe that I lie ? that I not am -not- capable of you to make

voir ce que je te promets ? Tiens ! petit entêté, prends cette
see this that I you promise ? Hold ! little stubborn (one) take this

lorgnette. Regarde les spectacles auxquels tu pourrais te mêler tous
lorgnette Watch the shows to the which you could yourself mix all

les jours ! »
the days !

Ce disant, il ramena sur se bedaine un étui qui pendait par une
This saying he brought back on his belly a case which hung by a
                  pulled

courroie à son côté et en tira une magnifique jumelle qu'il tendit
belt at his side and of it pulled a splendid twin that he extended
                                                        binoculars

à l'enfant.
to the child

Celui-ci la porta à ses yeux. Il distingua d'abord une grande salle
That one it carried to his eyes He distinguished of first a large room
                                              initially

où étaient rassemblés une multitude d'enfants. On leur distribuait toutes
where were gathered a multitude of children One them distributed all

sortes de friandises.
kinds of treats

Puis, on les revêtait d'habits magnifiques ; on les faisait monter
Then one them dressed with clothes magnificent ; one them made climb

dans de belles voitures tirées par de jolies chèvres blanches que
in -of- beautiful carriages pulled by -of- pretty goats white that

conduisaient de petits cochers coiffés de perruques poudrées, chaussés
drove -of- small coachmen capped with wigs powdery shod
were driven by

de grandes bottes à revers, couverts d'habits galonnés sur toutes les
with large boots at (the) side covered with clothes laced on all the

coutures.
seams

Puis, on les faisait monter dans des voitures plus solides, c'était la
Then one them made climb in -of the- carriages more solid it was the

plaine, la mer ; puis la montagne qu'ils grimpaient sur des mulets.
plain the sea ; then the mountain that they climbed on -of the- mules

Et puis des fêtes partout. On voyait qu'ils n'étaient occupés
And then -of the- festivals everywhere One saw that they not were busy

qu'à se distraire.
(other) than to themselves distract

Cependant Nono remarquait sur leur visage, par moments, un air de
However Nono noted on their face by moments an air of

contrainte et d'ennui, qu'il ne connaissait pas depuis qu'il était à
constraint and boredom that he not knew -not- since that he was at

Autonomie.
Autonomy (land)

Les scènes changeaient encore. Il voyait à nouveau une grande salle en
The scenes changed still He saw at new a large room in
                                     again

demi-cercle, garnie de grandes draperies aux franges d'or. Depuis le
semi circle furnished with large draperies to the fringes of gold From the
           decorated   with

plancher jusqu'au plafond, cette salle était divisée en loges garnies, elles
floor up to the ceiling this room was divided in lodges furnished they
                                                              decorated

aussi, de draperies et de franges d'or. Dans ces loges, des
also with draperies and with fringes of gold In these lodges -of the-

messieurs aux chemises éblouissantes de blancheur, en habits noirs, des
gentlemen to the shirts dazzling of whiteness in clothes black -of the-

femmes décolletées couvertes de diamants, des enfants
women with revealing necklines covered with diamonds -of the- children

richement habillés.
richly dressed

Au fond de la salle, sur des planches, une autre foule de gens,
At the back of the room on of the boards an other crowd of people

encore plus richement habillés, lui parut-il, se remuaient, se
still more richly dressed him appeared it themselves moved about themselves

trémoussaient au son d'une musique tantôt douce et mystérieuse,
jigged at the sound of a music sometimes sweet and mysterious

tantôt vive et alerte.
sometimes lively and alert

Nono, ébloui de tout ce mouvement, des lumières innombrables qui
Nono dazzled of all this movement of the lights countless which

éclairaient la salle, ôta, émerveillé, la jumelle de ses yeux.
lit the room removed marveled the twin from his eyes
marveling binoculars

— Eh bien ? questionna insidieusement le tentateur.
— Eh well ? questioned insidiously the tempter

— Oh ! que c'est beau ! » Et en lui-même, il se demanda s'il
— Oh ! what this is beautiful ! And in him self he himself asked if he
how

n'allait pas suivre l'homme.
not went -not- to follow the man
not would follow

Puis, voulant jeter un dernier coup d'œil, il porta à nouveau la
Then wanting to throw a last strike of eye he carried to new the
glance again

jumelle à sa vue. Mais l'ayant, par mégarde, changée de bout, ce fut un
twin to his sight But it having by inattention changed of end it was a
binoculars eyes reversed

horrible spectacle qu'il vit.
horrible spectacle that he saw

Il eut à peine le temps de distinguer des rues sales, tortueuses,
He had at pain/barely the time of to distinguish -of the- streets dirty winding

des maisons comme des casernes, aux logis sordides, habités par
-of the- houses like -of the- barracks to the/with the dwellings sleazy inhabited by

une population misérable, loqueteuse, aux figures souffrantes, occupée à
a population miserable ragged to the/with faces suffering occupied at

des besognes qu'il n'eut pas le temps de distinguer, mais qui
-of the- tasks that it/that there was not -not- the time of to distinguish, but which

lui semblèrent répugnantes.
him seemed disgusting

Cela n'eut que la durée d'un éclair. La jumelle lui fut violemment
That was not than the duration of a flash The twin/binoculars him was/were violently

arrachée des mains par le gros homme qui, d'une voix rude, lui dit
torn away from the hands by the fat man who with a voice hard him said

:

— Ne regarde pas de ce côté, ce n'est pas ton affaire, et ça
— Not look -not- from this side this not is -not- your business and that

n'en vaut pas la peine, du reste. »
not of it is worth -not- the trouble of the/for the rest

Nono, interloqué, fixait l'homme d'un air effrayé !
Nono speechless fixed the man with an air frightened !

Mais celui-ci avait repris sa mine doucereuse et ce fut d'une voix
But that one had resumed his looks sweetish and it was with a voice

pateline qu'il reprit :
wheedling that he continued :

— Je t'ai fait peur ; mais c'est que j'ai été effrayé moi-même.
— I you have made fear/afraid ; but it is that I have been frightened my self

C'est une pièce unique au monde, je ne donnerais pas cette lorgnette
This is a piece unique at the/in the world I not would give -not- this lorgnette

pour quoi que ce soit, et j'ai vu le moment où tu allais la
for what that it be and I have seen the moment where you went it

laisser échapper.
to let escape
        fall

Nono se demandait s'il avait réellement vu, ou si ce n'était pas
Nono himself asked if he had actually seen or if this not was -not-
                                                              more than

une illusion. Il se calma un peu, mais ses premières appréhensions
an illusion. He himself calmed a bit but his first apprehensions

lui étaient revenues. Il se recule de l'homme, et, d'une voix altérée,
him were returned He himself receded of the man and with a voice altered
    had

il cria : Hans ! Mab !
he shouted : Hans ! Mab !

— Que t'es bête, reprit l'homme, en essayant de lui prendre la
— What you are dumb continued the man in trying -of- him to take the
How

main, décide-toi, et je t'emmène. Mais fais vite, car je suis pressé
hand make a decision and I you take But make quickly because I am pressed
                                                                     in a hurry

!
!

On entendait la voix de Hans, Dick et Mab, qui appelaient leur
One heard the voices of Hans Dick and Mab who called their

camarade absent.
comrade absent

Et Nono reculant encore de l'homme, appela ses amis.
And Nono recoiling still from the man called his friends
                    even more

— Où donc te caches-tu ? fit la voix de Hans qui, cette fois,
— Where then you hide you ? made the voice of Hans who this time
                                said

paraissait tout près.
appeared all near

— Par ici, par ici, cria Nono.
— By here by here shouted Nono

Et il vit déboucher Hans d'un fourré, puis Dick, puis Mab d'un
And he saw come out Hans from a thicket then Dick then Mab from a

sentier voisin.
path neighboring

— Ce que tu nous as fait peur, firent-ils, tous ensemble. On te
— This that you us have made fear did they all together One you
How said they

croyait perdu. Voilà une heure que l'on te cherche. » Et tous lui
believed lost See there an hour that -it- one you searches And all him

sautèrent au cou.
jumped at the neck
around the

Le gros homme avait disparu.
The fat man had disappeared

Nono allait raconter à ses amis son aventure ; mais comme à un
Nono went to tell to his friends his adventure ; but as on a
wanted

moment donné, il avait été bien près de se laisser séduire et de
moment given he had been well near of himself to let seduce and of

suivre l'homme, il n'osa pas avouer à ses amis qu'il avait été
to follow the man he not dared -not- to confess to his friends that he had been

sur le point de les oublier et de les abandonner ; une fausse honte
on the point of them forget and of them abandon ; a false shame

le retint. Il résolut de taire son aventure, racontant seulement
him kept back He resolved of to be quiet about his adventure recounting only

qu'entraîné à la poursuite du sphinx il s'était égaré. Expliquant son
that dragged to the pursuit of the sphinx he himself was lost Explaining his

émotion par la crainte qu'il avait éprouvée en se voyant seul,
emotion by the fear that he had experienced in himself seeing alone

isolé, craignant de ne plus pouvoir rejoindre ses camarades.
isolated fearing of not (any)more to be able to rejoin his comrades

— Ah ! pas de danger que l'on t'oubliât, fit Hans ; nous aurions
— Ah ! no -of- danger that -it- one you forgot made Hans ; we would have
you forgets said

plutôt passé la nuit à te chercher. »
rather passed the night at you to search
searching you

Et comme les autres enfants appelaient, on se dirigea vers le
And like the other children called one oneself directed towards the
they themselves

gros de la colonne en répondant à leurs appels.
big of the column in answering to their calls
majority

Les dernières paroles de Hans furent un cruel reproche pour Nono qui
The last words of Hans were a cruel reproach for Nono who

sentit davantage son ingratitude à leur égard, s'accusant d'avoir voulu
felt more his ingratitude to their respect himself accusing of to have wanted

les quitter pour le premier inconnu venu.
them to leave for the first unknown (person) (having) come

Il fut de plus en plus persuadé qu'il devait taire son aventure,
He was of more in more convinced that he must be quiet about his adventure

persistant dans son mutisme à cet égard.
persisting in his mutism at this respect

En quoi il eut encore plus tort, car Solidaria l'aurait alors
In what he had still more wrong because Solidaria him would have then

prévenu que le gros monsieur n'était autre que Monnaïus, l'éternel
warned that the fat gentleman not was (any) other than Monnaïus the eternal

ennemi de Solidaria et de ses enfants : cela l'aurait mis sur ses
enemy of Solidaria and of her children : that her would have put on her

gardes, et lui aurait évité de plus grands malheurs par la suite.
guards and her would have avoided of more great misfortunes by the following
greater

Mais il est rare qu'une première faute n'en entraîne pas d'autres, et
But it is rare that a first fault not of it results -not- of others and
mistake in others

qu'un premier manque de confiance ne soit pas suivi d'un et
that a first lack of confidence not is -not- followed by one and

même de plusieurs mensonges.
(the) same of several lies

Les suites d'une première faute
The consequences of a first mistake

En regagnant Autonomie, Nono prit peu de part à la conversation. Il
In returning to Autonomy (land) Nono took bit -of- part to the conversation He
little in

réfléchissait à tout ce qu'il venait de voir.
thought to all this that he came of to see
of

Gamin de Paris, enfant d'ouvriers dont les plus grands voyages qu'ils
Kid of Paris child of workers of which the most great trips that they
biggest

pussent se permettre étaient une promenade au bois de Clamart
could themselves permit were a walk at the woods of Clamart

ou de Meudon, — c'était un événement lorsqu'on poussait jusqu'à celui
or of Meudon — it was an event when one pushed up to the one

de Verrières — il ne connaissait de la mer que les descriptions
of Verrieres — he not knew of the sea (other) than the descriptions

enthousiastes qu'il avait trouvées dans quelques livres. En fait de
enthusiastic that he had found in some books In fact of
Concerning

montagnes il ne connaissait que les buttes Chaumont et
mountains he not knew (other) than the hills (of) Chaumont and

Montmartre ; mais dans les mêmes livres, il avait lu la description de
Montmartre ; but in the same books he had read the description of

tableaux grandioses d'ascensions, il avait toujours, depuis, rêvé à de
scenes grandiose of ascents he had always since dreamed -to- of

semblables voyages. Aussi les suggestions du gros monsieur étaient-elles
similar trips So the suggestions of the fat gentleman were they

venues attiser ses désirs.
come to stir his desires

Puis, sans vouloir faire de morale, trop relative qu'elle est, changeant
Then without to want to do of moral too relative that she is changing
to preach morals

avec les latitudes, climats, mœurs et éducation — chose que mes petits
with the latitudes climates mores and education — thing that my small

lecteurs apprendront plus tard, lorsque, sortis de l'école ou du
readers will learn more late when out of the school or of the
later

lycée où on leur apprend un tas de choses fausses, ils
high school where one them learns a heap of things false they

éprouveront le besoin de refaire leur éducation eux-mêmes, pour se
will experience the need of to redo their education themselves for themselves

décrasser le cerveau des niaiseries qu'on leur aura enseignées ; —
to scrub the brain of the sillinesses that they them will have taught ; —

je le répète, sans vouloir faire de la morale, il faut reconnaître
I it say again without to want to make of the moral it is necessary to recognize
to preach morals

que lorsqu'on a fait quelque chose qu'on n'aurait pas dû faire, on
that when one has does some thing that one would not -not- had to to do one

est assez mal satisfait de soi-même. Et cela vous rend pointu et fort
is enough badly satisfied of oneself And that you makes sharp and very
rather

grincheux, parce que, au lieu de franchement avouer ses torts, on
grumpy because that at the place of frankly to confess ones wrongs one

aime mieux exhaler sa mauvaise humeur. C'est ce qui arriva à Nono.
loves better to exhale his bad mood This is this which arrived to Nono

Tourmenté par ses désirs, par le reproche de sa conscience — qui
Tormented by his desires by the reproach of his consciousness — which

n'est pas une voix mise au dedans de nous par un dieu que l'on
not is -not- a voice put at the inside of us by a god that -it- one

n'a jamais vu comme l'affirment les prêtres, mais bien une opération
not has ever seen like it affirm the priests but well an operation

de notre jugement qui nous indique que nous avons fait quelque
of our (own) judgment which us indicates that we have done some

chose qui n'est pas juste, — Nono resta taciturne jusqu'à l'arrivée à
thing who not is -not- right — Nono remained taciturn up to the arrival to

Autonomie, ne répondant que par monosyllabes à l'empressement
Autonomy (land) not answering (other) than by monosyllables to the friendliness

de ses amis.
of his friends

Il était donc dans un état très électrique, lorsqu'en dressant le couvert,
He was then in a state very electric when raising the cutlery

il alla se buter contre un des membres d'un groupe moins lié
he went himself to bump against one of the members of a group less bound

avec le sien. La pile d'assiettes qu'il tenait lui échappa des mains
with the his The pile of plates that he kept him escaped from the hands

et se brisa à terre.
and itself broke on earth
          the ground

Quoique ce fût sa faute à lui, Nono, qui avait marché sans faire
Though this was his fault to him Nono who had walked without to make
                    of   to pay

attention, l'autre ayant bien essayé de se garer, c'était une trop
attention the other having well tried of himself shelter it was a too
                                          to evade

bonne occasion d'épancher sa mauvaise humeur pour que Nono n'en
good opportunity to pour his bad mood for that Nono not of it

profitât pas :
should profit -not- :

— Fais donc attention, animal ! » et, furieux, il lui détacha un coup
— Make then attention animal !   and furious he him untied a strike
    Pay   gave

de poing.
of fist

Le pauvre en resta si interloqué qu'il ne sut que répliquer,
The poor (boy) of it remained so speechless that he not knew what to reply

s'attendant peu à cette algarade. Pleurant, il alla se réfugier près
expecting little -to- this outburst Weeping he went himself to hide near

de ses camarades habituels.
of his comrades usual

— Ho ! le méchant, fit Mab qui se trouvait là avec Hans, et
— Ho ! the mean made Mab who herself found there with Hans and
          you're mean said

avait assisté à la scène complète. C'est toi qui es allé te buter
had assisted at the scene complete It is you who are gone yourself bump
witnessed the whole scene has

contre lui, c'est toi qui as tort et tu le bats.
against him it is you who have wrong and you him hit
are

— Hé bien ! pourquoi se trouvait-il sur mon chemin ? » fit Nono
— Hey! well ! why himself was he on my way ? made Nono
said

rendu plus furieux encore, parce qu'il sentait bien que le reproche
rendered more furious still because that he felt well that the reproach
made

était mérité. »
was deserved

D'autant plus qu'en donnant le coup de poing, il avait entrevu Solidaria
Especially more as in giving the strike of fist he had glimpsed Solidaria

s'éloignant de lui, les yeux pleins de reproches.
herself moving away from him the eyes full of reproaches

Labor qui, au milieu des autres enfants, avait pour eux le visage
Labor who at the middle of the other children had for them the face

aussi aimable et avenant que d'habitude prenait, au contraire, lorsque
as pleasant and comely as of usual took at the contrary when

ses yeux se tournaient vers Nono, une physionomie dure, revêche
his eyes themselves turned towards Nono an aspect hard surly

et renfrognée qui le paralysait.
and scowling which him paralysed

— Eh bien, mauvaise tête, fit Biquette en intervenant, veux-tu bien
— Eh well bad head made Biquette while intervening want you well
said

vite aller t'excuser auprès de Riri, lui dire que c'est un moment
quickly to go yourself apologize close of Riri him to say that it is a moment

de vivacité, que ça ne t'arrivera plus ?
of vivacity (and) that that not you will happen more ?
(too much) liveliness

— N...on ! fit Nono revenu à son obstination, non, c'est de sa
— No ! made Nono (having) come back to his obstinacy no It is -of- his
said

145

faute.
fault

— Voyons ! Riri ne peut pourtant pas venir te demander pardon
— See ! Riri not can however -not- come you ask forgiveness

du coup de poing qu'il a reçu ? » fit Hans intervenant à son
of the strike of fist that he has received ? made Hans intervening at his
said

tour, et cherchant à tourner la chose en plaisanterie, afin de dérider
turn and searching to turn the thing in joke so of to cheer

Nono qu'il voyait s'ancrer de plus en plus dans son obstination.
Nono that he saw himself anchor -of- more in more in his obstinacy
and

— Hé, fit Nono, hargneux, je ne lui demande pas cela. Qu'il reste
— Hey! made Nono aggressive I not him request -not- that That he remains
said

où il est. Qui est-ce qui lui demande quelque chose ? »
where he is Who Is this who him requests some thing ?

À cette réponse, le visage des enfants qui entouraient Nono prit une
At this response the face of the children who surrounded Nono took an

expression sévère.
expression severe

Ils le regardèrent tout étonnés, ne comprenant rien à son attitude.
They him looked at all astonished not understanding nothing to his attitude
from

Mais comme il méritait une leçon, ils affectèrent de s'éloigner
But like he deserved a lesson they feigned of themselves to recede

de lui, et de ne plus lui adresser la parole.
from him and of not (any)more him to address the word

Cependant, avant de s'éloigner, Mab tenta un dernier effort :
However before of herself to move away Mab tried a last effort :

— Alors, c'est bien décidé ! Tu ne veux pas faire des excuses à
— Then It is well decided ! You not want -not- to make -of-the- excuses to

Riri ?
Riri ?

Nono secoua énergiquement la tête en signe de dénégation.
Nono shook vigorously the head in sign of denial

— Tu es un vilain. Je ne t'aime plus. » Et elle s'éloigna
— You are a villain I not love you (any)more And she herself moved away / departed

avec les autres.
with the others

Nono se trouva seul, isolé à sa table.
Nono himself found alone isolated at his table

Il tenta de faire contre mauvaise fortune bon cœur, et essaya de
He tried of to make against bad fortune good heart and tried of

goûter à une grappe de raisin excellent qui se trouvait devant lui,
to taste -to- a bunch of grapes excellent which itself found in front of him

mais sa poitrine oppressée refusa de laisser passer les quelques grains
But his chest choked refused of to let pass the few grains / pieces

auxquels il avait mordu. À la fin, n'y tenant plus, de gros
on the which he had bitten At the end not there holding more of big

sanglots sortirent de son gosier contracté, pendant qu'un flot de larmes
sobs went out of his throat contracted during that a flood / mass of tears

amères jaillissait de ses yeux. Il s'accouda sur la table, et pleura à
bitter sprayed of his eyes He leaned himself on the table and cried at

son aise.
his ease

Sa crise commençait à se calmer, lorsqu'il sentit deux bras entourer
His crisis began to itself calm when he felt two arms surround

son cou, pendant qu'on l'embrassait avec force.
his neck during that one him embraced with force

Et Mab, grimpée au dossier de sa chaise, lui disait à l'oreille :
And Mab climbed up at the back of his chair him said at the ear :

— Tu vois, ce que c'est de faire le méchant.
— You see this what this is of to do the mean (thing)

— On se rend malheureux soi-même, ajoutait Biquette qui lui avait
— One himself makes unhappy oneself added Biquette who him had

sauté sur les genoux.
jumped up on the knees

— Allons ! viens trouver Riri ; et que ça soit fini, fit Hans en
— Go ! come to find Riri ; and that that be finished made Hans in

l'entraînant par la main.
him dragging by the hand

Et, moitié de gré, moitié de force, ils l'entraînèrent à la table où
And half of liking half of force they him dragged to the table where

se tenait Riri. Les excuses faites, les deux enfants s'embrassèrent,
himself kept Riri The excuses made the two children each other embraced

se promettant d'être bons camarades à l'avenir, et de ne plus
each other promising of to be good comrades to the future and of not (any)more
in

se laisser aller à des mouvements irréfléchis de colère.
themselves to let go to of the movements unthinking of anger

Nono tira une belle toupie de sa poche qui, en tournant, donnait
Nono drew a beautiful top from his pocket which in turning gave

l'illusion d'un pantin, faisant toute sorte de sauts et de culbutes. Riri,
the illusion of a puppet making all kind of jumps and of somersaults Riri

ne voulant pas être en reste de générosité, lui donna une petite boîte,
not wanting -not- to be in rest of generosity him gave a little box
debt

œuvre de Labor, pouvant se mettre dans la poche et contenant un
artwork of Labor being able itself to put in the pocket and containing an

accordéon qui, sous les doigts, devenait un grand et bel instrument,
accordion which under the fingers became a large and beautiful instrument

duquel on pouvait tirer toutes sortes d'airs, non pas de ce son
of the which one could pull all kinds of tunes not -not- of this his

nasillard des accordéons ordinaires, mais comme si un orchestre complet
snuffling of the accordions ordinary but as if an orchestra complete

y eût été enfermé ; et sans que l'on sut la musique. Il
there had been locked up ; and without that -it- one knew the music It

suffisait de désirer l'air et d'appuyer sur les touches pour que,
sufficed of to desire the tune and of to press on the keys for that
was enough

aussitôt, l'air fût joué.
immediately the tune was played

La réconciliation faite, la gaîté reparut parmi tout ce petit monde
The reconciliation made the gaiety reappeared among all this little world

qu'avait attristé la dispute, et le repas continua plus gaiment qu'il
that had saddened the dispute and the meal continued more gaily than it

n'avait commencé. Jamais Labor n'avait semblé aussi avenant.
-not- had started Never Labor not had appeared so comely

Solidaria semblait lui sourire, lorsque Nono la regardait.
Solidaria seemed him to smile (to) when Nono her looked at

Comme tout le monde était fatigué, Amorata, sitôt levés de table,
As all the world was tired Amorata as soon as raised from (the) table

leur donna des nouvelles de leurs familles, puis on alla se
them gave -of the- news of their families then they went themselves

coucher.
to lay down

Mais, quoique sa réconciliation avec Riri l'eût un peu soulagé, Nono
But though his reconciliation with Riri him had a bit relieved Nono

était encore mécontent de ne pas avoir dit la vérité. Il dormit mal
was still unhappy of not -not- to have told the truth He slept badly

et eut le cauchemar.
and had the nightmare
        a

Tantôt il était en querelle avec ses amis et ceux-ci le chassaient
Sometimes he was in quarrel with his friends and these him chased

honteusement d'Autonomie. Ensuite, c'était le sphinx tête de mort qui,
shamefully from Autonomy Subsequently It was the sphinx head of death which

sous les traits du gros monsieur, venait se poser sur sa poitrine, lui
under the traits of the fat gentleman came itself pose on his chest him

montrant une foule de belles choses qui lui glissaient des doigts
showing a crowd of beautiful things which him slipped from the fingers

lorsqu'il voulait les saisir, et devenait si lourd, si lourd, que Nono
when he wanted them to seize and became so heavy so heavy that Nono

suffoqué perdait la respiration, se sentant aplati, avec la sensation
suffocated lost the breathing himself feeling flattened with the feeling

de ne plus être qu'une feuille de papier.
of not more be than a leaf of paper

Puis ensuite, il était entraîné dans un jardin plein de cette plante,
Then subsequently he was dragged along in a garden full of this plant

le muflier, vulgairement connue sous le nom de gueule-de-loup, et
the snapdragon vulgarly known under the name of maw-of-wolf and

dont la fleur a, en effet, quelque ressemblance avec un mufle de
of which the flower has in fact some resemblance with a muzzle of

bête.
beast

Ces fleurs étaient deux fois grandes comme lui, et de temps en
These flowers were two times large as him and from time in
larger than to

temps, elles s'ouvraient comme si elles allaient l'avaler. À la fin,
time they themselves opened as if they went him to swallow At the end

il en sortit de petits korrigans qui tous avaient la figure du gros
he of it got out with small korrigans who all had the figure of the fat

homme. Se prenant la main, ils dansaient en cercle autour de
man Each other taking the hand they danced in circle around -of-

Nono, cherchant à l'entraîner.
Nono searching to him drag along

Mais celui-ci se débattait, appelant à son secours Solidaria qui
But that one himself struggled calling to his help Solidaria who

accourait le délivrer, et les gueules de loup disparaissaient, se
rushed up him to deliver and the mouths of wolf disappeared themselves
to free

transformant en capucines, en aconit, dont les fleurs ressemblent à
transforming in nasturtiums in aconites of which the flowers resemble to

des casques.
-of- the helmets

Les korrigans se coiffaient de ces casques, se faisaient
The korrigans themselves capped with these helmets themselves made

des boucliers des feuilles rondes de la capucine, et se
-of-the- shields from the leaves rounds of the nasturtium and themselves

faisant	une	monture	de	dauphinelles	qui	figurent	un	Dauphin,	ils
making	a	mount	of	delphiniums	which	contained	a	Dolphin	they

se	précipitaient	sur	Nono,	semblant	vouloir	le	traverser	de	longues
themselves	rushed	on	Nono	seeming	to want	him	to cross	with	long

lances	qu'ils	avaient	à	la	main,	l'assaillant	de	tous	les	côtés,	et	à
spears	that they	had	at / in	the	hand	him assailing	from	all	the	sides	and	at

coups	si	multipliés	que	Solidaria	n'arrivait	plus	à	le	défendre.
blows	so	multiplied	that	Solidaria	not succeeded	(any)more	to	him	defend

L'enlèvement
The take away (The kidnapping)

Lorsque Nono se réveilla, le lendemain, il était brisé de fatigue
When Nono himself woke up the following day he was broken from exhaustion

et avait un fort mal de tête.
and had a strong ache of head
        big head ache

Il se leva, heureux d'échapper à l'obsession du cauchemar, espérant
He himself raised happy of to escape to the obsession of the nightmare hoping

que le mouvement et l'air frais du matin, et surtout une bonne
that the movement and the air fresh of the morning and especially a good

douche froide, dissiperaient sa migraine.
shower cold would dissipate his migraine

Lorsqu'il sortit de la piscine, ses amis le reçurent à bras ouverts,
When he got out of the swimming pool his friends him received at arms open
        with open arms

aucune allusion ne fut faite à l'incident de la veille.
any hint not was made to the incident of the evening before

Tout le monde était en l'air, car il s'agissait de commencer un
All the world was in the air because it itself dealt of to begin a
  Everyone   concerned

travail qui avait amené de longues discussions dans la colonie.
work who had led of long discussions in the colony
        to

Il s'agissait d'un pont à construire sur un ruisseau qui traversait un
It itself dealt -of- a bridge to build over a stream which crossed one
  concerned

des bois proche d'Autonomie. Les uns voulaient le construire en face
of the woods close of Autonomy The ones wanted it to build in front
        Some

de la route menant au palais, les autres voulaient l'élever en face
of the road leading to the palace the others wanted to raise it in front

d'un sentier menant derrière les serres.
of a path leading behind the greenhouses

Il faut ajouter aussi qu'ils n'étaient pas tout à fait d'accord
He is necessary adding also that they not were -not- all at fact of agreement
alltogether in agreement

sur la façon de le construire ; les uns le voulaient d'une façon, les
on the way of it to build ; the ones it wanted of one way the
some in one

autres d'une autre.
others of an other
in an

La discussion durait depuis que Nono était arrivé à Autonomie. C'était
The discussion lasted since that Nono was arrived at Autonomy It was
had

la veille de la promenade seulement que Liberta avait suggéré un
the evening before of the walk only that Liberta had suggested a

moyen d'en terminer.
means of with it to end

Les deux opinions avaient leurs raisons d'être. Les deux ponts pouvaient
The two opinions had their reasons of to be The two bridges could

être utiles aux endroits où l'on voulait les élever. Pourquoi, au
be useful to the locations where it one wanted them to raise Why at the

lieu de perdre leur temps en discussions, les deux camps ne
place of to lose their time in discussions, the two camps not

s'entendraient-ils pas pour en construire chacun un à la place qu'il
themselves heard they -not- for of it to build each one at the place that it
would they agree

désirait, et sur les plans qui leur convenaient ?
desired and on the plans which them convened ?

Une fois d'accord là-dessus, il leur serait facile de s'entendre
A time of agreement there upon it (to) them would be easy of themselves to hear
Once in agreement to agree

pour s'aider mutuellement dans le gros œuvre qui demanderait
for each other to help mutually in the great work which would ask
on

le concours de tous.
the along-run of all
help

L'idée de Liberta fut accueillie avec enthousiasme, et il avait été décidé
The idea of Liberta was received with enthousiasm and it had been decided

que chaque groupe travaillerait à son projet, quitte à s'aider
that each group would work at their project left to each other help

mutuellement lorsque l'importance des travaux l'exigerait.
mutually when the importance of the works it required

C'était ce matin que l'on devait commencer les terrassements, faire
It was this morning that -it- they must begin the earthworks to make

les premiers travaux nécessités par l'établissement des caissons pour la
the first works necessary by / for the establishment of the caissons / bases for the

construction des piles.
construction of the pillars

Nono travailla quelque temps, mais sa migraine ne l'ayant pas quitté,
Nono worked some time But his migraine not him having -not- left

il avertit ses amis qu'il prenait un peu de repos, et se dirigea
he warned his friends that he took a bit of rest and himself directed

vers un châtaignier qui se trouvait à quelque distance d'où
towards a chestnut (tree) which itself found at some distance from where

l'on travaillait, espérant y faire un petit somme qui le
-it- they worked hoping there to make a little nap which him

soulagerait.
would soothe

Étendu sous le châtaignier, il réfléchissait à son aventure de la
Stretched out under the chestnut tree he reflected on his adventure of the

veille, à ses parents, à son rêve de la nuit, lorsque son
evening before on his parents on his dream of the night when his

attention fut attirée par un mouvement qui se produisait à quelques
attention was attracted by a movement which itself produced at some

pas de lui.
steps from him

C'était le cadavre d'un mulot, qu'il avait aperçu avant de se
It was the corpse of a fieldmouse that he had perceived before of himself

coucher, qui s'agitait et se remuait. Nono, s'allongeant sur le
to lay down which itself moved and itself stirred Nono stretching himself on the

ventre, s'appuyant sur les coudes, allongea la tête dans cette direction,
belly leaning on the elbows stretched the head in that direction

et eut bientôt l'explication de ces mouvements insolites.
and had soon the explanation of these movements unusual

Cinq insectes, un peu moins longs qu'un hanneton, mais bien moins
Five insects, a bit less long than a cockchafer but well less

larges, de couleur noire, tachetés de bandes fauves, s'étaient glissée
wide of (a) color black speckled with bands savage themselves were crept
had

sous le corps du mulot, et là, s'aidant de leurs pattes,
under the body of the fieldmouse and there themselves helping with their paws

poussant de la tête, cherchaient à changer le corps de place.
pushing with the head were looking for to change the body of place

Nono reconnut dans ces insectes le coléoptère désigné sous le nom de
Nono recognized in these insects the beetle designed under the name of

nécrophore, à cause de son habitude d'enterrer les cadavres des animaux
necrophorus at cause of his habit of the bury the corpses of the animals

dont ses larves font leur nourriture.
of which his larvae make their food

À l'endroit d'où ils avaient enlevé le mulot, Nono reconnut
At the place from where they had taken away the fieldmouse Nono recognized

que la terre avait été déjà fouillée ; mais une large pierre plate
that the earth had been already rummaged ; but a wide stone flat

obstruait le fond. C'était l'impossibilité d'entamer cette pierre et de
obstructed the bottom It was the impossibility of to tame this stone and of

continuer la fosse qui, sans doute, avait décidé les nécrophores à
to continue the pit which without doubt had decided the necrophores to

changer le mulot de place.
change the fieldmouse of place

Ils le transportèrent ainsi une trentaine de centimètres plus loin,
They it transported thus a thirty-some of centimeters more far
farther

sachant tourner les obstacles qui auraient pu les entraver ; puis,
knowing to turn the obstacles which would have been able them hamper ; Then
to round

arrivés à l'emplacement propice, ils s'espacèrent autour du cadavre,
arrived at the location propitious they themselves spaced around of the corpse

et commencèrent à fouir la terre de leurs fortes pattes, la
and began to burrow the earth with their strong paws it

rejetant derrière eux, formant ainsi un talus qui s'élevait au
throwing back behind them forming thus a slope which itself rose at the
was rising

fur et à mesure que la fosse se creusait.
forum and to measure that the pit itself dug
the same was

Fortement intrigué, Nono les examinait, se demandant où ils
Strongly intrigued Nono them examined himself asking where they

voulaient en venir.
wanted of it come

Petit à petit, il voyait le corps du mulot s'enfoncer comme si la
Little by little he saw the body of the fieldmouse itself sink like if the

terre se dérobait sous lui. Au bout d'un certain temps, il avait
earth itself disappeared under him At the end of a certain time he had

complètement disparu à ses yeux. Les nécrophores sortirent alors de
completely disappeared to his eyes The necrophores went out then from

la fosse, y rejetant la terre pour combler le trou qu'ils avaient
the pit there throwing back the earth for to fill in the hole that they had

fait ; à la fin un petit renflement et la terre remuée indiquaient
made ; at the end a little bulge and the earth moved indicated

seuls le travail qui venait de s'accomplir.
only the work which came of itself to accomplish
had been accomplished

Les nécrophores partirent à la recherche d'une autre proie. Seul l'un
The necrophores left to the search of an other prey Alone -the- one

d'eux resta sur la fosse, faisant sa toilette, se passant les pattes
of them remained on the pit making his dress himself passing the paws

sur les élytres, sur ses antennes. On aurait dit un être très content
on the elytra over his antennas One would have said a being very satisfied

de lui, se frottant les mains de satisfaction.
of him(self) himself rubbing the hands of satisfaction

Et Nono, vaguement assoupi, le regardait faire, ne le voyant que
And Nono vaguely drowsy him watched make not him seeing than

comme à travers un brouillard.
like -at- through a fog

Puis il lui sembla que l'insecte grandissait, grandissait, que son ventre
Then it him seemed that the insect grew grew that his belly

s'élargissait, qu'il prenait forme humaine.
itself widened that he took (a) shape human

— Eh bien, as-tu réfléchi depuis hier ?
— Eh well have you reflected since yesterday ?

Nono, subitement tiré de sa torpeur, se dressa alarmé sur son
Nono suddenly pulled out from his torpor himself raised alarmed on his

séant.
behind

C'était le gros monsieur de la veille qui était debout devant lui,
It was the fat gentleman of the evening before who was upright in front of him

et lui parlait ; car l'astucieux Monnaïus n'abandonnait pas celui
and to him spoke ; because the clever Monnaïus not abandoned -not- the one

qu'il considérait déjà comme sa proie, et venait, à nouveau, essayer
that he considered already like his prey and came at new to try
                                                            again

ses tentatives de séduction, au risque d'être découvert par Solidaria.
his attempts of seduction at the risks of to be discovered by Solidaria

Ce n'est pas qu'il eût des sentiments hostiles à l'égard de Nono,
It not is -not- that he had of the feelings hostile at the regard of Nono

ni que les facultés de ce dernier le désignassent plus spécialement à
nor that the faculties of this last (one) him designated more specially to
        abilities

son choix. Seulement Monnaïus savait que s'il laissait trop la
his choice Only Monnaïus knew that if he let too (much) the

population d'Autonomie s'augmenter et devenir puissante, cette population
population of Autonomy itself increase and become strong this population

s'étendrait, se rapprocherait de ses États ; qu'il ne pourrait pas
itself would extend itself would approach of his States ; that he not could -not-

toujours, quel que fût le nombre de ses gendarmes et de ses
always what(ever) that was the number of his gendarmes and of his

douaniers, empêcher ses sujets d'avoir connaissance du genre de vie
customs officers prevent his subjects of to have acquaintance of the sort of life

que l'on y menait, ce qui serait d'un fâcheux exemple pour ses
that it they there led this which would be of a sad example for his

esclaves, que la force seule ne parviendrait plus à maintenir dans
slaves that the force alone not would succeed (any)more to maintain in

l'obéissance, lorsqu'ils apprendraient que l'on peut vivre heureux, sans
the obedience when they would learn that -it- they could live happy without

avoir des gens qui vous disent ce que vous avez à faire, et qui
to have -of the- people who you tell this that you have to do and who

vous y forcent au besoin.
you there (to) force at the need

Car, chez Monnaïus, la population était divisée en toutes sortes de
Because with Monnaïus the population was divided in all kinds of

classes de gens, dont les trois principales étaient : ceux qui jouissent
classes of people of which the three main were : those who enjoy

de tous les plaisirs et ne font rien, ceux qui travaillent et n'ont
-of- all the pleasures and not do nothing those who work and not have

aucun plaisir, et ceux qui forcent ces derniers à travailler pour ceux
any pleasure and those who force these last to work for those

qui ne font rien.
who not do nothing

Quel que soit le nombre de ceux-là, il est bien évident qu'ils
What that be the number of those there it is well obvious that they

n'auraient pas réussi à se faire obéir bien longtemps de ceux
not would have -not- succeeded to themselves make obey well (a) long time by those

qui se voyaient condamnés à passer leur existence à travailler
who themselves saw condemned to pass their existence at to work working

continuellement au milieu des privations, si l'habileté de Monnaïus et
continually at the middle of the privations if the skill of Monnaïus and
in the

de ses ministres n'y avait suppléé.
of his ministers not there had supplemented

Cette habileté avait été de faire croire aux gens que s'ils n'avaient
This skill had been of to make believe to the people that if they not had

pas des individus chargés de les fourrer en prison lorsqu'ils ne
-not- of the individuals charged of them shove in prison when they not

voudraient pas faire une chose qui ne leur plairait pas, il leur
would like -not- to do a thing which not them would please -not- it them

serait impossible de s'entendre, et d'être libres ; qu'ils se
would be impossible of themselves to agree and of to be free ; that they themselves

disputeraient, se battraient entre eux, et, finalement mourraient
would dispute themselves would fight between them and finally would die
each other

de faim.
from hunger

Puis, qu'il faut aussi une autre classe qui fasse la fête,
Then that it is necessary also an other class which makes the celebration

gaspille beaucoup de choses, pour que ceux qui sont forcée de les
wastes much -of- things for that those who are forced of them

produire, aient beaucoup de travail afin d'avoir un peu à manger.
to produce have much -of- work so of to have a bit to eat

On avait enseigné cela aux Argyrocratiens de père en fils depuis des
One had taught that to the Argyrocratiens of father in son since -of the-

milliers d'années. Aussi étaient-ils convaincus qu'il était impossible de
thousands of years Also were they convinced that it was impossible of

vivre autrement.
to live otherwise

Certes la baguette d'or de Monnaïus avait beaucoup de puissance, mais
Certainly the stick of gold of Monnaïus had a lot of power but

cette puissance était limitée. Il y avait des cas où elle lui
this power was limited It there had of the cases where she him
There were times

devenait inutile entre les mains.
became useless between the hands

159

Ainsi, il n'avait pu empêcher que quelques notions de la vie
Thus he not had been able to prevent that some notions of the life

d'Autonomie n'eûssent pénétré parmi ses sujets. Et, l'histoire
of Autonomy had -not- penetrated among his subjects. And the history

d'Argyrocratie rappelait trois ou quatre révolutions terribles, où les
of Argyrocratie recalled three or four revolutions terrible, where the

habitants, poussés par la misère, par un vague désir de mieux
inhabitants, pushed by the misery, by a vague desire of better

s'arranger entre eux, avaient failli se débarrasser de
to arrange themselves between them had (just) missed themselves to get rid of
to share with each other

leurs maîtres.
their masters

Mais ceux-ci avaient su profiter de l'ignorance de la foule, et su
But these had known to enjoy of the ignorance of the crowd, and known
managed

reprendre leur place à la tête de la nation, toujours sous le prétexte
to take again their place at the head of the nation, always under the pretext

qu'il faut bien qu'il y en ait qui forcent les gens à faire
that it is necessary well that it there of them has who force the people to do
that there are those

le contraire de ce qu'ils veulent pour que tout marche bien.
the contrary of this that they want for that all goes well

Aussi, Monnaïus était toujours en campagne pour enlever les habitants
Also, Monnaïus was always on (a) campaign for to take away the inhabitants
to kidnap

d'Autonomie, et les transporter dans ses états.
of Autonomy, and them transport in his States

Vous me direz, peut-être, que c'était là un moyen, justement, de
You me tell maybe that this was there a means exactly of

faire pénétrer chez lui la connaissance des mœurs d'Autonomie. Mais,
to make enter with him the knowledge of the mores of Autonomy But

comme je vous l'ai dit, la puissance de Monnaïus était limitée et, de
like I you it have said the power of Monnaïus was limited and of

deux maux, il choisissait le moindre.
two evils he chose the lesser

Les Argyrocratiens étaient tellement persuadés de l'excellence de leur genre
The Argyrocratiens were so confident of the excellence of their sort

de vie que, lorsqu'un des Autonomiens enlevés leur racontait
of life that when one of the (boys and girls of) Autonomy kidnapped them told

la vie qu'il menait auparavant, la foule le traitait de fou, de
the life that he led before the crowd him treated of insane as of

visionnaire et se moquait de lui. Jamais on n'avait vu les
visionary and himself made fun of of him Never one did not have seen the

hommes vivre autrement que, les uns obéissant, les autres commandant, il
men live otherwise than the ones obey the others command it

était impossible qu'il en fût autrement.
was impossible that it -of it- was otherwise

Il faut dire aussi, que, souvent, il s'en trouvait parmi les
It is necessary to say also that often it itself of them found among the
there were

Autonomiens qui trouvaient plus commode de s'arranger
(boys and girls of) Autonomy who found more easy of themselves to arrange
those who

de la façon de vivre des Argyrocratiens, ils se faisaient les
of the way of to live of the Argyrocratiens they themselves made the

flatteurs de ceux qui font travailler les autres, arrivaient à se
flatterers of those who make work the others arrived to themselves

glisser parmi eux, et ils étaient les premiers à tourner en ridicule
slip among them and they were the first to turn in ridicule

ceux des Autonomiens qui regrettaient et rappelaient les jours
those of the (boys and girls of) Autonomy who regretted and recalled the days

de liberté.
of freedom

Nono s'étant trouvé sur le chemin de Monnaïus, ayant montré un
Nono himself being found on the way of Monnaïus having shown a
himself having

penchant à se laisser séduire, celui-ci revenait à la charge. Mais
penchant to himself let seduce that one returned to the charge But

comme l'astucieux personnage avait vu qu'il ne fallait pas heurter
like the clever character had seen that it -not- was necessary not to hit
to hurt

les sentiments de l'enfant, ce fut de sa voix la plus doucereuse qu'il
the feelings of the child it was with his voice the most sweetish that he

continua :
continued :

— Tu es étonné de me voir ici, n'est-ce pas ? Mais Solidaria est ma
— You are surprised of me to see here is not this not ? But Solidaria is my
isn't it

meilleure amie ; étant venu la voir aujourd'hui, elle m'a dit que je
best friend ; being come her to see today she me has said that I

trouverais ici mon excellent ami Labor, et je suis venu lui serrer la
would find here my excellent friend Labor and I am come him to close the
to shake

main. Je t'ai reconnu en passant. Elle m'a même remis ce
hand I you have recognized while passing She me has even set back this

flacon à ton intention. Ton camarade Hans lui ayant dit que tu avais
bottle to your intention Your comrade Hans him having said that you had

mal à la tête. C'est une liqueur qu'elle a composée et qui va
bad to the head This is a liqueur that she has composed and which goes
ache in

faire disparaître ton mal de tête. »
to make disappear your ache of head

Nono, sans défiance, puisque la liqueur lui était envoyée par Solidaria,
Nono without distrust since the liqueur him was sent by Solidaria

avala le contenu du flacon, et, en effet, son mal de tête disparut
swallowed the contents of the bottle and in fact his ache of head disappeared

pour laisser place à une torpeur qui lui sembla être le summum du
for to let place to a torpor which him seemed to be the pinnacle of the

bien-être.
well be
well being

Mais la liqueur avait été fabriquée par Monnaïus, le prétendu bien-être
But the liqueur had been fabricated by Monnaïus the alleged well be
well being

dont jouissait Nono n'était dû qu'à un engourdissement du
of which enjoyed Nono not was owed (other) than to a numbness of the

cerveau qui l'empêchait de sentir et lui troublait la raison.
brain which him prevented of to feel and him troubled the reason
  distorted

Complètement revenu de ses alarmes, Nono s'était mis à causer avec
Completely come back from his alarms Nono itself was put to chat with
  itself had

Monnaïus, comme à un camarade.
Monnaïus like to a comrade

— Alors, chez toi, c'est plus beau qu'ici ?
— Then with you this is more beautiful than here ?

— Oh ! plus beau qu'ici, ça n'est pas tout à fait le mot. Mais
— Oh ! more beautiful than here that not is -not- all to fact the word But
  absolutely

enfin, c'est autre chose. Ça vaut la peine d'être vu.
enfin it is (an)other thing That is worth the pain of to be seen

— Comment se fait-il que Solidaria ne nous en ai jamais parlé ?
— How itself does it that Solidaria not (to) us of it has ever spoken ?
  can it be

— C'est que, vois-tu, Solidaria ne trouve rien de plus beau
— This is that see you Solidaria not finds nothing of more beautiful

qu'Autonomie ; à son avis il n'y a rien qui puisse rivaliser
than Autonomy ; to her opinion it not there has nothing which can rival
  in   there is

avec son petit royaume ; alors, tu comprends, pour elle le reste
with her little kingdom ; then you understand for her the rest

n'existe pas.
not exists not
does not exist

— Ah ! fit Nono, qui ne sentait, ne voyait, et ne raisonnait
— Ah ! made Nono who not felt not saw and not reasoned
  said

que comme à travers un brouillard, et ces belles choses,
(other) than like -at- through a fog and these beautiful things

comment viennent-elles, si personne ne travaille chez toi ?
how come they if no one not works with you ?

— Hé bien, tu l'as vu hier, il suffit d'avoir une baguette
— Hey! well you it have seen yesterday it is enough of to have a stick

d'or comme la mienne, et l'on a tout ce que l'on veut.
of gold like the mine and -it- one has all this that -it- one wants

— Bon, est-ce que tout le monde peut avoir de ces baguettes ? Si je
— Good Is this that all the world can have of these little sticks ? If I

te suivais, moi je n'en ai pas. Est-ce que j'aurais tout de même
you followed me I not of it have -not- Is this that I would have all of same

ces belles choses ?
these beautiful things ?

— Heu ! heu, fit Monnaïus embarrassé, craignant que sa liqueur n'ait
— Er ! er made Monnaïus embarrassed fearing that his liqueur not has
said not had

pas réussi à troubler complètement la raison de sa victime, il y
-not- succeeded to trouble completely the reason of his victim it there
distort

en a bien quelques-uns qui n'en ont pas, mais on leur donne ce
of it has well some who not of it have -not- but one them gives this

dont ils ont besoin ; s'ils ont de la volonté et savent
of which they have need ; if they have -of- the will and know

s'arranger, ils peuvent arriver à s'en procurer. »
themselves arrange they can arrive to themselves of it acquire
how to get around succeed acquire them

Nono, dont la raison vacillait de plus en plus, ne remarqua pas ce
Nono of which the reason flickered -of- more in more not noted -not- this
and

qu'avait de vague et d'embarrassé cette réponse. Cela ne se
that had -of- vague and -of- embarrassed this response. That not himself
that was

passait-il pas ainsi, du reste, à Autonomie, où chacun trouvait à
passed him -not- thus of the rest at Autonomy (land) where each found to
for the

satisfaire ses goûts, où l'on était plein de prévenance l'un pour
satisfy their tastes where -it- one was full of thoughtfulness the one for

l'autre ?
the other ?

— Ainsi, toi, tu me plais, continua Monnaïus, je veux faire quelque chose
— Thus you you me please continued Monnaïus I want to do some thing

pour toi. Je vais te mettre à même de te procurer une de ces
for you I go you put/make at same/capable of yourself to acquire one of these

baguettes. Tu vois que la mienne a, de place en place, des
little sticks You see that the mine has from place in place -of the-
here and there

bourgeons comme une branche d'arbre. Ces bourgeons, on les détache
buds like a branch of (a) tree These buds one them detaches

lorsqu'ils sont grands comme celui-là — et il en montrait un. — Et
When they are large like that one — and he of it showed one — And

ces bourgeons grandissent et deviennent baguettes à leur tour. Tiens !
these buds grow and become little sticks at their turn Hold !

je vais enlever celui-là, qui est mûr et te le donner. »
I go take away that one which is ripe and you it give

Ce disant, avec un couteau très affilé il détacha le bourgeon et le
This saying with a knife very sharp he detached the bud and it

tendit à Nono.
extended to Nono

Celui-ci le regardait curieusement, mais d'un œil trouble !
That one it watched with curiosity But with an eye troubled !
blurred

— Alors, il va grandir, comme cela, et j'aurai tout ce que je voudrai
— Then it goes grow like that and I will have all this that I will want

avec ?
with ?
with it

— Mais certainement, tu n'as qu'à le mettre de côté et il
— But certainly you not have (other) than to it to put of side and it

deviendra bientôt aussi grand que la canne d'où je l'ai arraché.
will become soon as large as the cane from where I her have ripped off

»

Nono mit le précieux bourgeon dans sa poche.
Nono put the valuable bud in his pocket

Monnaïus le prit par la main, lui disant :
Monnaïus him took by the hand him saying :

165

— Eh bien ! c'est dit, tu viens avec moi ? Allons trouver Solidaria qui,
— Eh well ! this is said you come with me ? Go find Solidaria who
that said Let's go

certainement, te donnera la permission.
certainly you will give the permission

— Je croyais que tu voulais voir Labor ? fit Nono qu'un reste de
— I believed that you wanted to see Labor ? made Nono that a rest of
said

raison soutenait encore.
reason supported still

— Pendant que nous causions, il est parti avec tes camarades, fit
— During that we conversed he is left with your comrades made
said

Monnaïus, en mettant sa baguette d'or entre le champ où travaillait
Monnaïus in putting his stick of gold between the field where worked

Labor et la vue de sa victime. »
Labor and the sight of his victim

Avisant un escargot qui se prélassait sur l'herbe, il le toucha de
Noticing a snail which himself lounged on the grass he it touched with

sa baguette, le transformant en un char enlevé par deux énormes
his stick it transforming in a chariot pulled by two enormous

chauve-souris de l'espèce vampire ; puis il poussa vivement Nono
bald-mice of the species vampire ; then he pushed strongly Nono
bats

dedans, y monta à côté de lui, et les chauves-souris s'envolèrent
in there there went up to side of him and the bald-mice flew
bats

dans la direction d'Argyrocratie.
in the direction of Argyrocratia

— Solidaria ! Liberta ! » ne put s'empêcher d'appeler Nono, malgré
— Solidaria ! Liberta ! not could help call Nono in spite of

l'état de somnolence dans lequel il se trouvait, en se sentant
the state of drowsiness in which he himself found in himself feeling

enlever.
to take away

Mais, quoique faible, cet appel instinctif de son protégé était allé frapper
But though weak this call instinctive of her protegee was gone to strike

douloureusement Solidaria au cœur. Levant les yeux au ciel, elle vit
painfully Solidaria at the heart Raising the eyes to the sky she saw

le char de Monnaïus.
the chariot of Monnaïus

— Vite ! vite ! fit-elle à Électricia, il nous faut arracher
— Quickly ! quickly ! she asked -to- Electricia it us is necessary to tear away

notre protégé des serres de Monnaïus ; va, vole, et arrête son char.
our protegee from the grasps of Monnaïus ; goe fly and stop his chariot

»

Plus rapide que la pensée, Électricia avait prit la forme d'un
More rapid than the thought Electricia had taken the shape of a

éclair qui illumina tout le ciel et alla foudroyer dans leur vol
lightning flash which lit all the sky and went to blast in their flight

les deux horribles bêtes qui emportaient Nono et son ravisseur.
the two horrible animals which carried away Nono and his abductor

Mais, hélas, si rapide qu'elle eût fait, le char était déjà sorti des
But alas as rapid as she had made the chariot was already gone out of the
been had

limites d'Autonomie, et Solidaria n'avait de puissance que là
edges of Autonomy and Solidaria did not have -of- power (other) than there

où elle était connue et respectée.
where she was known and respected

Monnaïus, se voyant près de ses États, changea son char en
Monnaïus himself seeing near of his States changed his chariot in

parachute qui le descendit tout doucement à terre, pendant que Nono
parachute which him descended all softly to earth during that Nono

s'était instinctivement agrippé à un cordage.
itself was instinctively clutched at a rope
itself had

Tous deux tombèrent au bord d'un ruisseau qui coupait la plaine en
All two fell at the edge of a stream which cut the plain in

deux. Monnaïus n'avait qu'à le franchir pour être dans ses États.
two Monnaïus did not have than to it to cross for be in his States

Avant qu'ils eussent atteint la terre, Électricia, de la part de
Before that they had reached the earth Electricia from the side of

Solidaria, était allée trouver la naïade du ruisseau qui consentit à
Solidaria was gone find the naiad of the stream who agreed to
tree spirit

gonfler ses flots afin de barrer la route au ravisseur.
inflate its waves so of to bar the road to the abductor

Le ruisseau se mit donc à bouillonner, à gonfler, franchissant ses
The stream itself set then to seethe to swell going over its
started

rives, s'épandant dans la plaine, la transformant en lac.
borders itself spreading in the plain it transforming in lake

Sans perdre une minute, Monnaïus ramassa à terre une moitié de
Without to lose a minute Monnaïus picked up on earth a half of
from the ground

coquille de noix, la jeta à l'eau, et, d'un coup de baguette, en
(a) shell of nuts it threw on the water and with a strike of stick of it

fit une barque légère, munie d'une voile triangulaire que l'on pouvait
made a boat light provided with a veil triangular that -it- one could

facilement manier.
easily handle

— Vite, fit-il à Nono, embarquons ! Labor nous attend de l'autre
— Quickly made he to Nono embark ! Labor us awaits of the other
said he get on on

côté. Et il désignait un homme qui ressemblait bien à Labor, mais à
side And he designated a man who resembled well to Labor but to

un Labor à l'aspect dur, féroce, repoussant et sordide.
a Labor at the appearance hard fierce repulsive and sordid

Cependant, trompé par les apparences, Nono sauta dans la barque. Alors
However deceived by the appearances Nono jumped in the boat Then

Monnaïus lui ordonna brutalement de manœuvrer la voile, pendant que
Monnaïus him ordered brutally of to maneuver the veil during that

lui se mettait à la barre.
he himself put at the bar

Nono, à moitié dégrisé par ce changement de ton, exécuta cependant
Nono -at- half sobered by this change of tone executed however

ce qui lui était ordonné, contemplant la figure de plus en plus
this which him was ordered contemplating the face -of- more in more and

cruelle du Labor qui l'attendait au rivage opposé. Mais il attribuait
cruel of the Labor which him awaited at the shore opposite But he attributed

ce changement de physionomie au mécontentement qu'éprouvait son
this change of aspect at the dissatisfaction that experienced his

ami de le voir quitter Autonomie sans le prévenir, et se
friend of him to see leave Autonomy (land) without him warn and himself

promettait de l'apaiser en lui racontant tout ce qui lui était arrivé.
promised of him to appease in him recounting all this which him was arrived / had happened

Ils étaient près d'atteindre le rivage, lorsque la barque venant frapper
They were near of reaching the shore when the boat coming to hit

contre un obstacle, s'ouvrit en deux, coulant à fond. Mais
against an obstacle itself opened in two flowing to (the) bottom But

Monnaïus eut vite fait de gagner la rive.
Monnaïus had quickly made of to win the shore

Cet obstacle, c'était Solidaria qui venait de le susciter, espérant, à la
This obstacle it was Solidaria who came of it to spark hoping at the

faveur du naufrage, se ressaisir de son protégé.
favor of the shipwreck herself to recover of her protegee

Et, de fait, nageant vigoureusement, elle s'approchait de Nono que la
And in fact swimming vigorously she herself approached of Nono that the

naïade maintenait au-dessus de l'eau. Elle allait le saisir, lorsque
naiad tree spirit kept above of the water She went him to seize when

Monnaïus étendit sa baguette, et Nono, comme attiré par un puissant
Monnaïus extended his stick and Nono like attracted by a powerful

aimant, glissa dans la direction de la baguette, échappant à l'étreinte
magnet slipped in the direction of the stick escaping at/from the embrace

de Solidaria qui ne pouvait aborder sur les États de Monnaïus.
of Solidaria who not could enter on the States of Monnaïus

Une des vertus de la baguette de Monnaïus, c'était d'exercer une
One of the virtues of the stick of Monnaïus it was to exercise an

attraction sur les matières dont elle était formée. Monnaïus, on se
attraction on the contents of which she was formed Monnaïus one himself

le rappelle, en avait détaché un rameau qu'il avait donné à Nono, et
it recalls of it had taken off a branch that he had given to Nono and

que celui-ci avait mis dans sa poche. Et la baguette de Monnaïus,
that that one had put in his pocket And the stick of Monnaïus

exerçant sa fatale attraction, avait entraîné le rameau et son
practicing its fatal attraction had dragged along the branch and its

possesseur.
owner

Celui-ci, dégrisé par le bain forcé qu'il venait de prendre, subissant
That one sobered by the bath forced that he came of to take undergoing

l'attraction dont il ne se rendait pas compte, vit la figure de
the attraction of which he not himself rendered -not- account saw the figure of

Solidaria désolée qui lui tendait les bras, mais s'obscurcissant, s'effaçant
Solidaria desolate who him stretched the arm but herself darkening herself fading

lentement, dans les brumes du lac agité.
slowly in the mists of the lake agitated

Il restait prisonnier de Monnaïus.
He remained (a) prisoner of Monnaïus
was now

L'accordéon enchanté
The enchanted accordeon

Lorsqu'il atteignit la rive, Nono tout trempé dut se déshabiller et
When he reached the shore Nono all drenched had to himself undress and

étendre ses habits au soleil pour les sécher.
spread out his clothes at the sun for them to dry
            in the

Monnaïus, Solidaria, Labor, tous avaient disparu. Il se trouvait seul
Monnaïus Solidaria Labor all had disappeared He himself found alone

au milieu d'une grande plaine désolée. Il lui était impossible de
at the middle of a large plain desolate It (to) him was impossible of
in the

se rendre compte où se trouvait Autonomie. À présent que
himself to render account where itself found Autonomy (land) At present that

l'engourdissement causé par le philtre était dissipé, sa raison lui
the numbness caused by the potion of charm was dissipated his reason him
                              had

revenait. Il comprenait qu'il était victime de Monnaïus, et son
returned He understood that he was victim of Monnaïus and his

prisonnier puisque Solidaria n'avait pu l'atteindre.
prisoner since Solidaria did not have been able to reach him

Il savait que, désormais, seul, il lui serait impossible d'y retourner.
He knew that from now on alone it him would be impossible of there to go back

Il n'en retrouverait le chemin que lorsqu'il aurait réussi à
He not of it would find back the way (other) than when he would have succeeded to

unir ses efforts à d'autres.
unite his efforts to of others
             withothers

Et cet enseignement de Solidaria, lui revint à l'esprit pendant qu'il
And this education of Solidaria him returned to the mind during that he

se séchait, regrettant amèrement de s'être laissé entraîner.
himself dried regretting bitterly of himself to be let drag away
                            Now and then

Aussi loin que sa vue pouvait s'étendre, c'était le roc, perçant de
As far as his sight could itself extend it was the rock piercing by

maigres bruyères. De loin en loin, de pauvres champs rompaient
thin heather From far in far -of- poor fields broke
Now and then

l'uniformité de la plaine.
the uniformity of the plain

Nono, une fois qu'il sentit ses habits secs, se rhabilla, la faim
Nono one time that he felt his clothes dry himself dressed again the hunger
once

commençait à le talonner. Mais ce n'était plus comme à Autonomie,
began to him claw But this not was (any)more like at Autonomy
bother in

où il n'y avait qu'à étendre la main pour cueillir quelque
where he not there had (other) than to extend the hand for to pick some
needed

fruit succulent. Autour de lui les ajoncs épineux et les genêts
fruit succulent Around of him the gorse thorny and the brooms
shrub

s'élevaient seuls au dessus de la bruyère.
themselves raised alone at the on top of the heather
were lifted above

Nono se mit en marche vers le côté de la plaine où il lui
Nono himself set in march towards the side of the plain where it him
started to walk

semblait voir loin, bien loin, quelques habitations.
seemed to see far well far some habitations
quite

Les champs près desquels il passait étaient entourés de haies formées
The fields near of which he passed were surrounded by hedges formed

d'arbustes épineux ; du reste, rien à y grappiller, le blé
from shrubs thorny ; of the rest nothing to there scrounge the grain
for the

commençant seulement à pousser. Les bourgeons des haies ne faisaient
starting just to push The buds of the hedges not made
grow did

que s'entrouvrir. Cela semblait annoncer le commencement
(other) than themselves between open That seemed to announce the beginning
half-open themselves

du printemps.
of the spring

Nono arriva enfin à une route plantée de quelques arbres, dont le
Nono arrived finally at a road planted with some trees of which the

feuillage commençait à pointer. Mais, eussent-ils été plus avancés, ils
foliage began to point bud But had they been more advanced they

n'auraient pu être d'aucune utilité à l'affamé, qui y reconnut
would not been able be of any utility to the hungry which there recognized

des ormes, des sycomores, des platanes, des acacias, mais aucun
-of the- elms -of the- sycamores of the planetrees of the acacias But no

arbre à fruit.
tree at fruit
with

En approchant des maisons, il vit bien quelques arbres en fleur,
While approaching -of- the houses he saw well some trees in flower
indeed

des cerisiers, lui sembla-t-il. Seulement, eussent-ils eu des fruits,
-of the- cherry trees him it seemed Only had they had of the fruits

pour en approcher il lui aurait fallu escalader des murs
for of them to approach it him would have been necessary to climb -of- the walls

ou des haies. Mais les murs étaient couronnés de tessons de
or -of- the hedges But the walls were crowned with shards of

bouteilles fort coupants, les haies se hérissaient d'épines qui
bottles very sharp the hedges themselves bristled with thorns which

ôtaient l'envie d'en tenter l'escalade.
took away the desire of them to try the climb
the wish

Il continua donc son chemin vers les maisons, espérant trouver là
He continued then his way towards the houses hoping to find there

de quoi boire et manger.
of what to drink and eat
something

À la première où il arriva, une petite fille était sur le seuil.
To the first (one) where he arrived a little girl was on the threshold

Croyant que c'était comme à Autonomie, il s'approcha pour la
Believing that it was like at Autonomy he -himself- approached for her

173

caresser et demander à manger, mais la gamine s'enfuit en poussant
caress and ask to eat but the lassie herself fled in pushing
ran away uttering

des cris de pintade.
-of the- cries of (a) guinea fowl

Et quelle différence avec Mab, Sacha, Biquette, et les autres enfants
And what difference with Mab Sacha Biquette and the other children

d'Autonomie ! Sale, mal peignée, la figure toute barbouillée, les jupons
of Autonomy ! Dirty badly combed the face all stained the petticoats

en loque, elle rappela à Nono ses petites voisines, lorsqu'il était chez
in rag(s) she recalled -to- Nono his small neighbors when he was with

ses parents.
his parents

Il continua donc son chemin vers une autre chaumière qu'il aperçut
He continued then his way towards an other cottage that he saw

un peu plus loin. Mais lorsqu'il voulut en approcher, un dogue
a bit more far But when he wanted -of- it approach a mastiff
farther

s'élança vers lui, aboyant furieusement. Nono n'eut que le temps
itself launched towards him barking furiously Nono not had than the time
just had

de s'éloigner.
of himself get away

Il s'avança vers une troisième, et s'adressant à un petit
He himself advanced towards a third and himself addressing to a little

garçon qui se trouvait sur le seuil, il lui demanda à manger.
boy who himself found on the threshold he him asked to eat

— M'man, fit l'enfant s'adressant à une jeune femme qui lavait
— Mom made the child himself addressing -to- a young woman who washed
said

du linge dans un baquet, au milieu de la chambre, c'est un p'tit
-of- the linen in a tub at the middle of the room this is a lil

garçon, y dit qu'il a faim.
boy there said that he has hunger
is hungry

— Encore un mendiant, fit la femme sans se déranger, si on
— Still a beggar made the woman without herself to bother if one
Yet another said

voulait donner à tous, on n'en finirait pas. Dis lui que l'on ne
wanted to give to all one not of it would end -not- Tell him that -it- one not

peut rien faire pour lui. »
can nothing do for him

Le cœur gros, Nono alla s'asseoir sur une grosse pierre, ses jambes
The heart big Nono went himself sit on a big stone his legs
Emotional

refusant de le porter plus loin, il se mit à méditer amèrement sur
refusing of him to carry more far he himself put to meditate bitterly on

les aventures qui lui survenaient, se rappelant les paroles de
the adventures which him occurred himself recalling the words of

Solidaria, lorsqu'elle l'avait introduit à Autonomie :
Solidaria when she him had introduced to (the country of) Autonomy :

« Je te mettrai aux prises avec les circonstances. Comme tu agiras,
I you will put at the grips with the circumstances Like you will act
height of

elles seront bonnes ou néfastes pour toi. — C'est donc toi qui, en
they will be good or adverse for you — This is then you who in

définitive, feras tes aventures, et les ornementeras par ta façon de
definitive will make your adventures and them will decorate by your way of

te comporter. »
yourself behave

Et, de fait, s'il avait été plus confiant, plus sage, il ne se serait
And of fact if he had been more confiding more wise he not himself would be
in

pas laissé enlever d'Autonomie, ni attirer dans un pays si ingrat.
-not- let take away from Autonomy nor draw in a country so ungrateful

— Décidément, se dit-il, je n'ai pas pris le bon chemin.
— Definitely himself said he I not have -not- taken the good way

Et fouillant machinalement dans sa poche, sa main y heurta
And searching mechanically in his pocket his hand there bumped into

quelque chose de carré. C'était la boîte que lui avait donnée Riri.
some thing -of- square It was the box that him had given Riri

Voulant s'assurer que l'eau n'avait pas détérioré, en y
Wanting himself to ensure that the water did not have -not- deteriorated in there

pénétrant, son instrument magique, il en tira l'accordéon et appuya
penetrating his instrument magic he from it drew the accordion and pressed

sur les notes. Aussitôt, l'accordéon grandit, jouant une valse entraînante.
on the keys Immediately the accordion grew playing a waltz catchy

Le petit garçon de la maison, qui l'avait suivi de loin,
The little boy of the house who him had followed from (a) distance

s'arrêta émerveillé d'entendre sortir d'une si petite boîte, une musique
himself halted marveled of to hear go out from a so little box a music
stopped marveling

faisant autant de bruit que celle des soldats de Monnaïus lorsque, par
making as much -of- noise as that of the soldiers of Monnaïus when by

hasard, ils venaient à traverser ce petit village perdu.
chance they came to cross this little village lost

D'autres enfants du village, attirés par la musique, étaient accourus,
Of others children of the village attracted by the music were rushed
Other came rushing

sortant des maisons, arrivant de la route ; c'était comme une nichée
leaving -of- the houses arriving by the road ; it was like a brood

de petits lapins. Il y en avait de toutes les tailles et de toutes
of small rabbits It there of them had of all the sizes and of all

les couleurs. Ils eurent bientôt fait un demi-cercle devant Nono et
the colors They had soon made a semi circle in front of Nono and

sa musique. Nono satisfait de voir son instrument en bon état,
his music Nono satisfied of to see his instrument in good state

s'arrêta d'en jouer et fît mine de le remettre dans sa boîte.
himself halted of on it to play and made (a) gesture of it to put back in his box
stopped

Les enfants demandèrent qu'il leur jouât encore un air.
The children asked that he them played still a tune
another

Mais le musicien guignait avidement une grosse tartine de pain qu'un
But the musician eyed greedily a big slice of bread that one

des enfants tenait à la main.
of the children kept at the hand
in

Le premier garçon qu'il avait abordé, se rappelant la demande de
The first boy that he had entered himself recalling the request of
encountered

Nono, lui dit :
Nono him said :

— Fais-nous encore de la musique, t'auras la tartine.
— Make us still of the music you will get the tartine

— N'est-ce pas Zidore, fit-il en s'adressant au propriétaire de
— Not is this -not- Zidore made he while himself addressing to the owner of
Isn't it said he

la tartine, que tu lui donneras ton pain au garçon s'il nous fait
the tartine that you him will give your bread to the boy if he us makes

encore de la musique ? »
still of the music ?

Celui-ci se gratta la tête, mais finit par tendre sa tartine à
That one himself scratched the head But ended by to tender his tartine to
to hand over

Nono qui se mit à y mordre goulûment.
Nono who himself set to there bite greedily
started to bite it

Et, faisant à nouveau fonctionner l'accordéon, il régala ses auditeurs
And making to new function the accordion he entertained his audience
again

d'un nouvel air, en prenant le temps de dévorer sa tartine.
with a new tune in taking the time of to devour his slice with sweet spread

Lorsqu'il eut jugé leur avoir donné assez de musique pour leur pain,
When he had judged them to have given enough -of- music for their bread
having

il voulut se lever, emportant sa boîte, car il voyait que le soleil
he wanted himself to raise carrying his box because he saw that the sun

s'approchait de l'horizon.
herself approached of the horizon

Mais les enfants lui redemandèrent encore un air. Et il ressortit sa
But the children him demanded again still a tune And he took out again his

musique en disant que, leur faire plaisir, il allait encore jouer un
music in saying that them to make pleasure he went still to play a

morceau, mais qu'il était temps qu'il se remît en route.
piece but that it was time that he himself to set again on (the) road

Et lorsque l'air fut joué, il remit la boîte dans sa poche, pour
And when the tune was played he put back the box in his pocket for

partir.
leave

Mais ce n'était pas le compte de ses auditeurs qui lui demandèrent
But this not was -not- the account of his audience who him asked

de faire jouer encore la musique.
of to make to play still the music

— Non, vraiment, je ne puis pas, car il faut que je me remette
— No really I not can -not- because it is necessary that I me set again

en route, fit Nono.
in road made Nono
        said

Et comme les enfants insistaient.
And as the children insisted

— La nuit va arriver, je ne sais pas où je suis. Non je ne peux
— The night goes arrive I not know -not- where I am Not I -not- can

pas rester plus longtemps. Il faut que je parte.
-not- stay more long It is necessary that I leave

Les figures commencèrent à devenir hargneuses.
The faces began to become peevish

— Hé ! va donc, teigneux, fit un des garçons.
— Hey! ! go then scabby made one of the boys
                    said

— A-t-il l'air de faire son malin, avec sa musique ! fit un autre.
— Has-it he the air of to make his malignant with his music ! made an other
                                                                    said

— Si je voulais en avoir une, mon papa m'en achèterait une bien
— If I wanted of it to have one my daddy me of it would buy one well

plus belle, renchérit une petite fille en loques.
more beautiful added a little girl in tatters

Et, ramassent des cailloux, ils allaient faire un mauvais parti à Nono,
And picking of the pebbles they went to make a bad action to Nono
                                        to do   thing

lorsque, heureusement pour lui, une femme sortit d'une des maisons,
when fortunately for him a woman got out from one of the houses

fit la chasse aux galopins, en saisissant un par l'oreille.
made the chase to the urchins in gripping one by the ear
chased away the

— Après qui en as-tu, encore, chenapan ! fit-elle.
— After who in have you still scoundrel ! she asked

— C'est pas moi, m'man, hurla le vaurien. C'est les autres qui voulaient
— It is -not- me mom howled the rascal It is the others who wanted

que le garçon leur fasse encore de la musique. »
that the boy them makes still of the music
more

La femme lâcha l'oreille de son garnement, et s'approcha de Nono,
The woman left the ear of her scamp and herself approached of Nono

lui demandant qui il était, d'où il venait, où il allait.
him asking who he was from where he came where he went

Nono lui raconta ses aventures, sa vie à Autonomie, sa rencontre avec
Nono him told his adventures his life at Autonomy his meeting with
in

le gros monsieur, son enlèvement, son naufrage, et son isolement dans
the fat gentleman his removal his shipwreck and his isolation in
abduction

ce pays inconnu.
this country unknown

Mais la pauvre campagnarde n'avait jamais entendu parler d'Autonomie.
But the poor rural lady did not have ever heard speak of Autonomy

Pour elle, le gros monsieur devait être quelque Bohémien qui enlevait
For her the fat gentleman must be some Bohemian who took away
gypsy

les enfants pour en faire des petits mendiants.
the children for of them to make -of the- small beggars

— Hélas, mon pauvre enfant, fit-elle apitoyée, je ne connais pas le
— Alas my poor child she asked pitying I not know -not- the

beau pays dont tu me parles. Je n'ai jamais entendu parler de
beautiful country of which you me speak I not have ever heard speak of

179

choses semblables que dans les contes de fées, et, si vraiment tu
things similar that in the (fairy)tales of fairies and so really you

viens d'un pays si magnifique, je te plains certes, car ici, c'est
come of a country so splendid I you pity certainly because here it is

bien différent de ce que tu me racontes.
well different of this that you me tell

Il faut travailler beaucoup pour gagner peu. Le pays est pauvre,
It is necessary to work a lot for to earn (a) little The country is poor

tu n'as aucune chance de trouver quelqu'un qui veuille te prendre.
you not have any fortune of to find someone who wants you take

Ton travail ne paierait pas ta nourriture.
Your work not will pay -not- your food

Le mieux que tu puisses faire, c'est de te rendre à Monnaïa, la
The best that you can do it is of you to hand over to Monnaïa the

capitale qu'habite notre roi Monnaïus. Là on y emploie des
capital that inhabits our king Monnaïus There one there employs -of the-

enfants de tous les âges, comme domestiques, ou dans les usines. Là,
children of all the ages like servants or in the factories There

tu auras quelque chance de gagner ta vie.
you will have some fortune of to earn your life

Attends-moi. Je reviens. »
Wait for me I come back
          will come back

Et se dirigeant vers sa chaumière, elle en revint avec un gros
And herself directing towards her cottage she from it returned with a big

cagnon de pain, un peu de fromage, et une tasse de lait qu'elle fit
piece of bread a bit of cheese and a cup of milk that she made

boire au pauvre exilé.
drink to the poor exile

— Mets ce pain et ce fromage dans ta poche, continua la femme,
— Put this bread and this cheese in your pocket continued the woman

ça te servira pour continuer ta route. Tu n'as qu'à suivre ce
that you serves for to continue your road You not have than to to follow this

chemin, jusqu'à ce que tu arrives sur une route plus grande, tu
way / up to / this / that / you / arrived / on / a / road / more / large / you

tourneras à gauche et tu suivras cette nouvelle route pendant quelque
will turn / to / (the) left / and / you / will follow / this / new / road / during / some

temps. Tu rencontreras bien quelque passant pour t'indiquer lorsqu'il
time / You / will meet / well / some / passer by / for / to tell you / when it

faudra changer. »
will be necessary / to change (road)

Nono eut bien envie de pleurer lorsqu'il vit confirmer ses craintes d'être
Nono / had / well / envy / of / to cry / when he / saw / confirm / his / fears / of to be

transporté en Argyrocratie, mais refoulant ses larmes, il remercia la
transported / in / Argyrocratie / but / repulsing / his / tears / he / thanked / the

bonne femme et lui demanda s'il lui faudrait marcher longtemps
good / woman / and / her / asked / if it / him / would be necessary / to walk / (a) long time

pour atteindre Monnaïa. Il fut tout à fait consterné lorsqu'elle lui eut
for / to reach / Monnaïa / He / was / all / to / fact / appalled / when she / him / had

dit qu'il n'y arriverait qu'après de longues journées de
said / that he / not there / would arrive / (other) than after / -of- / long / days / of

marche.
march

Le cœur bien gros, il dit adieu à la femme et se remit en
The / heart / well / big / he / said / farewell / to / the / woman / and / himself / set again / in

marche pour Monnaïa.
march / for / Monnaïa

Sur la route
On the road

Il y avait déjà plusieurs jours que Nono était en route, ayant vécu
It there had already (for) several days that Nono was in road having lived
It was   on the

de quelques croûtes de pain dues à la commisération que sa jeunesse
of some crusts of bread due to the commiseration that his youth
    pity

soulevait chez quelque campagnarde compatissante.
raised with some rural person compassionate
    compassionate farmer

Il marchait depuis le matin, n'ayant mangé qu'un morceau de
He marched since the morning, not having eaten (other) than a piece of

pain qu'on lui avait donné chez un paysan qui, pris de pitié à la
bread that one him had given with a peasant who, taken of pity at the

vue de son jeune âge, avait consenti à le laisser passer la nuit sur
sight of his young age, had granted to him to let pass the night on

le foin, dans sa grange.
the hay, in his barn

Il avait faim, il était bien las, et il faisait presque nuit déjà
He had hunger he was well weary and it made almost night already
    was hungry   was

lorsqu'il atteignit une ferme non loin de la route qu'il suivait.
when he reached a farm not far from the road that he followed

À son approche, deux dogues qui étaient à l'attache, aboyèrent après lui,
At his approach, two mastiffs who were at the leash barked after him

faisant tous leurs efforts pour lui sauter dessus. Nono, craintif,
making all their efforts for him to jump on top Nono, apprehensive
    to jump him on top

n'osant plus avancer, se tenait indécis à la porte qu'il
not daring (any)more to move forward himself kept undecided at the gate that he

n'osait franchir.
not dared to cross

Un valet, occupé à tasser du fumier dans la cour, vint vers lui
A servant occupied to pile up -of- the manure in the yard came towards him
farmhand

et lui demanda ce qu'il voulait.
and him asked this that he wanted
what

Le jeune voyageur lui expliqua qu'il se rendait à Monnaïa et
The young traveller him explained that he himself rendered to Monnaïa and
went

demandait qu'on voulut bien lui faire l'aumône d'un morceau de pain
asked that one wanted well him to make the alms of a piece of bread
whether they to give the grace

et lui donner asile pour la nuit.
and him to give asylum for the night

— Heu ! fit l'homme, le maître n'est pas donnant, et je doute
— Er ! made the man the master not is -not- giving and I doubt
said

fort qu'il veuille te recevoir. Attends là, tout de même, je vais
strongly that he wants you receive Wait there all of same I go

aller lui demander. »
to go him ask

Nono, qui depuis qu'il était en Argyrocratie, avait appris plus d'une
Nono who since that he was in Argyrocratie had learned more than one

fois, au grand déplaisir de son appétit, que l'on ne donne rien
time at the large displeasure of his appetite that -it- one not gives nothing

pour rien dans le pays de Monnaïus, ajouta :
for nothing in the country of Monnaïus added :

— Dites-lui que, s'il a des enfants, je leur ferai de la musique
— Tell him that if he has -of-the- children I them will make -of- the music

à la veillée pour les amuser. »
at the evening-gathering for them to amuse

Et il sortit l'accordéon de sa boîte et se mit à jouer un
And he got out the accordion from his box and himself set to play a

pas redoublé.
step intensified
lively tune

Depuis qu'il était en marche, son accordéon lui avait valu ainsi
Since that he was in march his accordion him had been worth thus

quelques écuellées de soupe, une place dans la grange. Mais ce n'était
some spoonfuls of soup a place in the barn But this not was

que dans les fermes isolées, dans les petits villages loin de toute
(other) than in the farms isolated in the small villages far of all

communication, où les distractions sont rares. Dans les bourgs un peu
communication where the distractions are rare In the towns a bit

importants, sa musique avait peu de succès, et il devait, le plus
important his music had little of success and he must the most

souvent, se coucher le ventre creux, en quelque renfoncement, dans
often himself lay down the belly hollow in some recess in

l'encoignure d'une porte.
the corner of a door

— Bon, je vais le dire au maître, fit l'homme, qui disparut.
— Good I go it say to the master made the man who disappeared
said

— Rentre, fit-il en revenant, et en apaisant les chiens. Et il
— Enter made he in coming back and in appeasing the dogs And he
said he when he came back

conduisit le voyageur dans une grande salle noire, enfumée, meublée
led the traveller in a large room black smoky furnished

seulement d'une grande table au milieu ; une maie dans un coin,
only with a large table at the middle ; a dung heap in a corner
in the

un buffet plus loin, au plafond pendaient des pièces de lard, des
a buffet more far at the ceiling hung -of the- pieces of bacon -of the-

jambons, des oignons, de l'ail et des graines dans leur cosse.
hams -of the- onions -of- -the- garlic and -of the- seeds in their pod

Un feu de sarment brillait dans une grande cheminée au fond de la
A fire of branch(es) gleamed in a large fireplace at the back of the

salle. Près du feu, sous le manteau de la cheminée, était un vieux
room Near of the fire under the mantel of the fireplace was an old (man)

de quatre-vingts ans au moins. C'était le père du fermier.
of eighty years at the least It was the father of the farmer

Non loin de la cheminée, le fermier fumait sa pipe. Son fils, un gars
Not far from the fireplace the farmer smoked his pipe His son a boy

d'une trentaine d'années, s'occupait à réparer une hotte en osier.
of a thirty-some of years himself occupied to repair a basket in wicker

La fermière, dans des écuelles alignées devant elle, taillait du
The farmer woman in -of the- bowls aligned in front of her carved -of the-

pain pour la soupe qui bouillait dans une marmite pendue à la
bread for the soup which boiled in a pot hung at the

crémaillère dans l'âtre. La bru raccommodait le linge de la
rack and pinion in the hearth The daughter-in-law mended the linen of the

famille.
family

Deux enfants, — ceux du fils, — un petit garçon et une petite fille,
Two children — those of the son — a little boy and a little girl

s'amusaient à faire des constructions avec des chènevottes.
enjoyed themselves to make -of the- constructs with -of the- shives

— C'est toi, fit le fermier d'une grosse voix bourrue, qui demandes à
— This is you made the farmer with a big voice gruff who requests to
said

coucher ?
lay down ?

— Oui, monsieur, fit Nono un peu intimidé.
— Yes Sir made Nono a bit nervous
said

— Et où est-elle la musique dont tu as promis de nous jouer
— And where is she the music of which you have promised of us to play

? Je ne t'en vois pas.
? I not you for it see -not-
I don't see it on you

Nono sortit sa boîte de sa poche, et en tira son accordéon dont il
Nono got out his box of his pocket and of it drew his accordion which he

joua.
played

Les enfants abandonnèrent du coup leurs chènevottes pour venir
The children abandoned of the strike their shives for to come
immediately

écouter le merveilleux instrument.
hear the wonderful instrument

Les grandes personnes, qui ne devaient pas avoir de grandes
The large people who not must -not- have -of- great
    adults

distractions dans cette ferme qui était quelque peu isolée, semblèrent
distractions in this farm which was some bit isolated seemed

y prendre autant de plaisir que les petits.
there to take as much of pleasure as the small

Une grosse servante, qui venait de traire les vaches, et rentrait avec
A big servant girl who came (back) of to milk the cows and returned with

un seau plein de lait, s'écria :
a bucket full of milk exclaimed :

— Matin ! que c'est biau ! On dirait les musiqueux de
— Morning ! that this is beautiful ! One would say the music of
    {dialect for beau}   {dialect for musique}

cheux nous, lorsqu'avec leur violon et le cornet à piston, ils font
those us when with their violin and the horn at piston(s) they make
{dialect for chez}

danser la jeunesse. »
dance the youth

Mais la fermière, qui venait de tremper la soupe, s'écria :
But the farmer woman who came of to dip the soup cried :

— Allons à table les enfants ! après souper vous aurez le temps
— Go to (the) table -the- children ! after supper you will have the time

d'écouter la musique. »
of to listen (to) the music

Une place, près de l'âtre, fut désignée à Nono, et on lui tendit
A place near of the hearth was designated to Nono and one him extended

une écuelle de soupe qu'il dut manger sur ses genoux, pendant que
a bowl of soup that he had to eat on his knees during that

les habitants de la ferme prenaient place autour de la table.
the inhabitants of the farm took place around of the table

Nono, ayant fini sa soupe tenait son écuelle, embarrassé, ne sachant
Nono having finished his soup kept his bowl embarrassed not knowing

où la poser, guignant de l'œil une appétissante platée de choux et
where it to put eyeing with the eye an appetizing plateful of cabbages and

de lard que la fermière venait de tirer de la marmite, espérant
of bacon that the farmer woman came of to pull from the pot hoping

qu'on lui en offrirait une petite part.
that one him of it would offer a little part

Mais lorsque la fermière eut fait la tournée de la table, le plat
But when the farmer woman had made the turn of the table the plate

était vide, et Nono, poussant un gros soupir, comprit qu'il n'avait
was empty and Nono pushing a big sigh understood that he did not have
uttering

plus rien à espérer de la générosité de ses hôtes.
more nothing to hope from the generosity of his hosts

Cependant, la bru, le voyant suivre des yeux chaque bouchée
However the daughter-in-law him seeing follow with the eyes each bite

qu'ils portaient à leur bouche, vint lui apporter un morceau de pain,
that they carried to their mouth came him bring a piece of bread

et un verre de cidre aigrelet.
and a glass of cider tart

Quand le fermier fut rassasié, il ferma son couteau, et tout le monde
When the farmer was satiated he closed his knife and all the world
everyone

se leva : la table fut desservie, la vaisselle lavée dans l'eau que
himself raised : the table was unserved the dishes washed in the water that
themselves raised cleaned

l'on avait mis à chauffer dans la marmite d'où l'on avait
it one had put to warm in the pot from where -it- one had

tiré la soupe, le lard et les choux. Les domestiques allèrent aux
pulled out the soup the bacon and the cabbages The servants went to the

étables s'assurer que les bestiaux ne manquaient de rien. Puis,
cowsheds themselves to assure that the cattle not lacked of nothing Then

un à un, ils revinrent s'asseoir près du foyer, sans rien dire, les
one by one they came back to sit down near of the hearth without nothing to say the

yeux perdus dans le vague.
eyes lost in the vague

187

Les enfants ayant réclamé la musique, Nono les en régala.
The children having reclaimed the music Nono them with it entertained

Puis, le fermier que la digestion semblait rendre un peu plus aimable,
Then the farmer that the digestion seemed to render a bit more pleasant
who

le questionna, lui demandant d'où il venait ? où il allait ?
him questioned him asking from where he came ? where he went ?

Nono avait eu plus d'une fois l'occasion de remarquer qu'en
Nono had had more than one time the opportunity of notice that in

Argyrocratie on tenait absolument à savoir ce qu'étaient les gens avant
Argyrocratie one kept absolutely to know this what were the people before
wanted

de leur venir en aide.
of them to come in aide

Ce fut donc une nouvelle occasion pour lui de raconter ses aventures.
This was then a new opportunity for him of to tell his adventures

Mais le vieux fermier, qui n'avait pas sourcillé lorsque Nono lui
But the old farmer who did not have -not- blinked when Nono him

avait mentionné l'histoire de l'oiseau parlant, des abeilles se
had mentioned the story of the bird speaking of the bees themselves

transformant en belles dames, des carabes venant offrir des
transforming in beautiful ladies of -the- beetles coming to offer -of the-

fraises, partit d'un accès de fou rire qui lui secouait le ventre,
strawberries left with an access of mad laughter which him shook the belly
attack

lorsque le narrateur en arriva au séjour d'Autonomie où chacun
when the narrator of it arrived at the stay of Autonomy where each one

travaillait comme il l'entendait, se reposait quand il lui plaisait, où
worked like he it agreed himself rested when it him pleased where

les fruits appartenaient à tous, où tous pouvaient prendre autant qu'ils
the fruits belonged to all where all could take as much as they

voulaient dans la récolte, où l'on était toujours plein de prévenances
wanted in the harvest where -it- one was always full of attention

l'un pour l'autre.
the one for the other

Le fermier riait de si bon cœur qu'il manqua de s'en étrangler,
The farmer laughed of so good heart that he lacked of himself of it strangle
almost choked

ce qui lui occasionna une quinte de toux. Lorsque l'accès fut un
this which him occasioned a fifth of cough When the attack was a
fit

peu calmé :
bit calmed :

— As-tu jamais entendu parler d'un pays comme cela ? fit-il à son
— Have you ever heard speak of a country like that ? made he to his
said he

fils.
son

— Dame ! non.
— Lady ! No

— Heu, heu, ça irait bien ici, s'il n'y avait personne pour
— Er Er that would go well here if it not there had anyone for
if there was

commander !
to command !

— Et s'il fallait attendre que les voisins viennent nous aider à
— And if it was necessary to wait that the neighbors come us help to

labourer, sûrement que nous attendrions fort longtemps, répliqua le fils.
plow surely that we would wait for (a) very long time replied the son

— Tandis qu'il ne manquerait pas de monde pour la récolte, s'il
— While that it not would miss -not- of world for the harvest if it
that no one would miss

fallait qu'elle fût à la disposition de qui en voudrait.
was necessary that she was to the disposition of who of it would like

— M'est avis, reprit le fils, que tout cela ne me semble pas
— Me is opinion continued the son that all that not me appears -not-
I'm of the opinion

bien net. Le fieu cependant est bien trop jeune pour mentir et savoir
well clean The kid however is well too young for to lie and to know

inventer des histoires. Il doit avoir le cerveau un peu fêlé ; alors
to invent of the stories He must have the brain a bit cracked ; so

189

il dit ce qui lui vient, sans savoir. »
he says this which him comes without to know

Nono sentait confusément que si le fermier eût été en peine de trouver
Nono felt confusedly that if the farmer had been in pain of to find
in trouble

des bras pour l'aider à cultiver ses champs, c'est que, précisément, il
of the arms for him to help to cultivate his fields it is that exactly he

prétendait en conserver pour lui tout le profit. Mais, trop jeune
claimed of it to preserve for him(self) all the profit. But too young

pour bien démêler ses propres idées et trouver les expressions justes
for well to unravel his own ideas and to find the expressions righteous
to discern

pour répliquer, il se tut, très mortifié qu'on le crût un peu
for to reply he himself silenced very mortified that one him believed a bit

fou.
crazy

— Alors, tu dis comme ça, reprit le fermier, qu'il n'y avait pas
— Then you say like that continued the farmer that it not there had -not-
that there was no

d'argent à Autonomie, que chacun prend ce qu'il veut ? Mais comment
of silver at Autonomy that each takes this that he wants ? But how
silver

paie-t-on les archers pour vous défendre des voleurs ?
pays one the archers for you to defend from the thieves ?

— Je n'ai jamais vu d'archers, ni entendu parler de voleurs.
— I not have ever seen -of- archers nor heard speak of thieves

— Vous n'aviez pas de soldats, pas de messiers, ni d'archers du
— You not had -not- -of- soldiers not -of- gentlemen nor archers of the
{monsieurs}

guet ? Tu nous en contes. Vous vous seriez continuellement
look-out ? You us of it (make) tales You yourself would be continually

battus pour avoir les meilleurs fruits.
fought for to have the best fruits

— Ça n'est jamais arrivé pendant que j'y étais. — Je ne me suis
— That not is ever arrived during that I there was — I not me am
happened have

battu qu'une fois. Ce n'était pas pour des fruits, mais parce
fought (other) than one time This not was -not- for -of- the fruits but because

que j'étais de mauvaise humeur. Mais j'ai été si malheureux, que je me
that I was of bad mood But I have been so unhappy that I me

suis bien promis de ne plus recommencer.
am well promised of not (any)more to start again

— Et ça ne t'ennuyait pas de travailler ? Allons, avoue-le : sans la
— And that not you bored not -of- to work ? Go admit it : without the

crainte de Solidaria et de Labor, tu te serais bien reposé plus
fear of Solidaria and of Labor you yourself would be well rested more

d'une fois, au lieu d'aller travailler avec les autres ?
than one time at the place of to go work with the others ?

— Oh ! non, je me serais au contraire fort ennuyé, s'il m'avait
— Oh ! no I myself would be at the contrary strongly bored if it me had
                                         very much

fallu rester à ne rien faire.
been necessary to stay to not nothing to do
                            anything

Le fermier secoue la tête d'un air incrédule, faisant remarquer combien
The farmer shakes the head with an air incredulous making notice how much

tout cela était improbable, des enfants aimant le travail, malheureux de
all that was unlikely of the children desiring the work unhappy of

s'être disputés.
themselves to be disputed
to have argued

— Si les deux tiens, continua-t-il, regrettaient quelquefois de s'être
— If the two hold, continued he regretted sometimes of themselves to be
         here   to have

battus, ça ne leur arriverait pas si souvent ; d'autant plus qu'il
beaten that not them would arrive -not- so often ; especially more that he
fought   not if there

n'y a que quelques paires de taloches qui arrivent, sinon à les
not there has -that- some pairs of cuffs which arrive if not to them
          are

mettre d'accord, à les faire taire tout au moins.
put of agreement (than) to them make be quiet all at the least
     in agreement

— Il est de fait que si nous n'étions pas là, ils se
— It is of fact that if we were not -not- there they themselves

disputeraient tout les deux comme deux pies-grièches, fit le fils, en
would dispute all the two like two shrikes made/said the son in

regardant d'un air satisfait les deux petits qui écoutaient, ouvrant
watching with an air satisfied the two small (ones) who listened opening

des yeux grands comme des portes cochères, pendant que la mère
of the eyes large like of the doors (for) coaches during that the mother

les attirait contre elle, les embrassant.
them pulled against her them kissing

— Moi, aussi, fit Nono, chez mes parents j'étais tout le temps à me
— Me also made Nono with my parents I was all the time to me

disputer avec ma sœur. Ça n'empêche qu'à Autonomie, personne n'avait
dispute with my sister That not hinders that at Autonomy no one not had

envie de se disputer.
envy of themselves to dispute
the desire to argue with each other

— Tout ça, mon garçon, fit le fermier, ce sont des idées folles. Si
— All that my boy made/said the farmer these are of the ideas mad If

personne n'était forcé de travailler, tout le monde voudrait se
no one -not- was forced -of- to work all the world would like himself

reposer. Il faut des gens raisonnables pour mettre la paix parmi
to rest It is necessary of the people reasonable for to put the peace among

ceux qui ne le sont pas. Quand tu auras vécu ici, parmi les gens
those who not it are -not- When you will have lived here among the people

d'Argyrocratie, quand tu seras plus en âge de saisir les choses, tu
of Argyrocratie when you will be more in age of to seize the things you

comprendras qu'il ne peut en être autrement.
will understand that it not can of it be otherwise

— C'était autrement à Autonomie, soupira Nono.
— It was otherwise/different at Autonomy sighed Nono

— Pourtant, not'maître, fit un des valets, si on s'en rapporte à
— However our master made/said one of the servants/farmhands if one oneself of it brings back to

nos anciens, qui le tiennent de leurs anciens, qui le tenaient
our elders who it take from their elders who it held
get got

eux-mêmes des leurs, il paraîtrait que la terre n'a pas toujours
themselves from -the- theirs it would appear that the earth not has -not- always

appartenu aux seigneurs ; qu'il y a eu une époque où elle
belonged to the lords ; that it there has had a time where she
that there was

appartenait à tous, que l'on s'en partageait les produits. En ces
belonged to all that -it- one himself of it shared the products. In these

temps-là, les gens n'étaient pas forcés de travailler pour des maîtres
time -there- the people not were -not- forced of to work for of the masters

rapaces. Ils pouvaient manger à leur faim.
rapacious They could eat to their hunger

— Des bêtises, des radotages de vieux, trancha le fermier. Avez-vous
— Of the fooleries of the drivel of old cut the farmer. Have you

entendu parler de cela, père ? fit-il en élevant la voix, s'adressant
heard speak of that father ? made he in raising the voice himself addressing
said he

au vieux qui, sous la cheminée, restait toujours silencieux.
to the old (man) who under the fireplace remained always silent

Et comme le vieux secouait la tête en signe de dénégation :
And as the old (one) shook the head in sign of denial :

— De tous temps, il y a eu des propriétaires et des fermiers
— Of all times it there has had -of the- owners and -of the- farmers
there have been

qui ont pris soin de la terre, faisant vivre ceux qu'ils employaient. Si
who have taken care of the earth making to live those that they employed If

ça avait été comme tu dis, si les gens s'en étaient si bien
that had been like you say if the people itself of it were so well

trouvés, ils seraient restés comme ils étaient. Tout ça, ce sont
found they would be remained like they were All that these are

des racontars de fainéants, qui voudraient vivre à ne rien faire.
-of- the gossips of loafers who would like to live to not nothing do
anything

— Ah ! moi, je ne sais pas, fit le valet. Je répète ce que j'ai
— Ah ! me I not know -not- said the servant I repeat this that I have

entendu dire.
heard say

— Tu répètes alors des bêtises. Ça a été toujours comme ça est,
— You repeat then of the fooleries It has been always like that is

et ça sera toujours comme ça.
and that will be always like that

— Allons, fit-il en s'adressant à Nono, joue-nous encore un air de
— Go made he in himself addressing to Nono play us still a tune of
  said he

musique avant d'aller nous coucher, ça vaudra mieux que de raconter
music before of to go us lay down that will be worth better than of to tell

des sornettes.
-of the- silly talks

Nono s'exécuta. Puis chacun fit ses préparatifs pour aller se
Nono complied Then each made their preparations for to go themselves

reposer. Le valet emmena le musicien à l'étable, où il couchait
to rest The servant took along the musician to the stable where he lay down

lui-même, lui fit une place dans la paille fraîche qu'il avait éparpillée
him self him made a place in the straw fresh that he had scattered

dans un coin, près du coffre à avoine.
in a corner near of the chest to oat
                                  withoats

Nono, brisé de fatigue, s'endormit aussitôt, rêvant à Autonomie.
Nono broken of exhaustion himself slept immediately dreaming to Autonomy
                          fell asleep   of

L'arrivée à Monnaïa
The arrival at Monnaïa

Quand il s'éveilla le lendemain, quoique un peu remis de sa
When he himself awoke the following day though a bit set back from his

fatigue, il avait encore les membres bien moulus, et serait resté
exhaustion he had still the members well ground and would be remained
                         arms and legs   broken   would have

volontiers dans la paille si fraîche. Mais il savait que prolonger son
willingly in the straw so fresh. But he knew that to extend his

vagabondage sur les routes, c'était prolonger la misère et les fatigues.
vagrancy on the roads it was to extend the misery and the exhaustions

Il avait hâte d'atteindre Monnaïa, dont il se savait tout près
He had hurry of to attain Monnaïa of which he himself knew all near

maintenant, et où il espérait trouver du travail.
now and where he hoped to find -of the- work

Il sortit donc de l'étable et se trouva dans la cour. Les hommes
He got out then from the stable and himself found in the yard The men

étaient partis aux champs. Seule la jeune femme du fils restait
were left to the fields Only the young woman of the son remained
had

occupée à distribuer du grain aux poules, canards, oies et dindons
occupied to distribute -of the- grain to the hens ducks geese and turkeys

qui gloussaient autour d'elle, accourant de toutes parts.
who clucked around -of- her running up from all parts

Nono lui souhaita le bonjour.
Nono her wished the good-day

— Ah ! c'est toi, petit. Te voilà parti ?
— Ah ! It is you little (one) You see there left ?

Elle courut à la maison, en revint avec deux tartines bien beurrées
She ran to the house of it returned with two slices of bread well buttered

:
:

— Prends, la route est encore longue. Bonne chance, mon petit gars. »
— Take the road is still long Good fortune my little boy

Et, une fois de plus, notre pauvre ami se trouva sur le grand
And one time -of- more our poor friend himself found on the large
long

chemin bien triste et bien esseulé. Mais il finissait par s'habituer
road well sad and well lonely But he ended by himself to accustom
quite quite

au mauvais sort, et ce fut d'un pas ferme qu'il se remit en
to the bad fate and it was with a step firm that he himself set again on

route.
(the) road

Il marchait depuis plusieurs heures déjà, lorsque la faim se fit
He marched since several hours already when the hunger itself made

sentir. Il alla s'abriter sous un gros chêne qui se dressait non
feel He went himself shelter under a big oak which itself drew up not

loin du chemin, et se mit en posture de dévorer ses deux
far from the road and himself put in posture of to devour his two
readiness

tartines. Mais, à la première bouchée, il sentit que la soif le
slices of bread But at the first bite he felt that the thirst him

prenait ; il chercha autour de lui s'il n'apercevrait pas quelque ruisseau
took ; he sought around of him if he not perceived -not- some stream

pour se désaltérer, et ne tarda pas à entendre les glouglous
for himself quench (the thirst) and not delayed -not- to hear the gurgles

d'une source qui tombait d'un rocher, à pic, aux bord de la route,
of an spring which fell from a rock to peak at the side of the road

dans une petite vasque que l'eau, en tombant, avait fini par creuser
in a little bowl that the water in falling had finished by to dig

dans la pierre.
in the stone

Lorsqu'il eut étanché un peu sa soif, il allait retourner sous son chêne,
When he had quenched a bit his thirst he went to go back under his oak

lorsque, à quelques pas de la fontaine, il vit une taupe, couverte de
when at some steps from the fountain he saw a mole covered of
in

sang, faisant tous ses efforts pour atteindre son trou.
blood making all his efforts for to reach his hole

Ému de pitié à la vue de la triste situation de la pauvre bête,
Moved with pity at the sight of the sad situation of the poor animal

Nono la prit et alla laver sa blessure à la fontaine, la débarrassant
Nono him took and went to wash his wound at the fountain him ridding

du sang et de la boue qui couvrait son pelage si doux et si
of the blood and of the mud which covered his coat so soft and so

soyeux.
silky

Fort embarrassé de savoir quoi mettre sur la blessure, il mâcha
Very embarrassed of to know what to put on the wound he chewed

quelques miettes de pain, qu'il colla ensuite dessus, à l'aide d'une
some crumbs of bread that he stuck subsequently on top at the help of a
with

petite bande de toile qu'il déchira de son mouchoir, et la porta
little band of canvas that he tore from his tissue and it carried

ensuite près de son trou, où, cahin, caha, elle s'engouffra aussi
subsequently near of his hole where chugging caha she herself engulfed as
as good as it got herself got in

prestement qu'elle put.
nimbly as she could

Un peu reposé, ayant fini sa deuxième tartine, Nono reprit sa
A bit rested having finished his second slice of bread Nono continued his

route.
road

Mais, quelque diligence qu'il fit, il lui fut impossible d'atteindre
But whatever diligence that he made it him was impossible of reaching

Monnaïa ce jour-là. La nuit le surprit en pleine campagne, loin de
Monnaïa this day there The night him surprised in full countryside far from

tout village, de toute ferme où il pût demander l'asile ; il
all village from all farm where he could ask for shelter ; he

résolut de s'abriter sous une meule de blé qu'il aperçut dans
resolved of himself to shelter under a millstone of grain that he saw in

un des champs qui bordaient la route.
one of the fields which lined the road

Quelqu'un avait dû s'y abriter déjà, car des gerbes avaient
Someone had had to himself there shelter already because -of the- sheaves had

été déplacées, laissant un vide qui permettait de s'y mettre
been displaced leaving an emptiness which allowed of himself there to put
a hole

à l'abri de la fraîcheur de la nuit. Nono se glissa dans cette
to the shelter from the freshness of the night Nono himself slipped in this

cachette improvisée, et s'endormit, harassé, le ventre creux, les deux
hiding-place improvised and fell asleep weary the belly hollow the two

tartines du matin ayant fait tout autant de chemin que lui.
slices of bread of the morning having made all as much of way as he

La nuit fut particulièrement froide. Quand Nono s'éveilla le matin,
The night was particularly cold When Nono himself awoke the morning
awoke

il était transi ; la faim lui tiraillait l'estomac. Il essaya de la
he was benumbed ; the hunger him tugged the stomach He tried of it

calmer en mâchant quelques grains de blé qu'il égrena des épis
to calm in munching some grains of grain that he shelled from the ears

arrachés aux gerbes près de lui. Il en mit quelques-une dans sa
snatched to the sheaves near of him He of them put some in his
from the

poche pour tromper sa faim en route, et reprit sa marche vers
pocket for to deceive his hunger on (the) road and continued his march towards

la capitale, dont il ne tarda pas à deviner le voisinage, les
the capital of which he not delayed -not- to guess the neighborhood the

voyageurs devenant moins rares sur la route.
travelers becoming less rare on the road

Les voitures aussi devenaient plus nombreuses. On les voyait, chargées
The carriages also became more numerous One them saw loaded

de denrées, s'y diriger, tandis que d'autres en revenaient vides ou
with food itself there direct while that -of- others of it came back empty or

chargées de meubles, de machines, d'étoffes, de toutes sortes de
loaded with furniture with machines with cloths with all kinds of

choses qui annonçaient un trafic important et une industrie très
things which announced a traffic important and an industry very

développée.
developed

Les maisons étaient plus fréquentes le long de la route. Commençant à
The houses were more frequent the long of the road Starting to
along

se montrer de loin en loin, elles finissaient par se tenir les
itself show from far in far they ended by themselves keep the
here and there

unes aux autres, pour ne s'arrêter qu'à une centaine de
ones to the others for not themselves halt (other)than at a hundred of
stop

mètres des murs de Monnaïa.
meters from the walls of Monnaïa

Arrivé là, Nono se trouva sur un plateau élevé d'où il pouvait
Arrived there Nono himself found on a plateau raised from where he could

découvrir tout l'espace devant lui.
discover all the space in front of him

En bas, dans une plaine immense, la capitale d'Argyrocratie étalait ses
In low in a plain immense the capital of Argyrocratie spread its

maisons, ses faubourgs ; dressait les coupoles de ses palais, les tours
houses its outskirts of town ; drew up the cupolas of its palaces the towers

dont ils étaient flanqués, les clochers, les aiguilles, les flèches de ses
of which they were flanked the steeples the needles the arrows of its

églises. C'était un fouillis de murs, de toits, de lucarnes et de fenêtres
churches It was a mess of walls of roofs of skylights and of windows

où l'œil avait peine à se reconnaître.
where the eye had trouble to itself recognize
find back

Nono s'arrêta pour contempler cette ville qui l'effrayait d'avance,
Nono himself halted for to contemplate this city which him frightened beforehand
stopped

ne sachant à quel sort inconnu il allait se trouver livré. Il
not knowing to what fate unknown he went himself to find delivered He
he would be

resta ainsi quelque temps absorbé dans cette contemplation. Il jeta un
remained thus some time absorbed in this contemplation He threw a

dernier regard de regret derrière lui, sur le chemin parcouru, sa pensée
last look of regret behind him on the road traveled his thought

allant à Autonomie, à ses camarades, à ses parents qu'il ne
going to Autonomy to his comrades to his parents that he not

reverrait peut-être plus jamais, et se mit à descendre vers
would see again maybe (any)more ever and himself set to go down towards

la route qui le mènerait aux portes de la ville.
the road which him would lead to the doors of the city

Quelques instants après il était à la tête du pont-levis qui donnait
Some moments after he was at the head of the drawbridge which gave

accès dans la ville qu'enceignait un mur crénelé, flanqué de tours,
access in the city that encircled a wall crenellated flanked with towers
to

carrées ou rondes, celles-ci surmontées de toits en poivrière.
square or round these overcome by roofs in (form of) pepper pot

Au haut de ces tours, flottait la bannière de Monnaïus, un grand
At the height of these towers floated the banner of Monnaïus a large

pavillon jaune semé de taches rouge en formes de larmes ; au centre
flag yellow sown with spots red in forms of tears ; at the center

était brodée en noir, les ailes éployées, une chauve-souris, de l'espèce
was embroidered in black the wings outspread a bald-mouse of the species
bat

vampire, comme celles qui avaient enlevé Nono d'Autonomie.
vampire like those who had taken away Nono from Autonomy

Le mur était séparé lui-même de la plaine par un large fossé plein
The wall was separated it-self from the plain by a wide ditch full

d'eau. Le pont-levis sur lequel s'engageait Nono était commandé par
of water The drawbridge on which himself engaged Nono was commanded by
stood overlooked

une grande tour carrée, servant de poste aux hommes d'armes qui
a large tower square serving of post to the men of weapons who
soldiers

défendaient la porte. Une lourde herse de fer, levée en ce moment,
defended the gate A heavy harrow of iron gotten up in this moment

était prête à s'abattre en cas de surprise.
was ready to itself beat down in case of surprise

En passant sur le pont, Nono vit une longue file de voitures chargées
In passing on the bridge Nono saw a long row of carriages loaded

de denrées, et de toutes sortes de matériaux, qui stationnaient. Une
of food and of all kinds of materials which stood still A

paysanne qui marchait, deux paniers aux bras, fut accostée par deux
peasant woman who marched two baskets on the arm was accosted by two

êtres habillés de vert. Ils avaient un corps humain, mais ce corps était
beings dressed of green They had a body human but this body was
in

surmonté d'une tête de fouine.
mounted by a head of (a) weasel

À vrai dire, était-ce bien une tête de fouine ? était-ce une tête
At true to say Was it well a head of (a) weasel ? Was it a head
indeed

humaine ? C'est ce que Nono aurait été fort embarrassé de décider.
human ? It is this that Nono would have been very embarrassed of to decide

C'était l'une ou l'autre, selon la façon dont on les envisageait.
It was the one or the other according to the way of which one them considered

Ils fouillèrent dans les paniers qui contenaient des poules, des
They searched in the baskets which contained -of the- hens -of the-

lapins, des légumes. Après avoir bien tout retourné, les deux êtres
rabbits -of the- vegetables After to have well all returned the two beings

inscrivirent quelque chose sur un carnet, en détachèrent la moitié de
inscribed some thing on a notebook of it detached the half of
registered

la page, la remirent à la paysanne qui leur donna quelques pièces
the page it handed to the peasant woman who them gave some pieces

de monnaie qu'elle avait tirées de son mouchoir, et passa.
of money that she had pulled from his kerchief and passed

Après elle, ce fut un voyageur qui arrivait sa valise à la main. Les
After her it was a traveller who arrived his suitcase at the hand The

deux êtres à figure de fouine la lui firent ouvrir, en éparpillèrent le
two beings at face of weasel it him made open in scattering the
with

contenu sur le sol, mêlant linge propre et linge sale, puis ils firent
contents on the ground mixing linen clean and linen dirty then they made

une marque à sa valise, et passèrent à un autre.
a mark on his suitcase and passed to an other

D'autres êtres, habillés de même, toujours à double physionomie, visitaient
Of others beings dressed of same always at double aspect visiting
Other the

les voitures, ne les laissant pénétrer qu'après en avoir vérifié
the carriages not them letting enter (other) than after of them to have verified

le contenu et tiré quelque argent de ceux qui les conduisaient.
the contents and pulled out some silver of those who them drove

Nono, qui n'avait aucun paquet, passa sans qu'il lui fût rien dit,
Nono who not had any package passed without that it him was nothing said

mais on l'inspecta des pieds à la tête, pour s'assurer qu'il
but one him inspected from the feet to the head for himself to ensure that he

ne dissimulait rien sous ses vêtements.
not concealed nothing under his clothes

Des soldats montaient la faction de distance en distance. Ceux qui
Of the soldiers rose the watch from distance in distance Those who
kept up

attendaient leur tour de prendre la faction étaient devant la porte
awaited their turn of to take the watch were in front of the door

du corps de garde, fumant, riant, jouant. Il y en avait de
of the body of guard smoking laughing playing It there of them had -of-
There were

plusieurs sortes.
several kinds

Parmi ceux qui montaient la faction, les uns étaient armés de longues
Among those who rose the watch the ones were armed with long
went up some

piques. Un sabre suspendu à un baudrier pendait à leur côté. Une
pikes A saber suspended to a sling hung at their side A

cuirasse de fer leur protégeait le buste, un casque surmonté d'une
cuirass of iron them protected the chest a helmet mounted by a

plume leur ombrageait la tête. Ce devaient être les vieilles troupes, ils
feather them shaded the head This must be the old troops they

avaient des moustaches grises.
had of the mustaches gray

Mais, chose curieuse, comme ceux qui fouillaient les passants, comme le
But thing curious like those who searched the passersby as it

remarquerait encore Nono, sur tous les types qu'il rencontrerait dans la
noticed still Nono on all the types that he would meet in the

ville, ces soldats avaient une double physionomie : humaine et animale.
city these soldiers had a double aspect : human and animal

À certains moments, lorsqu'on les regardait, leur figure faisait penser
At certain moments, when one them watched their face made to think

au mufle du tigre que, parfois, Nono avait aperçu au Jardin des
at the muzzle of the tiger that sometimes Nono had perceived at the Garden of the

Plantes.
Plants

D'autres, plus jeunes, étaient armés d'arbalètes, couverts seulement d'une
Of others more young were armed with crossbows covered only with a
Others

casaque de buffle, sur la tête un chaperon, avec une plume de
(jockey) jersey of buffalo on the head a cap with a feather of

faucon sur le côté. Leur double physionomie était moins cruelle. Ils
falcon on the side. Their double aspect was less cruel They

rappelaient à Nono les bouledogues qu'il avait, plus d'une fois, aperçus
recalled to Nono the bulldogs that he had more than one time perceived

dans des voitures de bouchers.
in -of- the carriages of butchers

Il y avait bien d'autres variétés encore, mais il avait hâte de pénétrer
It there had well of others variations still but he had hurry of to enter
indeed other

dans l'intérieur de la ville, et ce fut d'un pas délibéré qu'il
in the interior of the city and it was with a step deliberate that he

s'engagea	sur	la	large	route	qui	y	menait.
himself engaged	on	the	wide	road	which	there	led
went							

Une promenade dans Monnaïa
A walk in Monnaia

De loin, la ville lui avait semblé magnifique ; mais, maintenant, à
From far the city him had appeared splendid ; but now to

droite, à gauche, il voyait des ruelles étroites, ténébreuses, bordées
(the) right to (the) left he saw -of the- streets narrow dark lined

de bicoques branlantes, suant la misère et la saleté, et qui
with shacks rickety sweating the misery and the dirt and which

contrastaient avec la route qu'il suivait, belle, large et plantée
contrasted with the road that he followed beautiful wide and planted

d'arbres.
with trees

Cependant, en avançant, ces ruelles misérables faisaient peu à peu place
However in advancing these streets wretched made bit by bit place

à des rues plus larges, plus aérées, bâties de maisons plus propres.
to -of the- streets more wide more airy built with houses more clean

Et enfin il arriva à une voie plus large encore, qui s'étendait
And finally he arrived at a way more wide still which itself extended

à perte de vue. Elle était plantée de plusieurs rangées d'arbres de
at loss of sight She was planted with several rows of trees of
as far as the eye could see It on

chaque côté. Des ronds-points garnis de grands bassins, du centre
each side -Of the- roundabouts decorated with large basins of the center
pools at the

desquels s'élevaient de magnifiques gerbes d'eau se rencontraient
of which themselves rose -of- splendid sheaves of water themselves encountered
rose sprays were located

de loin en loin. Autour de ces bassins des corbeilles de fleurs aux
of far in far Around of these basins of the baskets of flowers to the
at intervals with

couleurs variées reposaient la vue, en rompant l'uniformité.
colors varied rested the sight in breaking the uniformity

De magnifiques équipages, dans lesquels se prélassaient de belles
-Of- splendid carriages in which themselves lounged -of- beautiful

dames et de beaux messieurs, défilaient conduits par des cochers
ladies and -of- beautiful gentlemen filed by led by -of the- coachmen

aux livrées éclatantes, tirés par de superbes chevaux qui piaffaient et
at the coats bright pulled by -of- great horses who pranced and
with

redressaient la tête orgueilleusement.
raised up straight the head proudly

Si Nono n'avait pas, en traversant le pays, vu tant de misère,
If Nono did not have -not- in traversing the country seen so much -of- misery

il aurait cru à la réalisation des promesses du gros monsieur.
he would have believed at the realisation of the promises of the fat gentleman
in

Mais il était payé pour savoir ce que cachait ce beau spectacle.
But he was paid for to know this that hid this beautiful spectacle
had suffered

Malgré les riches costumes des beaux messieurs, malgré les falbalas
In spite of the rich dresses of the beautiful gentlemen in spite of the furbelows

des dames, malgré qu'à première vue quelques-unes semblassent très
of the ladies in spite of that at first sight some seemed very

jolies, la vision rapide qu'il en eut était que ce monde-là ressemblait
pretty the vision rapid that he of it had was that this world there resembled
these people there

un peu aux pourceaux qu'il avait vus à l'engrais dans les étables
a bit -to- the swine that he had seen at the fattening in the cowsheds

de sa nourrice.
of his wet nurse

Nono descendit une des allées en admirant ce qui se passait
Nono descended one of the walkways while admiring this which itself passed
happened

autour de lui. Là, sous les arbres, assises sur des chaises, de
around -of- him There under the trees seated on -of the- chairs -of-

grosses femmes joufflues, coiffées de larges rubans, enveloppées de
fat women chubby coiffed with wide ribbons wrapped with

grands manteaux, avaient autour d'elles de petits enfants richement
great coats had around of them -of- small children richly

habillés, jouant avec des jouets luxueux.
dressed playing with -of-the- toys luxurious

Plusieurs de ces femmes portaient en leurs bras les bébés trop jeunes
Several of these women carried in their arms the babies too young

pour marcher ou jouer avec les autres, et par instants, leur donnaient
for to walk or to play with the others and by moments them gave

à téter. Notre promeneur reconnut qu'il avait là, devant lui, les
to suck Our walker recognized that it had there in front of him the

enfants des personnages qui étaient dans les équipages. Les femmes qui
children of the characters who were in the carriages The women who

les gardaient, n'étaient que les bonnes ou les nourrices. Il lui semblait
them guarded not were than the good-wives or the nurses It him seemed

trouver dans leurs traits une vague ressemblance avec la Blanchette de
to find in their traits a vague resemblance with the Blanchette of
{cow}

Mab, mais elles paraissaient bien moins douces, par exemple.
Mab but they appeared well less sweet for example

Dans les chalets qui se dressaient au milieu des bosquets, on
In the chalets which themselves rose at the middle of the groves one
in the

vendait des jouets, des gâteaux et friandises de toute sorte. Nono,
sold -of-the- toys -of-the- cakes and treats of all kind(s) Nono

qui avait oublié sa faim, absorbé par ce qu'il voyait, la sentit se
who had forgotten his hunger absorbed by this that he saw the felt himself

réveiller à la vue des gâteaux. Mais il avait appris qu'en Argyrocratie
wake up at the sight of the cakes But he had learned that in Argyrocratie

il faut avoir de l'argent pour obtenir quelque chose, et il
it is necessary to have -of- -the- money for to obtain some thing and he

n'en avait pas.
not of it had not
any

Il pensa à son accordéon, et alla se poster près d'un groupe
He thought to his accordion and went himself to post near of a group
of

d'enfants, égrenant ses morceaux les plus entraînants. Mais aucun ne
of children fingering his pieces the most catchy But none -not-

fit attention à sa musiquette ; il dut tristement la remettre dans sa
made attention to his little music ; he had to sadly it put back in his

poche, et se contenter de ramasser un gâteau qu'un de ces petits
pocket and himself content of to pick up a cake that one of these small

enfants avait jeté après y avoir mordu.
children had thrown after there to have bitten
                          of it

En reprenant sa marche, il vit quelques autres enfants qui voulurent
In taking (up) again his march he saw some other children who wanted

se mêler aux jeux des petits enfants bien habillés ; mais
themselves mix to the games of the small children well dressed ; but
        with the

comme leurs habits étaient quelque peu en ruine, les autres les
as their clothes were some bit in ruin the others them

repoussèrent dédaigneusement, pendant que leurs bonnes poussaient des
repulsed disdainfully during that their good-wives pushed of the
                                                        uttered

meuglements, scandalisées de voir que de petits déguenillés avaient le
lowing shocked of to see that -of- small ragged (ones) had the

toupet de vouloir se mêler au troupeau dont elles avaient la
nerve of to want themselves to mix to the herd of which they had the

garde. Et un soldat qui se promenait, habillé de noir, avec des
guard And a soldier who himself walked dressed of black with -of the-

broderies rouges, une grande épée au côté, allant et venant, dans les
embroideries red a large sword at the side going and coming in the

allées, courut aux petits guenilleux, menaçant de les mener en prison
walkways ran to the small ragged (ones) threatening of them to lead in prison
                                                                to take

s'ils ne déguerpissaient pas de là.
if they not skedaddled -not- from there

Plus loin Nono vit une femme en loques, traînant deux marmots
More far Nono saw a woman in tatters dragging two brats
Farther

à sa suite, un troisième en bas âge, en ses bras, semblait implorer la
at her following a third in low age in her arms seemed to implore the
behind her

pitié de beaux messieurs et de belles dames qui passaient
pity of (the) beautiful gentlemen and of (the) beautiful ladies who passed

sans la regarder, ni faire attention à ses lamentations.
without her to look at nor to make attention to her lamentations

Cependant, une belle madame, jeune, s'arrêtait pour lui mettre quelque
However a beautiful Madam young herself halted for her to put some
stopped

chose dans la main. Mais un des soldats en tunique noire, avec une
thing in the hand But one of the soldiers in tunic black with a

face tenant de l'homme, du lévrier et de la fouine, vint prendre
face holding of the man of the greyhound and of the weasel came to take
having

la malheureuse par le bras, lui disant brutalement :
the unhappy by the arms her saying brutally :

— Je vous y prends, ce coup-ci, à mendier. Allez, suivez-moi chez
— I you there take this time around to beg Go follow me with
to

le prévôt et, de là, en prison. »
the provost and from there in prison

Et malgré les cris de ses petits, malgré ses bêlements — en la
And in spite of the cries of her small (children) in spite of her bleating — in her

regardant, Nono lui voyait une vague ressemblance avec les moutons
watching Nono him saw a vague resemblance with the sheep

qu'il avait vu mener à l'abattoir — il l'entraîna.
that he had seen to lead to the slaughter — he her dragged away

Nono continua sa route.
Nono continued his road

Il arriva à une grande place, au centre de laquelle se dressait un
He arrived at a large square at the center of which itself drew up a

monument de la destination duquel il lui fut impossible de se
monument of the destination of the which it him was impossible of himself

rendre compte. On ne pouvait du reste en approcher, protégé qu'il
to render account One not could of the rest of it approach protected that it

était par une enceinte de bornes, reliées entre elles par des chaînes.
was by a enclosure of bollards linked between them by of the chains
each other

À l'extrémité de cette place, on apercevait un château crénelé, surmonté
At the far end of this square one saw a castle crenellated mounted

d'un haut donjon au faîte duquel flottait l'étendard d'Argyrocratie.
with a high keep at the top of the which floated the standard of Argyrocratie

Nono comprit que c'était là le palais royal. Il était bondé de
Nono understood that it was there the palace royal It was crowded with

soldats à face de tigre, mais plus richement habillés, plus formidablement
soldiers at face of tiger, but more richly dressed more wonderfully
with

armés que ceux qui gardaient la ville.
armed than those which guarded the city

De ce château protégé par un large fossé garni de palissades, il était
Of this castle protected by a wide ditch furnished with palisades it was

défendu d'approcher. Des sentinelles faisaient circuler les promeneurs.
forbidden of to approach -Of the- sentries made go around the walkers

Au-dessus de la porte un écusson sculpté dans la pierre reproduisait
Above of the door an escutcheon carved in the stone reproduced

les armes de Monnaïus, avec sa devise: « Argent prime Droit. »
the weapons of Monnaïus with his motto Silver primes Right
Money goes before Law

Nono tourna à gauche, et se trouva dans une rue qui allait en
Nono turned to (the) left and himself found in a street which went in

se rétrécissant. Il ne tarda pas à entrer dans un quartier aux
itself narrowing He not delayed -not- to enter in a quarter to the
with

ruelles étroites, aux maisons noircies et décrépites, habitées par une
streets narrow to the houses blackened and decrepit inhabited by a
with

population très misérable.
population very miserable

La fatigue et la faim le contraignirent à s'asseoir sur une borne.
The exhaustion and the hunger him forced to himself sit on a bollard

Là, comme il se laissait aller à son désespoir, et que,
There as he himself let go to his despair and as

machinalement, il palpait toutes ses poches dans l'espérance d'y
mechanically he palpated all his pockets in the hope of there

retrouver quelque croute égarée, il sentit le rameau d'or que Monnaïus
to find back some crust strayed he felt the branch of gold that Monnaïus

lui avait remis pour le décider à le suivre, et qu'il avait
him had set back for him to decide to him follow and that he had

totalement oublié.
totally forgotten

Il le sortit et l'examina, mais, contrairement à la promesse de
He it got out and it examined but in contrary to the promise of

Monnaïus, le rameau n'avait pas grandi. Tel il l'avait reçu, tel il
Monnaïus the branch did not have -not- grown As he it had received so it

était resté, rendu seulement un peu plus luisant par le frottement de
was remained rendered only a bit more shining by the friction of
had

la poche.
the pocket

Mais peut-être avait-il quand même les propriétés d'un plus grand ?
But maybe had he when even the properties of one more large ?
nevertheless that was larger

Et Nono désira des repas pantagruéliques pour assouvir sa faim,
And Nono wished -of the- meals pantagruelian for to satiate his hunger

des lits moelleux pour reposer ses membres endoloris, des chars
-of the- beds soft for to rest his members aching -of the- chariots

enchantés pour le ramener chez ses parents, à Autonomie, le tirer
enchanted for him to bring with his parents to Autonomy him pull (out)
to

de ce pays de peines et de misères.
of this country of pains and of miseries

Mais il resta sur la borne toujours aussi dure, sans la moindre
But he remained on the bollard always so hard without the least

croûte de pain à se mettre sous la dent. Monnaïus l'avait trompé
crust of bread to himself to put under the tooth Monnaïus him had deceived
between the teeth

sur	tous	les	points,	et,	dans	son	dépit,	il	fut	sur	le	point	de	jeter
on	all	the	points	and	in	his	spite	he	was	on	the	point	of	to throw

au	loin	son	rameau.
at the	distance away	his	branch

Mais	en	levant	les	yeux	il	aperçut	une	petite	boutique	d'orfèvre	où
But	in	raising	the	eyes	he	saw	a	little	shop	(of a) goldsmith	where

pendaient	en	montre	des	objets	d'or	et	d'argent.	Puisque,	dans	ce
hung	in	watch	-of- the	objects	of gold	and	of silver	Since	in	this

pays,	on	semblait	attacher	tant	de	prix	à	ces	métaux,	Nono	pensa
country	one	seemed	to attach	so much	of	price	to	these	metals	Nono	thought

qu'il	pourrait	peut-être	tirer	quelque	monnaie	de	son	morceau	d'or	;
that he	could	maybe	pull	some	money	from	his	piece	of gold	;

il	se	dirigea	vers	la	boutique	de	l'orfèvre.
he	himself	directed	towards	the	shop	of	the goldsmith

Celui-ci	était	à	son	établi.	C'était	un	petit	vieux,	au	nez	courbé
That one	was	at	his	workbench	It was	a	little	old (man)	at the with the	nose	bent

en	bec	d'oiseau	de	proie	;	il	était	en	train	de	raccommoder
in	(a) beak	(of) bird	of	prey	;	he	was	in	train process	of	to mend

un	pendant	d'oreille.	Il	leva	les	yeux	sur	le	visiteur,	mais	à	sa	mise,
a	pendant an earring	of ear	He	raised	the	eyes	on	the	visitor	but	at	his	set

jugeant	bien	que	ce	n'était	pas	comme	acheteur	qu'il	se	présentait,
judging	well	that	this	not was	-not-	as	buyer	that he	himself	presented

ce	fut	d'un	ton	fort	bourru	qu'il	lui	demanda	ce	qu'il	voulait.
it	was	with a	tone	very	surly	that he	him	asked	this	what he	wanted

—	Nono	lui	présenta	son	rameau	d'or,	demandant	s'il	voulait	le
—	Nono	him	presented	his	branch	of gold	asking	if he	wanted	it

lui	acheter.
(from) him	buy

L'orfèvre,	le	regardant	d'un	air	soupçonneux,	s'enquit	d'où	il
The goldsmith	it	watching	with an	air	suspicious	himself inquired	from where	he

le	tenait.
it	had

Nono lui expliqua en quelles circonstances Monnaïus le lui avait
Nono him explained in which circumstances Monnaïus it him had

remis. Et, espérant en avoir un meilleur prix, il eut bien soin de
handed over And hoping of it to have a best price he had well care of

lui faire ressortir que c'était de la baguette de ce monarque
him to make come out again clear that It was from the stick of this monarch

qu'il était détaché, et de lui détailler les propriétés merveilleuses qui,
that it was taken off and of him to detail the properties wonderful which

selon sa promesse, devaient y être attachées.
according to his promise must there be attached

Mais l'orfèvre prit un air dédaigneux, en soupesant le rameau. Il
But the goldsmith took an air disdainful in weighing the branch He
assumed

expliqua à Nono que quelques Argyrocratiens possédaient bien de ces
explained to Nono that some Argyrocratiens had well of these
indeed

baguettes merveilleuses ; mais, pour que ces baguettes possédassent la
little sticks wonderful ; but for that these little sticks possessed the

propriété précieuse de se reproduire elles-mêmes, il fallait que
property precious of themselves to reproduce themselves it was necessary that

des génies esclaves y fussent attachés. Sans ces génies, les
of the genies slaves there were attached Without these genies the

baguettes ne valaient plus que comme or, et n'avaient d'autre propriété
little sticks not were worth more than like gold and not had of other property

que de pouvoir s'échanger contre d'autres objets. Si Nono voulait
than of to be able to exchange themselves against -of- other objects If Nono wanted

lui laisser son rameau, il lui en donnerait deux grandes pièces
(with) him leave his branch he him for it would give two large pieces

d'argent, et encore, il ne gagnerait rien dessus ; c'était seulement par
of silver and still he not would earn nothing on top ; it was only by

pitié pour sa jeunesse ; — ce qui était faux, il y gagnait dix fois
pity for his youth ; — this which was false he there won ten times

les deux pièces d'argent ; — mais Nono, qui n'avait aucune notion de
the two pieces of silver ; — but Nono who did not have any notion of

la valeur, prit avec satisfaction les deux pièces d'argent, et courut chez
the valor took with satisfaction the two pieces of silver and ran with to

le boulanger s'acheter du pain.
the baker himself to buy -of- the bread

Une vieille femme qui vendait des pommes venant à passer, il en
An old woman who sold -of the- apples coming to pass he of them

acheta quelques-unes, et, un peu réconforté, il songea qu'il lui
bought some and a bit comforted he thought that it him

faudrait se mettre en quête d'un gîte pour la nuit.
would be necessary himself to put in quest of a home for the night

Il trottinait donc par les rues, cherchant l'enseigne d'une hôtellerie,
He trotted then through the streets searching the sign of a hotel

lorsque des cris attirèrent son attention. C'était un petit garçon de
when -of the- cries attracted his attention It was a little boy of

cinq à six ans qui avait roulé sur la chaussée, une voiture arrivait
five to six years (old) who had rolled on the road a carriage arrived

au galop sur lui. La mère, paralysée par la vue du danger que
at the gallop on him The mother paralyzed by the sight of the danger that

courait son enfant, levait les bras au ciel, poussant des cris d'effroi,
ran her child raised the arms at the sky pushing uttering of the cries of fright

sans pouvoir faire un pas à son secours.
without to be able to make a step to his help

Nono, d'un bond, fut sur lui et eut le temps de l'enlever, tous
Nono with a jump was on him and had the time of him to take away all

deux roulant dans le ruisseau, mais sains et saufs, car la voiture
two rolling in the stream gutter but healthy and sound because the carriage

avait passé sans les atteindre.
had passed without them to reach

Lorsqu'ils se relevèrent, la mère était sur eux, les accablant
When they themselves raised again the mother was on them them overwhelming

de caresses, riant et pleurant tout à la fois.
with caresses laughing and weeping all at the (same) time

Comme le jeune sauveteur s'était sali dans le ruisseau, la mère
As the young rescuer himself was went out in the stream the mother
gutter

l'emmena chez elle. Elle habitait une petite échoppe, en face, où le
took him with her She lived in a little shop in face where the
opposite

père rapetassait les habits du voisinage.
father fixed up the clothes of the neighborhood

Le père, anxieux, en les voyant tout bouleversés, s'informa de ce
The father anxious in them seeing all upset himself informed of this

qui s'était passé.
which itself was passed
itself had happened

La mère, encore tout en larmes, raconta l'accident et présenta le
The mother still all in tears told the accident and presented the

sauveur de leur enfant.
savior of their child

Le père remercia sommairement Nono, puis se mit à quereller
The father thanked summarily Nono then himself put to quarrel with

l'enfant, le traitant d'insupportable, de mauvais garnement, l'accusant de
the child him dealing of unbearable of bad scamp him accusing of

ne pas savoir se tenir tranquille et d'être toujours en mouvement,
not -not- to know himself to keep quiet and of to be always in movement

ne sachant quoi inventer pour contrarier ses parents. Et, finalement, il
not knowing what to invent for to upset his parents And finally he

l'envoya s'asseoir dans un coin avec une paire de taloches qu'il lui
him sent himself to sit in a corner with a pair of cuffs that he him
to sit

détacha.
untied
dealt

La mère fit déshabiller Nono pour laver ses habits. Pendant qu'ils
The mother made undress Nono for to wash his clothes During that they

séchaient, Nono dut, encore une fois, faire le récit de ses malheurs,
were drying Nono had to still one time make the story of his misfortunes
tell

et expliquer comment il se faisait qu'il se trouvait seul dans les
and explain how it itself made that he himself found alone in the
had come to be

rues de Monnaïa, à la recherche d'un gîte et d'un emploi.
streets of Monnaïa at the search of a home and of an employment

Les habitants de l'échoppe s'extasièrent sur les merveilleux récits qu'il
The inhabitants of the shop went into ecstasies on the wonderful stories that he

leur fit d'Autonomie, se faisant donner mille explications sur
them made of Autonomy themselves making give (a) thousand explanations on
told

les plus intimes détails.
the most intimate details

Le tailleur raconta que, quelquefois, par des ouvriers de passage, il
The tailor told that sometimes by -of- the workmen of passage he

en avait déjà entendu parler ; mais que, jusqu'à ce jour, cela lui
of it had already heard speak ; but that up to this day that him

semblait tellement fabuleux qu'il ne pouvait y voir que des contes
seemed so much fabulous that he not could there see than of the (fairy)tales

bons tout au plus à distraire l'imagination.
good all at the more to distract the imagination

Et pendant qu'il parlait, Nono qui l'examinait, lui et sa femme, leur
And during that he spoke Nono who examined him him and his wife them

retrouvait cette physionomie de mouton qu'il avait déjà remarquée chez
found back this aspect of sheep that he had already noticed with

la guenilleuse conduite au poste.
the beggar led at the post
prison

Enfin, s'étant consultés, l'homme et la femme proposèrent à Nono
Finally each other being consulted the man and the woman proposed to Nono
having each other

de le garder avec eux. Il aurait le gîte et la nourriture assurés.
of him to keep with them He would have the home and the food assured

Il aiderait le tailleur qui lui apprendrait son métier. S'il était assidu
He would help the tailor who him would learn his trade If he was assiduous

au travail, on lui donnerait par la suite une petite paie.
at the work one him would give by the following a little pay

Nono	accepta	avec	joie.	Il	était	tiré	de	peine.	Le	tailleur	y
Nono	accepted	with	joy	He	was	pulled out	of	trouble	The	tailor	there(by)

économisait	un	ouvrier.
economized	a	worker
saved out		

L'instruction de Nono se continue

The instruction of Nono itself continues

Nono fut réveillé de bonne heure, le lendemain, par le tailleur pour
Nono was woken up of good hour the following day by the tailor for
(early)

se mettre au travail. L'ayant fait asseoir à côte de lui, sur
himself to put to the work Him having made sit to (the) side of him on

son établi, il lui apprit à se croiser les jambes pour tenir moins
his workbench he him learned to himself cross the legs for to keep less

de place. Puis il lui donna deux morceaux de drap à coudre ensemble,
of place Then he him gave two pieces of cloth to sew together
(room)

lui montrant comment il fallait qu'il tînt sa pièce, comment il
him showing how it was necessary that he held his piece how it

fallait piquer et tirer l'aiguille.
was necessary to prick and pull the needle

Pour varier le travail, il l'envoya, dans la journée, porter chez des
For to vary the work he him sent in the day to carry with -of- the
to

clients quelques costumes qu'il venait de terminer.
customers some dresses that he came of to end
had just finished

Quand vint le soir, Nono ne s'était pas arrêté une minute, sauf
When came the evening Nono not itself was -not- stopped a minute except
had

pour manger, ce qui se faisait très rapidement, pour se
for to eat this which himself made very quickly for himself
he did

remettre aussitôt au travail.
to put again immediately to the work

Il était exténué.
He was exhausted

Et les repas ?
And the meals ?

Adieu les bons fruits, les bonnes chatteries d'Autonomie. Le soir,
Farewell -the- good fruits -the- good titbits of Autonomy The evening

une mauvaise soupe, faite de légumes parcimonieusement mesurés, avec
a bad soup made of vegetables parsimoniously measured with
scarcely added

une léchette de graisse dedans, quelques tranches de pain bis, et
a thin little slice of fat in there some slices of bread brown and

c'était tout. À midi, quelques pommes de terre, auxquelles aux jours de
that was all At noon some apples of earth to the which at the days of
potatoes to which

bombance on ajoutait un petit morceau de lard ou de viande de qualité
feast one added a little piece of bacon or of meat of quality

inférieure.
inferior

Ce n'était pas que le tailleur et sa femme fussent de mauvaises gens,
It not was -not- that the tailor and his wife were -of- bad people

c'était leur ordinaire que Nono partageait. Ni qu'ils fussent avares,
it was their ordinary that Nono shared Neither that they were scrooges
usual fare

et désireux de thésauriser. Les vivres étaient chers à Monnaïa, les loyers
and desirous of to hoard The rations were dear at Monnaïa the rents

accablants, et le travail mal payé. Il fallait s'exténuer de travail
overwhelming and the work badly paid It was necessary to extenuate of to work

et rester sur sa faim pour pouvoir joindre les deux bouts.
and to stay on ones hunger for to be able to join the two ends
to survive

C'était là l'existence de tous ceux qui étaient forcés de travailler pour
That was there the existence of all those who were forced of to work for

les autres.
the others

Et encore, expliqua le tailleur, lui se trouvait relativement heureux,
And still explained the tailor him himself found relatively happy

son métier lui permettant d'avoir affaire directement à la clientèle.
his trade him permitting of to have business directly to the customer base

Mais ceux qui étaient forcés d'aller travailler dans les usines — et il
But those who were forced of to go work in the factories — and he

lui montra de grands bâtiments sans fenêtres, éclairés seulement par
him showed -of- great buildings without windows lit only by

un vitrage placé sur le toit, et dominés par de grandes cheminées
a glazing placed on the roof and dominated by -of- large chimneys

toujours fumantes — ceux-là, leur peine était encore pire. Enfermés toute
always smoking — those ones their pain was still worse Locked in all

une journée, surveillés par des intendants, toujours talonnés par la
a day watched by -of- the stewards always harassed by the

crainte du maître, ils devaient produire toujours, produire sans cesse,
fear of the master they must produce always produce without stop

sans oser lever la tête une minute, sans pouvoir parler entre
without to dare to raise the head a minute without to be able to speak between

eux, car à la moindre infraction au règlement, on leur imposait
them because at the least offense at the rules one them imposed

une retenue sur leurs salaires.
a deduction on their wages

Ces usines appartenaient aux individus que Nono avait vu se
These factories belonged to the individuals that Nono had seen himself

promener dans de si beaux équipages. On ne les voyait jamais à
walk in of so beautiful carriages One not them saw ever at

l'usine. C'étaient des sortes d'intendants, pris parmi les ouvriers, et
the factory There were of the kinds of stewards taken among the workmen and

que l'on payait un peu plus pour cela, qui prenaient leurs intérêts, et
that it one paid a bit more for that who took (up) their interests and

surveillaient le travail.
surveilled the work

Nono qui eut l'occasion de rencontrer de ces intendants
Nono who had the opportunity of encounter -of- these stewards

par la suite, leur trouva une physionomie partie humaine, partie loup,
by the following them found a aspect part human part wolf
subsequently

partie chien de berger.
part dog of shepherd

Ceux qui ne possédaient pas d'usines étaient propriétaires de champs,
Those who not had -not- of factories were owners of fields

de bois, et de prés à la campagne qu'ils donnaient à cultiver à
of woods and of meadows at the countryside that they gave to cultivate to
in

d'autres intendants qui faisaient travailler les paysans. Quand ceux-ci
of other stewards who made work the peasants When these
other

avaient moissonné, vendangé, venait l'intendant du maître qui
had reaped vintaged came the steward of the master who
harvested the fields harvested the grapes

prenait la meilleure partie de la récolte, leur laissant à peine de quoi
took the best part of the harvest them letting at pain of what
barely

ne pas crever de faim.
not -not- to starve from hunger

D'autres possédaient des maisons. — Celui auquel appartenait celle
Of others had -of the- houses — The one to which belonged that one
Others

où logeait le tailleur, en possédait à lui tout seul plus de
where stayed the tailor of them possessed to him all alone more than

cent dans Monnaïa. — Et ceux qui n'avaient pas de maison,
(a) hundred in Monnaïa — And those who not had -not- -of- (a) house

étaient forcés de payer ce qu'on leur demandait pour avoir le droit
were forced of to pay this that one them asked for to have the right

d'habiter un petit coin.
of to live in a little corner

D'autres n'avaient ni usines, ni champs, ni maisons, mais ils
Of others not had neither factories nor fields nor houses but they
Others

achetaient aux uns pour revendre aux autres, prélevaient un bénéfice
bought to the ones for to sell to the others levied a profit
from the

sur chaque opération. À la fin ils devenaient énormément riches ainsi.
on each operation At the end they became enormously rich this way

Et Nono hochait la tête, se demandant si les génies esclaves qui
And Nono shook the head himself asking if the genies slaves which

faisaient la puissance des baguettes d'or, n'étaient pas ceux qui
made the power of the little sticks of gold not were -not- those who

travaillaient à l'usine, aux champs, payant la dîme pour manger,
worked at the factory at the fields paying the dime for to eat

se vêtir, se distraire, se loger.
themselves dress themselves distract themselves stay
                                                   live in a house

Vous me direz que voilà des raisonnements bien profonds pour un
You me tell that see there of the reasonings well deep for a

petit bonhomme de neuf ans. Mais c'est que Nono commençait à avoir
little good man of nine years But this is that Nono began to have

vu pas mal de choses, et l'expérience mûrit, plus vite que les
seen not bad -of- things and the experience matures more quickly than the
       a few

années encore.
years still
      even

Les journées se passaient ainsi, causant et travaillant.
The days themselves passed thus chatting and working

Nono fit aussi connaissance de la ville, en allant rapporter le travail
Nono made also acquaintance with the city in going to bring back the work

chez les clients, ou chercher les marchandises chez les fournisseurs.
with the customers or to seek the merchandise with the suppliers
to

Parfois aussi, le dimanche, lorsque le travail ne pressait pas trop,
Sometimes also the Sunday when the work not pressed -not- too (much)

le tailleur sortait pour promener son enfant, Nono l'accompagnait. On
the tailor left for to walk his child Nono him accompanied One

faisait ainsi quelques promenades dans les beaux quartiers, admirant les
made thus some walks in the beautiful quarters admiring the
                                                       blocks

richesses entassées dans les magasins.
riches piled up in the shops

Et, avec le temps, le jeune apprenti faisait des progrès dans son
And with the time the young apprentice made -of the- progress in his

nouveau métier, se rendant utile au ménage, et l'ordinaire
new trade himself making useful at the household and the ordinary
the living standard

s'améliorait insensiblement. Un jour que le tailleur avait pu mettre
was improving imperceptibly A day that the tailor had been able to put

une pièce d'or de côté, il donna à Nono une piécette d'argent. C'était
a piece of gold of side he gave to Nono a small coin of silver It was
a-

un grand acte de générosité qu'il lui sembla accomplir, quoique la
a large act of generosity that he him seemed to accomplish though the

pièce remise à Nono ne représentait que la vingtième partie de ce que
piece shed to Nono not represented than the twentieth part of this that

celui-ci lui économisait.
that one him economized
saved out

Ce n'était pas un mauvais homme, nous le savons déjà. Mais faisant
This not was -not- a bad man we it know already But making

travailler Nono, il lui semblait tout naturel d'en tirer profit. N'était-ce
work Nono he him seemed all natural of of it to pull profit Not was this

pas comme cela que ça se pratiquait en Argyrocratie ?
-not- like this there what that itself practiced in Argyrocratie ?

Si le travail continuait à abonder, il pourrait prendre un autre apprenti,
If the work continued to abound he could take an other apprentice

puis des ouvriers, et en gagnant sur l'un et sur l'autre, il
then -of the- workmen and in earning on the one and on the other he

s'enrichirait lui aussi, et n'aurait qu'à choisir, soit à acheter une
himself will enrich him as well and would not than to choose be it to buy a

maison, soit à créer une usine. Et lorsque ces pensées le
house be it to create a factory And when these thoughts him

tourmentaient, il semblait à Nono que la partie ovine de sa physionomie
tormented it seemed to Nono that the part sheep of his aspect

faisait place à celle d'un vautour.
made place to that of a vulture

Au cours d'une de ces conversations, Nono lui expliqua la remarque
At the course of one of these conversations Nono him explained the observation

qu'il avait faite lors de son arrivée à Monnaïa : les doubles et triples
that he had made then of his arrival to Monnaïa : the double and triple

physionomies qu'il avait observées chez ses habitants.
countenances that he had observed with its inhabitants
of

Le tailleur lui expliqua que ces diverses physionomies commençaient à
The tailor him explained that these various countenances began to

se dessiner lorsque les individus faisaient le choix d'un métier ou
themselves draw when the individuals made the choice of a trade or

d'un emploi. Les enfants, par exemple, se ressemblaient tous.
of an employment The children by example themselves resembled all

Pour ce qui était des soldats, Monnaïus les choisissait parmi les
For this who was of the soldiers Monnaïus them chose among the

enfants d'ouvriers et de paysans. Une fois habillés d'uniformes, leur
children of workers and of peasants One time dressed of uniforms their

physionomie commençait à prendre la ressemblance d'un boule-dogue.
aspect began to take the resemblance of a bulldog

Ceux qui ne pouvaient pas acquérir cette physionomie étaient envoyés
Those who not could -not- acquire this aspect were sent

au loin, dans des pays inconnus, d'où ils revenaient rarement.
to the far in of the countries unknown from where they came back rarely
far away countries

D'autres ne tardaient pas à mourir, ne pouvant traverser cette crise
Of others not delayed -not- to die not being able to cross this crisis
Others

qui transformait leur physionomie.
which transformed their aspect

C'était là, la première mue. Ils prenaient ensuite facilement la
It was there the first moult They took subsequently easily the
moulting

physionomie de tigre qu'ils devaient ensuite garder toute leur vie.
aspect of (the) tiger that they must subsequently keep all their life
lives

Cependant, à l'armée, il y en avait qui n'arrivaient jamais à prendre
However, at the army it there of it had who not arrived ever to take
there were those

complètement cette physionomie. Ils prenaient celle de la fouine, du
completely this aspect They took that of the weasel of the
appearance

lévrier, du basset. On en faisait alors des employés aux gabelles,
greyhound of the basset One of them made then of the workers at the gabels

des exempts. Il y avait une espèce d'exempts qui ne portaient pas
of the policemen It there had a kind of policemen who not carried -not-
There were

d'uniforme, et qui avaient pour mission de se mêler à la
-of- uniform and who had for mission of themselves to mix at the

population dans les rues, aux ouvriers dans les ateliers, au cabaret,
population in the streets to the workmen in the workshops at the cabaret
with the

et de rapporter tout ce qu'ils entendaient aux ministres de
and of to bring back all this that they heard to the ministers of

Monnaïus. Ceux-là prenaient une physionomie partie basset, partie furet ;
Monnaïus Those ones taking an aspect part basset part ferret ;

comme le putois, ils dégageaient une odeur puante qu'ils n'arrivaient à
like the polecat they emanated a smell stinking that they not arrived to

cacher qu'à force de précautions. Mais il fallait une grande
hide than at force of precautions But it was necessary a large

habitude des physionomies pour les distinguer.
habit of the countenances for them to distinguish
experience with the appearances

Du reste, toutes ces différences de physionomies finissaient par devenir
Of the rest all these differences of countenances ended by to become
appearances

insensibles à l'œil ; l'habitude arrivait à les rendre insaisissables aux
insensitive to the eye ; the habit arrived at them to render elusive to the

habitants du pays. Il y en avait très peu qui fussent à même
inhabitants of the country It there of them had very few who were at even
There were of them capable

de les discerner. Nono, lui-même, lorsqu'il aurait habité un peu
of them to discern Nono him self when he would have lived a bit

plus longtemps le pays, ne saurait plus les reconnaître.
more long time (in) the country not would know (any)more them to recognize
   longer

Chez les maîtres, ces particularités se faisaient sentir un peu plus
With the masters, these particularities themselves made feel a bit more

tôt, et c'était toujours à quelque animal féroce qu'ils finissaient par
early and it was always to some animal fierce that they ended by

ressembler : loup, aigle, vautour, panthère, serpent, etc.
to resemble : wolf eagle vulture panther snake etc

Ceux qui prenaient des faces de loups, tigres, panthères, devenaient
Those who taking of the faces of wolves tigers panthers became

officiers dans l'armée de Monnaïus. Ceux dont l'aspect devenait
officers in the army of Monnaïus. Those of which the appearance became

celui de vautours, de hyènes, de chacals, étaient nommés conseillers au
the one of vultures, of hyenas, of jackals, were appointed advisors at the

Parlement. Ils étaient chargés de débarrasser Monnaïus de ses ennemis,
Parliament. They were charged of to get rid Monnaïus of his enemies

ou de ceux qui ne se conformaient pas à ses ordonnances ;
or of those who not themselves conformed -not- to his prescriptions ;

d'envoyer en prison ceux que l'âge et les infirmités empêchaient de
of to send in prison those that the age and the infirmities prevented of

travailler, et dont la présence sur les routes aurait mis en péril
to work and of which the presence on the roads would have put in peril

la tranquillité de ceux qui ne faisaient rien. Il y en avait qui
the tranquility of those who not did nothing It there of them had who
   There were of them

prenaient des physionomies de paons, de dindons ; ils garnissaient la
took of the countenances of peacocks of turkeys ; they decorated the

cour de Monnaïus.
court of Monnaïus

Ceux qu'il avait vu avec l'apparence de pourceaux étaient ceux qui,
Those that he had seen with the appearance of swine were those who

ne s'adonnant à aucune besogne, se contentaient de boire,
not themselves engaged to any task themselves satisfied of to drink
   with

manger, dormir et se promener.
to eat / to sleep / and / themselves / to stroll around

Il y avait bien d'autres variétés, mais leur nombre était si grand qu'il
It / there / had / well indeed / of others other / variations / But / their / number / was / so / large / that it

était impossible à Nono de les retenir toutes ; celles-là étaient les
was / impossible / to / Nono / of / them / to retain to remember / all / ; / those ones / were / the

principales.
main (ones)

Nouveaux malheurs
New troubles

Le	temps	passa,	et	Nono	s'habituait	peu	à	peu	à	son	nouveau
The	time	passed	and	Nono	himself habituated / got used	bit	by	bit	to	his	new

genre	de	vie,	travaillait	toujours	aussi	dur,	privé	de	toutes	les
sort	of	life	worked	always	as	hard	deprived	of	all	the

satisfactions,	alors	que	la	richesse,	la	joie	et	les	plaisirs	étaient	une
satisfaction	as	that	the	wealth	the	joy	and	the	pleasures	were	an

éternelle	provocation	à	ceux	qui	n'avaient	pour	eux	que
eternal	provocation	to	those	who	not had	for	themselves	(anything other) than

le	travail	et	la	misère.
the	work	and	the	misery

Les	seuls	bons	moments	de	notre	héros	étaient	ceux	où	un	groupe
The	sole	good	moments	of	our	hero	were	those	where	a	group

d'amis	du	tailleur	venaient	passer	la	veillée	avec	eux.	Parmi	eux,
of friends	of the	tailor	came	pass	the	vigil	with	them	Among	them

il	y	en	avait	deux	ou	trois	avec	lesquels	il	sympathisait	davantage,
it	there	of them	had	two	or	three	with	which	he	sympathized	more
		There were									

et	chose	singulière,	quoique		Monnaïens,		Nono,	ne	leur	trouvait
and	thing	singular	although	(they were)	Monnaïens		Nono	not	them	found

pas	cette	physionomie	moutonnière	si	caractérisée	chez	son	patron	et
-not-	this	aspect	sheeplike	so	characterized	with	his	boss	and

la	plupart	des	Argyrocratiens.
the	largest part	of the	Argyrocratiens

Quand	il	leur	racontait	les	joies	d'Autonomie,	la	douceur	de	Labor,
When	he	them	told	(of) the	joys	of Autonomy	the	softness	of	Labor

les	prévenances	de	Solidaria,	tous	l'écoutaient	ravis,	mais	plus	ou	moins
the	attention	of	Solidaria	all	him listened to	thrilled	but	more	or	less

incrédules, ou affirmant que cela était bien pour Autonomie, mais que
unbelieving or affirming that that was well for Autonomy (land) but that

ce genre de vie serait impossible pour les Argyrocratiens,
this sort of life would be impossible for the Argyrocratiens

qu'il fallait des riches pour faire travailler les pauvres — c'est
that it was necessary of the rich for to make work the poor — it is
that rich people were necessary

ce que ne se gênaient pas de faire les riches Argyrocratiens
this that not themselves were embarrassed -not- of to do the rich Argyrocratiens

— puis des lois, des gens d'armes, et des prisons pour ceux
— then -of- the laws -of- the people -of- weapons and of the prisons for those

qui avaient mauvaise tête.
who had bad head
wrong ideas

D'autres renchérissaient.
Of others went further
Others

— S'il n'y avait pas d'exempts ni d'archers du guet, on vous
— If it not there had -not- of policemen nor of archers of the look-out one you
If there were no policemen archers

assassinerait dans les rues, pour vous voler le peu d'argent que vous
would murder in the streets for you to steal the bit of silver that you

avez !
have !

Et Nono songeait que ces pauvres diables n'avaient jamais quatre sous
And Nono thought that these poor devils not had ever four nickels

vaillants dans leur poche.
worth in their pocket

Seuls, les deux ou trois que Nono avait remarqués protestaient, demandant
Alone the two or three that Nono had remarked protested asking

pourquoi il ne serait pas possible de vivre comme les
why it not would be -not- possible of to live like the

Autonomiens alors que l'on consentait bien à travailler quatorze
(boys and girls of) Autonomy then that -it- one consented well to work fourteen
since

heures par jour, pour un salaire dérisoire.
hours per day for a salary derisory

— Parce que l'on y est forcé, répliquaient les autres.
— Because that -it- one there is forced retorted the others

— Vous savez bien qu'il y en a qui naissent fatigués, répondit une
— You know well that it there of it has who are born weary answered one
that there are those

fois le bel esprit de la bande.
time the beautiful mind of the band

Et tous d'éclater de rire.
And all of to burst of laugh
burst out in laughter

Parfois, Nono essayait de répondre, mais le plus souvent, devant
Sometimes Nono tried of to answer but the most often in front of

l'ignorance et la bêtise de ces gens qui croient résoudre une
the ignorance and the stupity of these people who believed to resolve a

question par un trait d'esprit, il se taisait, jugeant inutiles les
question by a trait of spirit he himself kept silent judging useless the

meilleures raisons. Il se réservait pour ses trois favoris ; alors, là,
best reasons He himself reserved for his three favorites ; then there

c'étaient des conversations, des discussions qui n'en finissaient
there were -of- the conversations -of- the discussions which not of it ended

plus, surtout les jours de liberté.
(any)more especially the days of freedom

Et peu à peu, ces discussions se répandirent dans le voisinage.
And bit by bit these discussions themselves spread in the neighborhood

Il venait des habitants des autres quartiers pour écouter raconter
It came of the inhabitants from the others quarters for to hear tell
There the blocks

les jolies histoires du pays d'Autonomie.
the pretty stories from the country of Autonomy

Et tous trouvaient cela joli, tous auraient aimé à vivre dans un pays
And all found that nice all would have loved to live in a country

comme celui-là ; mais il y en avait peu qui dissent: « Nous
like that one ; but -it- there of them had few who said We
were

pourrions vivre comme cela si nous voulions. » S'il s'en trouvait un
could live like that if we wanted If it himself of it found one
If there was one

pour le suggérer, presque tous se trouvaient d'accord pour le
for it to suggest almost all themselves found of agreement for him
in agreement

trouver légèrement « toc-toc », une expression monnaïenne pour
to find lightly knock knock an expression monnaïenne for

exprimer qu'un homme ne possède pas toutes ses facultés cérébrales.
to express that a man not possesses -not- all his faculties of the brain

Cependant ces conversations chez le tailleur ne furent pas sans
However these conversations with the tailor not were -not- without

transpirer dans la ville. Elles faisaient parfois l'objet des discussions
sweat in the city They made sometimes the subject of the discussions

à la sortie des ateliers, au cabaret. Cela vint aux oreilles du
at the exit of the workshops at the cabaret That came to the ears of the

prévôt, et un beau jour — un vilain matin, plutôt — le domicile
provost and one beautiful day — an ugly morning rather — the home

du tailleur fut envahi par les exempts du prévôt. Tout fut bouleversé,
of the tailor was invaded by the policemen of the provost All was knocked over

mis sens dessus dessous.
put sense on top below
turned upside down

Les exempts s'emparèrent de quelques lettres que le tailleur avait
The policemen themselves empowered -of- some letters that the tailor had
seized

reçues de parents qui habitaient la province, et où on lui donnait
received from parents who dwelt in the province and where one him gave

des nouvelles de la famille, de le vache et du cochon. Le chef
of the news of the family of the cow and of the pig The chef

des exempts hocha le tête d'un air grave en les lisant, et assura
of the policemen shook the head with an air serious in the reading and assured

que cela devait signifier quelque chose, disant au tailleur qu'il ne le
that that must mean some thing saying to the tailor that he not him

laissait en liberté que grâce aux bons renseignements qu'il avait
let in freedom than thanks to the good information that he had

recueillis sur son compte.
collected on his account

Puis, au cours de ses recherches, ayant trouvé une demi-douzaine de
Then at the course of his researches, having found a half-dozen of

numéros de la Gazette officielle d'Argyrocratie, il les fit joindre au
numbers of the Gazette official of Argyrocratie he them made join to the

dossier, hochant encore la tête, et trouvant que cela devenait grave, très
file nodding still the head and finding that that became serious very

grave ! Puis, lorsqu'on eut bien saccagé le mobilier du pauvre tailleur,
serious ! Then when one had well trashed the furniture of the poor tailor

les exempts se retirèrent, emmenant Nono qui était accusé d'avoir
the policemen himself withdrew leading Nono who was accused of to have

voulu troubler l'ordre public par des histoires de nature à exciter les
wanted to trouble the order public by -of- the stories of nature to excite the

citoyens les uns contre les autres, et le tailleur fut averti qu'on le
citizens the ones against the others and the tailor was warned that they him

laissait libre, mais qu'il devait se tenir à la disposition de la
let free But that he must himself keep at the disposition of the

justice.
justice

Couvert de chaînes, Nono fut emmené à la prison de la prévôté,
Covered of/in chains Nono was taken to the prison of the provost

enfermé dans un cachot éclairé par une lucarne laissant pénétrer le jour,
locked up in a dungeon lit by a skylight letting enter the day

mais l'empêchant de voir dehors.
but preventing him of to see outside

Le prisonnier, une fois seul, se laissa tomber sur une grosse pierre
The prisoner one time alone himself let fall on a big stone

placée en un coin de son cachot et se mit à réfléchir
placed in a corner of his dungeon and himself put to think

sérieusement sur les événements qui lui arrivaient à la façon d'une
seriously on the events which him arrived at/in the way of an

avalanche de tuiles. La pensée de ses parents, de ses frères et
avalanche of roof tiles The thought of his parents of his brothers and

sœurs, lui revint plus vive en ce moment, et des larmes amères
sisters him returned more lively in this moment and -of the- tears bitter

vinrent lui brûler les paupières à la pensée qu'il ne les verrait
came him to burn the eyelids at the thought that he not them would see

peut-être plus.
maybe (any)more

Dans la journée, un geôlier lui apporta une cruche d'eau et un pain
In the day a gaoler him brought a jug of water and a bread

noirâtre, amer et à moitié moisi. Nono que l'angoisse étreignait, ne
blackish bitter and to half moulded Nono that the anxiety clutched not

se sentant aucune faim, n'y toucha pas, du reste.
himself felt any hunger not there touched -not- of the rest
not it for the

Quand vint la nuit, il se jeta sur une botte de paille que l'on
When came the night he himself threw on a bunch of straw that -it- one

avait jetée dans un coin, et finit par s'y endormir très tard,
had thrown in a corner and ended by himself there fall asleep very late

non sans avoir pleuré encore au souvenir de tous ceux qu'il aimait,
not without to have cried still at the memory of all those that he loved

au séjour d'Autonomie qu'il avait perdu par sa faute.
at the stay of Autonomy that he had lost by his fault

Son sommeil fut troublé par des cauchemars horribles, qui le
His sleep was troubled by -of the- nightmares horrible which him

réveillaient tout tremblant, trempé de sueur.
awoke again all trembling drenched of sweat

Tantôt, il était traîné devant des bêtes horribles, habillées de
Sometimes he was dragged in front of of the animals horrible dressed with

longues robes noires et rouges, coiffées de bonnets carrés, elles ouvraient
long robes black and red coiffed of caps squares they opened

des gueules menaçantes, faisant mine de se jeter sur lui pour
of the mouths threatening making looks of themselves to throw on him for

le   dévorer.
him   to devour

Tantôt   c'était   le   roi   Monnaïus   qui,   sous   les   traits   d'un   Nécrophore
Sometimes   it was   the   king   Monnaïus   who   under   the   traits guise   of a   Necrophorus

venait   creuser   le   terre   sous   lui,   comme   pour   l'enterrer   vivant   ;   ou   bien,
came   dig   the   earth   under   him   like   for   him to bury   alive   ;   or   well

sous   les   traits   du   vampire   de   ses   armoiries,   venait   lui   sucer   le   sang.
under   the   traits guise   of the   vampire   of   his   (coat of) arms   came   him   suck   the   blood

Nono,   paralysé   par   une   force   inconnue,   sentait   la   vie   s'écouler   lentement
Nono   paralyzed   by   a   force   unknown   felt   the   life   itself flow   slowly

de   ses   veines,   sans   pouvoir   opposer   aucune   résistance.
from   his   veins   without   to be able   to oppose   any   resistance

Il   se   réveilla   le   lendemain   tout   courbaturé.
He   himself   woke up   the   following day   all   aching

Dans   le   courant   de   la   journée,   deux   gardes   armés   de   hallebardes
In   the   course   of   the   day   two   guards   armed   with   halberds

vinrent   le   prendre   dans   son   cachot,   l'emmenèrent   à   travers   de
came   him   to take   in   his   dungeon   him took along   -at-   through   -of-

nombreux   couloirs,   lui   firent   monter   un   nombre   incalculable   d'escaliers,   et
numerous   corridors   him   made   climb   a   number   incalculable   of stairs   and

le   firent   enfin   pénétrer   dans   une   grande   pièce   où,   autour   d'une   table,
him   made   finally   enter   in   a   large   room   where   around   of a   table

se   tenaient   assis   deux   personnages.   Nono   se   crut   encore   dans
themselves   held   seated   two   characters   Nono   himself   believed   still   in

son   rêve,   en   reconnaissant   ses   bêtes   de   la   nuit.
his   dreams   in   recognizing   his   animals   of   the   night

Celui   qui   paraissait   le   maître   avait   une   tête   de   chacal   ;   il   exhalait
The one   who   appeared   the   master   had   a   head   of   jackal   ;   he   exhaled

une   odeur   repoussante.   Le   prisonnier   devina   qu'il   était   devant   un   des
a   smell   repulsive   The   prisoner   divined   that he   was   in front of   one   of the

conseillers   du   Parlement,   chargé   de   procéder   à   l'instruction   de   son
advisors   of the   Parliament   charged   with   to proceed   to   the instruction the decision   of   his

affaire.
affair
case

L'autre personnage avait devant lui du papier, de l'encre et
The other character had in front of him -of the- paper -of- -the- ink and

des plumes ; on devinait le greffier. Sa physionomie rappelait celle de
-of the- feathers ; one guessed the clerk His aspect reminded that of
pens

ces insectes que l'on appelle bousiers et dont le nom définit le
these insects that -it- one calls dung beetles and of which the name defines the

genre de vie.
sort of life

On fit asseoir le prisonnier devant l'homme à la tête de chacal.
One made sit the prisoner in front of the man at the head of jackal
with

Et celui-ci, d'une voix pédante, lui demanda ses noms et prénoms.
And that one with a voice pedantical him asked his names and first names

— Puisque vous m'avez fait arrêter, vous devez savoir qui je suis, fit
— Since you have me made arrest you must know who I am made
said

Nono avec candeur.
Nono with candor

— Dans votre intérêt, je vous engage à être respectueux de la justice.
— In your interest I you engage to be respectful of the justice
order

Savez-vous pourquoi vous êtes arrêté ?
Know you why you are arrested ?

— J'attends que vous me l'appreniez.
— I wait that you me it learn
tell it

— Ne faites pas l'ignorant, vous savez bien que vous avez poussé
— Not make -not- the ignorant you know well that you have pushed
pretend to be committed

à la désobéissance des lois, à l'irrespect de notre auguste
-to- the disobedience of the laws -the- the disrespect of our august

monarque, prêché la révolte contre nos saintes institutions. »
monarch preached the revolt against our holy institutions

Nono se demanda un instant s'il n'était pas un horrible criminel. Il
Nono himself asked a moment if he not was -not- a horrible criminal he

resta silencieux.
remained silent

— Vous voyez, vous n'osez pas répondre. Allons, mon enfant, un bon
— You see you not dare -not- to answer Go my child a good

mouvement, avouez, il vous en sera tenu compte, fit le chacal d'une
movement avow it you of it will be held account made the jackal with a
confess

voix papelarde.
voice sanctimonious

— Votre auguste souverain est un gredin qui m'a abominablement
— Your august sovereign is a bandit who me has abominably

trompé pour m'enlever d'Autonomie, répondit avec conviction Nono qui
deceived for take me away from Autonomy answered with conviction Nono who
to kidnap me

avait les nerfs agacés par la voix de fausset du chacal. Et j'ai
had the nerves frustrated by the voice of falsetto of the jackal And I have

toujours désiré sortir de votre sale pays pour retourner à ma chère
always desired to go out of your dirty country for to go back to my dear

Solidaria. »
Solidaria

Le chacal leva les deux pattes au ciel.
The jackal raised the two paws at the sky

— Gardes, cria-t-il, assurez-vous de ce criminel, reconduisez-le dans son
— Guards cried he assure-yourself -of- this criminal lead him back in his
get

cachot. Son affaire est claire maintenant. »
dungeon His business is clear now

De longs jours se passèrent sans que Nono vît personne. Une
-Of- long days themselves passed without that Nono saw anyone One

fois seulement un personnage en robe noire, avec une petite bavette sous
time only a character in dress black with a little bib under

le menton, vint lui rendre visite, sous le prétexte de lui parler de
the chin came him to render visit under the pretext of him to speak of
to give

ce qui lui arriverait après qu'il serait mort.
this which him would happen after that he would be dead

Nono qui souffrait de l'isolement, de l'immobilité, de l'incarcération, et
Nono who suffered from the isolation from the immobility from the incarceration and

était beaucoup plus occupé de ce qui lui arriverait de son vivant,
was much more occupied with this which him would happen of his alive
while living

le pria de le laisser tranquille. La physionomie du personnage, du
him asked of him to leave in peace The aspect of the character of the
for the

reste, lui ayant plutôt inspiré de l'antipathie, car dans cette
rest him having rather inspired of the antipathy because in this

physionomie, il y avait un peu de celle des personnages des
aspect it there had a bit of that of the characters of the
there was

équipages, mais aussi de la blatte et du cafard.
carriages but also of the roach and of the cockroach

Chaque jour son geôlier lui apportait son pain et sa cruche d'eau,
Each day his gaoler him brought his bread and his jug of water

sans dire une parole. Nono pensait devenir fou, tant lui était
without to say a word Nono thought to become insane so much him was

terrible cet isolement et ce silence. Il regrettait d'avoir mis l'homme
terrible this isolation and this silence He was sorry of to have put the man

noir à la porte.
(in) black at the door

Que faisaient son père et sa mère ? Savaient-ils où il était ? Et
What did his father and his mother ? Knew they where he was ? And

ses amis d'Autonomie ? que pensaient-ils de lui ? Et son ami le
his friends of Autonomy ? what thought they of him ? And his friend the

tailleur, ne l'avait-on pas inquiété à cause de lui ? Peut-être, lui aussi
tailor not had it him -not- worried at cause of him ? Maybe him also
be-

était-il arrêté, sa famille dans la misère ? Toutes ces questions restaient
was he arrested his family in the misery ? All these questions remained

sans réponse, et revenaient sans cesse se poser à son esprit.
without response and came back without stop themselves to pose to his mind

tourmenté.
tormented

Pour les chasser de son cerveau, le prisonnier se promenait de
For them to chase (away) from his brain the prisoner himself walked of

long en large dans sa cellule en comptant les dalles, mais cela
long in wide in his cell while counting the slabs but that

n'empêchait pas ses pensées de lui revenir en foule.
not prevented -not- his thoughts of him to return in crowd

Puis bientôt fatigué de cet exercice, il allait s'asseoir sur sa pierre, la
Then soon tired of this exercise he went himself sit on his stone the

tête entre les mains, se posant toujours les mêmes questions. Mais
head between the hands (to) himself posing always the same questions But

l'impatience le remettait vite debout pour recommencer sa promenade
the impatience him handed over quickly upright for to start again his walk
would hand over

d'ours en cage.
of bear in cage

Le jugement
The judgment

Des — jours — et — des — jours — se — passèrent — encore. — Puis — un — matin
-Of the- — days — and — -of the- more — days — themselves — passed — still — Then — one — morning

quatre — piquiers — vinrent — le — chercher, — lui — firent — traverser — un — couloir
four — pikemen — came — him — to seek — him — made — cross — a — corridor

souterrain, — monter — un — escalier, — traverser — des — couloirs — et — entrer — enfin
underground — climb — a — staircase — cross — -of the- more — corridors — and — enter — finally

dans — une — grande — salle — pleine — de — monde.
in — a — large — room — full — of — world / people

D'autres — soldats — avec — des — piques, — comme — ceux — qui — l'avaient — conduit,
Of other / Other — soldiers — with — -of the- — pikes — like — those — who — him had — led

étaient — disséminés — aux — quatre — coins — de — la — salle.
were — spread — at the — four — corners — of — the — room

On — fit — entrer — le — prisonnier — dans — une — espèce — de — compartiment — installé
One — made — enter — the — prisoner — in — a — kind — of — compartment — installed

sur — un — des — côtés — de — la — salle, — en — face — de — lui, — un — autre — compartiment
on — one — of the — sides — of — the — room — in — face — of — him — an — other — compartment

où — se — tenaient — douze — notables — Monnaïens, — présentant — toute — sorte
where — themselves — held — twelve — notables — Monnaian from Monnaia — presenting — all — kind

de — types : — paon, — buse, — vautour.
of — types : — peacock — buzzard — vulture

Au — fond, — sur — une — estrade, — une — espèce — de — comptoir, — avec — une — sorte — de
At the — back — on — a — dais — (was) a — kind — of — counter — with — a — kind — of

tribune — sur — la — droite — de — ce — comptoir, — près — de — la — ménagerie — où
tribune — on — the — right — of — this — counter — near — of — the — menagerie — where

étaient — enfermés — les — notables — Monnaïens.
were — locked in — the — notables — Monnaian from Monnaia

Dans le fond de l'estrade, bien en arrière du comptoir, d'autres
In the back of the dais well in back of the counter -of- other

Monnaïens, appartenant à l'aristocratie. Les variétés de types était si
Monnaians belonging to the aristocracy The variations of types was so

nombreuses qu'un moment, Nono se crut au
great that one moment Nono himself believed (to be) at the

Jardin des Plantes.
Garden of the Plants
{here: Zoo}

La première moitié de la salle était garnie d'une variété de Monnaïens
The first half of the room was furnished with a variety of Monnaians
filled

habillés de robes noires ; ils ressemblaient à des pies ou à
dressed with robes black ; they resembled to -of- the magpies or to

des perroquets.
-of- the parrots

Au fond de la salle, séparée par une balustrade, des Monnaïens
At the back of the room separated by a balustrade -of- the Monnaians

appartenant aux classes misérables. Là, dominait la ressemblance avec
belonging to the classes wretched There dominated the resemblance with

le mouton, le bœuf et l'âne.
the sheep the cows and the donkey

À une autre espèce de tribune près de Nono, se tenait un autre
At an other kind of tribune near -of- Nono himself kept an other

être de l'espèce qu'il avait vue chez le chacal qui avait procédé à
being of the species that he had seen with the jackal who had processed to

son interrogatoire.
his examination

Lorsque Nono fut casé dans son coin, un être à physionomie de
When Nono was encased in his corner a being to (the) aspect of
with

corbeau, faisant les fonctions d'huissier, glapit d'une voix de crécelle : La
(a) crow making the functions of bailiff yelped with a voice of (a) rattle : The
fulfilling

Cour !
Court !

Et   aussitôt,   sur   l'estrade,   parurent   quatre   messieurs   dont   trois   habillés
And   immediately on   the dais   appeared   four   gentlemen   of which three dressed

de   robes   noires,   le   quatrième   d'une   robe   rouge,   coiffés   de   bonnets
with robes   black   the   fourth   with a   dress red   capped   with   caps

carrés,   avec   de   larges   galons   d'or.
square   with   -of- wide   stripes of gold

L'habillé   de   rouge   qui   ressemblait   à   un   vautour   prit   place   à   la
The dressed   with   red   which resembled   -to-   a   vulture   took   place   at   the
The one dressed in

petite   tribune   près   des   notables.   Les   trois   noirs   qui   ressemblaient
little   tribune   near   of the notables   The   three   black (ones)   who   resembled

l'un   à   un   épervier,   un   autre   à   un   émouchet,   le   troisième   à   une
the one   to   a   sparrowhawk   an   other   to   a   goshawk   the   third   to   a

buse,   allèrent   s'asseoir   derrière   ce   que   Nono   avait   pris   pour   un
buzzard   went   themselves sit   behind   this   that   Nono   had   taken   for   a

comptoir.
counter

L'être   à   physionomie   de   bousier   qui   se   trouvait   dans   la
The being   to   (the) aspect   of   (a) dung beetle   who   himself   found   in   the
              with

tribune   près   de   l'accusé,   se   leva   avec   une   poignée   de   feuilles   de
tribune   near   of   the accused   himself   raised   with   a   fist   of   leaves   of

papier   à   la   main,   et   commença   la   lecture   de   ce   qui   y   était
paper   at   the   hand   and   started   the   reading   of   this   which   there   was
         in

écrit.   C'était   l'acte   d'accusation   contre   Nono.
written   It was   the act   of indictment against   Nono

Puis   quand   ce   fut   fait,   celui   qui   était   au   milieu   du   comptoir
Then   when   this   was   done   the one   who   was   at the   middle   of the   counter
                                                             in the

procéda   à   l'interrogatoire   de   l'accusé,   le   menaçant   de   peines   sévères
proceeded   to   the interrogation of   the accused   him   threatening   of   pains   severe
             with   punishments

s'il   se   montrait   aussi   irrespectueux   qu'il   avait   été   à   l'instruction.
if he   himself   showed   as   disrespectful   as he   had   been   at   the instruction
                                                                                    the decision

241

Nono fut abasourdi. Comment s'était-il montré irrespectueux, alors
Nono was thunderstruck How had he himself shown disrespectful then
since

qu'il n'avait fait que répondre selon ce qu'il pensait ?
that he not had made than answer according to this that he thought ?

Après la constatation de son état civil, le président lui demanda :
After the ascertainment of his state civil the president him asked :

— Reconnaissez-vous avoir parlé devant plusieurs Argyrocratiens d'un
— Do you recognize to have spoken in front of several Argyrocratiens of a

pays appelé Autonomie, où, selon vous, les fruits de la terre
country called Autonomy where according to you the fruits of the earth

seraient communs à tous, où il n'y aurait pas de lois,
would be common to all where it not there would have -not- -of- laws
there would be

pas de prévôts, pas de chevaliers du guet, où chacun serait libre
not of provosts not of knights of the watch where each would be free
no no

d'agir comme il l'entend ?
of to act like he it hears ?
it wants

— Certainement, puisque c'est là où j'étais quand j'en ai été
— Certainly since this is there where I was when I from it have been

enlevé par ce menteur de Monnaïus pour m'amener dans son sale
taken away by this liar -of- Monnaïus for me to bring in his dirty

pays où je n'ai eu que de la malechance et de la misère.
country where I not have had (other) than of the mischance and of the misery
bad luck

— Messieurs les notables, vous entendez avec quel cynisme l'accusé
— Gentlemen the notable you hear with what cynicism the accused

avoue son crime, glapit l'homme rouge en claquant du bec. Et, de
confesses his crime yelped the man red in slamming with the beak And of

plus, il se rend coupable du crime de lèse-majesté.
more he himself makes guilty of the crime of treason

— Reconnaissez-vous, continua le président, avoir excité vos auditeurs à
— Do you recognize continued the president to have excited your audience to

la révolte en les engageant à s'entendre entre eux pour
the revolt in them engaging to themselves to agree between them for

se passer des maîtres qui les font vivre, des lois qui les
themselves to pass of the masters who them make live from the laws which them
to get rid

protègent ?
protect ?

— Je ne sais pas si leurs maîtres les font vivre, ni si leurs lois
— I not know -not- if their masters them make live nor if their laws

les protègent, mais ce que je sais, c'est qu'à Autonomie nous
them protect but this that I know it is that at Autonomy (land) we

n'avions pas de tout cela et nous étions bien plus heureux. Je l'ai
not had -not- of all that and we were well more happy I it have

dit en effet, parce que c'était la vérité.
said in fact because that it was the truth

L'homme rouge continuait à faire claquer ses lèvres qui s'allongeaient
The man red continued to make flap his lips which themselves stretched

en bec de rapace.
in beak of predator

— C'est bien, vous pouvez vous asseoir, fit le président. Par vos
— This is well you can yourself sit made the president By your
said

aveux, votre crime est flagrant, nous pourrions nous en tenir là ;
confessions your crime is flagrant we could ourselves of it keep there ;

mais comme nous représentons la justice, nous ne voulons pas qu'il
but like we represent the justice we not want -not- that it

reste aucun doute dans l'esprit de messieurs les notables ; nous allons
remains any doubt in the mind of gentlemen the notables ; we go

entendre quelques témoins qui viendront déposer de ce qu'ils ont
hear some witnesses who will deposit of this that they have
tell

entendu.
heard

Le premier appelé fut un des trois préférés de Nono, qui
The first called was one of the three favorites of Nono who

fit preuve de courage, en essayant de prendre sa défense, excipant de
made evidence of courage in trying of to take his defense pleading of
showed

la bonne foi de Nono, qui ne faisait que raconter ce qu'il avait
the good faith of Nono who not did (other) than tell this that he had

vu. Et après tout, il n'était pas si criminel de soupirer après un sort
seen And after all it not was -not- so criminal of to sigh after a fate

meilleur. Parfois, l'existence était dure aux travailleurs d'Argyrocratie.
better Sometimes the existence was hard to the workers of Argyrocratie

Alors, l'homme rouge se leva, s'adressant aux notables :
Then the man red himself raised himself addressing to the notables :

— Vous voyez, messieurs, l'influence néfaste des discours du malfaiteur
— You see gentlemen the influence harmful of the speech of the malefactor

que vous avez à juger. Vous voyez combien il était temps d'arrêter ses
that you have to judge You see how much it was time to stop his

menées séditieuses qui menacent de pervertir le bon sens de nos
conducts seditious which threaten of to pervert the good sense of our

populations si tranquilles jusqu'à présent. C'est jusque dans le sanctuaire
populations so quiet up to (the) present It is until in the sanctuary

sacré de la justice que l'on ose venir répéter de semblables
sacred of the justice that it one dares to come repeat -of- similar

blasphèmes. Je demande une peine sévère contre le témoin qui, pour
blasphemies I request a punishment severe against the witness who for

sauver l'accusé, ne craint pas de fausser son serment en altérant la
to save the accused not feared -not- of to distort his oath in altering the

vérité. Du reste, des notes qui me sont fournies par le grand
truth Of the rest of the notes which me are provided by the large
For the have been

prévôt, me montrent cet homme comme très dangereux et un hardi
provost me show this man as very dangerous and a bold

propagateur des mensonges qui menacent de troubler notre admirable
propagator of the lies which threaten of to trouble our admirable

ordre social.
order social

L'ami de Nono fut condamné à cinq ans de prison séance tenante.
The friend of Nono was condemned to five years of prison session tending
during the session

Le tailleur fut appelé ensuite. Interrogé sur les circonstances où il
The tailor was called subsequently Interrogated on the circumstances where he

avait recueilli Nono, il raconta comment il l'avait connu.
had collected Nono he told how he him had known

— L'accusé n'a-t-il pas tenu, chez vous, des propos subversifs,
— The accused not has he -not- held with you -of the- proposals subversive

contraires au bon ordre public, au respect de nos institutions ?
contrary to the good order public at the respect of our institutions ?

demanda le président. À ce sujet, je vous ferai remarquer combien
asked the president At this topic I you will make notice how much

vous avez été coupable envers l'auguste majesté de notre sublime
you have been guilty towards the august majesty of our sublime

souverain, en tolérant chez vous des propos pareils, en recueillant ce
sovereign in tolerating with you -of- the proposals similar in receiving this

serpent qui ne pensait qu'à créer le désordre. Aussi, dans votre
snake who not thought (other) than to create the disorder Also in your

intérêt, je vous engage à être sincère et à dire tout ce que vous
interest I you engage to be sincere and to say all this that you
order

savez contre le misérable qu'attend le châtiment qu'il mérite. Votre
know against the miserable that awaits the punishment that he deserves Your

devoir de bon citoyen et de bon patriote était d'avertir de suite le
duty of good citizen and of good patriot was to warn of following the
immediately

grand prévôt.
great provost

Le tailleur sembla hésiter un moment, son regard se porta, comme
The tailor seemed to hesitate a moment his look himself carried like

malgré lui, sur Nono, mais s'en éloigna vivement, et ce fut d'une
in spite of him on Nono But himself of it removed strongly and it was with a

voix hésitante qu'il déclara que, par reconnaissance à Nono d'avoir
voice haltingly that he declared that by gratitude to Nono of to have

sauvé son enfant, il l'avait pris chez lui ; même qu'il n'avait pas à
saved his child he him had taken with him ; even that he not had -not- to

se plaindre de son travail. Que, en effet, l'accusé avait souvent
himself complain of his work That in effect the accused had often

raconté des histoires invraisemblables sur Autonomie, mais que, trompé
told -of the- stories unbelievable on Autonomy but that deceived

par son air candide, il n'avait pas cru au premier moment à
by his air candid he did not have -not- believed at the first moment to

la criminalité de ses intentions. Qu'il en demandait pardon au
the criminality of his intentions That he of it asked forgiveness to the

tribunal, promettant d'être plus clairvoyant à l'avenir.
court promising of to be more farseeing to the future
in

Et il se retira sans avoir osé regarder Nono.
And he himself withdrew without to have dared to look at Nono

Les suivants qui furent appelés étaient plusieurs de ceux qui avaient
The following who were called were several of those who had

assisté aux causeries, et ce fut sous la frayeur de partager le sort
assisted to the talks and this was under the fright of to share the fate

de l'accusé qu'ils déposèrent en le sens que leur dicta le
of the accused that they deposed in the sense that them dictated the
stated

président.
president

Et l'audition des témoins étant close, l'homme rouge se leva et
And the hearing of the witnesses being closed the man red himself raised and

prit la parole.
took the word

Il parla longuement de l'ordre magnifique qui présidait aux destinées
He spoke (a) long (time) of the order magnificent which presided to the destinies

du peuple soumis à Monnaïus ; parla de la bienfaisance de ceux
of the people submitted to Monnaïus ; (he) spoke of the beneficence of those

que la fortune avait comblé de ses dons ; de leur sollicitude pour les
that the fortune had filled with its gifts ; of their solicitude for the

malheureux, de leur ingéniosité à procurer du travail à ceux qui
unhappy of their ingenuity to acquire -of the- work for those who

n'avaient que leurs bras pour toute ressource.
not had (other) than their arms for all resource
as a

Il vanta les justes lois qui mettaient la propriété à l'abri des
He boasted the righteous laws which put the property at the shelter of the

déprédations de ceux qu'animent les mauvais instincts de rapine, de
depredations of those that enlivened the bad instincts of robbery of

paresse et d'envie ; exalta les vertus de patience et d'abnégation des
laziness and of envy ; exalted the virtues of patience and of abnegation of the

travailleurs, leur sobriété, leur économie, et leur dévouement à leur
workers their sobriety their economy and their dedication to their
budgeting

souverain et à leurs différents maîtres.
sovereign and to their different masters

Puis il parla ensuite contre ces gens sans aveu qui veulent
Then he spoke subsequently against these people without admission who want

troubler ce bel ordre de choses, de ces misérables sans feu ni
to trouble this beautiful order of things of these wretched (ones) without fire nor

lieu, venus on ne sait d'où, qui voudraient se vautrer dans
place come one not knows from where who would like themselves to wallow in

toutes les orgies sans rien produire ; qui, ne se sentant pas
all the orgies without nothing to produce ; who not themselves feeling -not-

le courage de travailler ni d'économiser, ne rêvent que de
the courage of to work nor of to save not dream (other) than of

s'emparer des biens de ceux qui, à force de patience, de
themselves to empower of the goods of those who at force of patience of

travail, d'ordre et d'économie, — ou les ayant reçus en héritage de
work of order and of economy — or them having received in heritage of
of savings

leurs ancêtres, — réussissent à se faire une place parmi ceux que
their ancestors — succeed to themselves make a place among those that

récompensent la fortune et le travail.
reward the fortune and the work

Puis, enfin, abordant ce qui concernait Nono, il fit voir que ce
Then finally approaching this which concerned Nono he made see that this

tableau enchanteur du soi-disant pays d'Autonomie, n'était qu'une
scene enchanting of the supposed country of Autonomy not was (other) than a

violente satire contre les institutions si justes, si saines d'Argyrocratie,
violent satire against the institutions so righteous so healthy of Argyrocratie

n'avaient qu'un but, faire croire aux travailleurs qu'ils pouvaient
not had than one goal to make believe -to- the workers that they could

se passer de maîtres — énorme absurdité qui se réfutait
themselves pass of masters — enormous absurdity which itself refuted
as

d'elle-même — contre laquelle on ne saurait être trop sévère — en
of itself — against which one not would know to be too severe — in

ce qu'elle tendait à faire croire aux travailleurs qu'on les frustrait
this that she stretched to make believe to the workers that one them frustrated
held back

du fruit de leur travail, les excitant ainsi contre ceux qui les font
from the fruit of their work them exciting thus against those who them make

vivre et sans lesquels il n'y aurait que misère et barbarie.
live and without which it not there would have (other) than misery and barbarity
there not would be

Puis il terminait en démontrant que l'accusé au lieu de chercher à
Then he ended in showing that the accused at the place of to seek to
instead

mériter l'indulgence du tribunal, avait au contraire poussé le cynisme
deserve the indulgence of the court had at the contrary pushed the cynicism

à son comble, en parlant de l'auguste monarque en termes irrespectueux.
at its peak in speaking of the august monarch in terms disrespectful

Il se rassit en demandant la peine de mort contre l'accusé.
He himself sat again in asking the pain of death against the accused
punishment

Un des personnages habillés de noir à tête de perroquet et qui était
One of the characters dressed of black to head of parrot and who was
in with

assis à une table devant Nono, se leva à son tour.
seated at a table in front of Nono himself raised at his turn

Lui aussi proclama la grandeur du pays d'Argyrocratie, l'austérité et la justice de ses lois, la légitimité des biens de ceux qui les possédaient, la patience et la force des classes laborieuses qui contribuaient tant à la prospérité générale.

À la vérité, les histoires de Nono, par leur excessive hardiesse, pouvaient devenir un danger contre l'ordre établi en troublant quelques esprits faibles. Mais, son client lui semblait ne pas avoir saisi toute la portée de ce qu'il disait. Je ne le crois pas tout à fait responsable, conclut-il. De plus, je prierai messieurs de la Cour, et messieurs les notables de prendre son âge en pitié. Je fais appel à votre indulgence.

Et il se rassit au milieu des bravos de la salle qui avait aussi énergiquement applaudi le discours de l'homme rouge.

Les notables se retirèrent pour délibérer. Un moment après, ils revinrent apportant un verdict de culpabilité, mitigé de circonstances atténuantes.

Les trois hommes du comptoir se consultèrent. Nono fut
The three men of the counter each other consulted Nono was

condamné aux travaux forcés à perpétuité.
condemned to the works forced at perpetuity

Atterré, il fut ramené à son cachot, où il succomba à
Dismayed he was taken back to his dungeon where he succumbed to

l'accablement. Il s'assit sur sa pierre et y resta cloué par
the dejection He sat on his stone and there remained nailed down by

l'angoisse. Des larmes brûlantes coulèrent de ses paupières. La nuit
the anxiety -Of the- tears burning flowed from his eyelids The night

vint sans qu'il s'en aperçut.
came without that he himself of it saw

À la fin, le désespoir le prit si fort qu'il résolut de mourir. Se
At the end the despair him took so strong that he resolved of to die Himself

levant d'un bond, il voulut se briser la tête contre le mur. Mais
raising with a jump he wanted himself break the head against the wall But

un rayon de lune qui pénétrait par la lucarne vint le frapper au
a ray of moon which penetrated by the skylight came him hit at the / in the

visage et l'arrêta dans son élan. Sur ce rayon il vit glisser une
face and him stopped in his momentum On this ray he saw slip a

jeune femme au visage radieux, enveloppée d'une clarté douce faisant
young woman at the / with the face radiant wrapped of a / in a light sweet making

ressortir le vert de sa robe.
come out / shine the green of her dress

— Je suis l'Espérance, dit-elle, je suis envoyée vers toi par Solidaria qui
— I am the Hope said she I am sent to you by Solidaria who

ne peut se hasarder dans les États de Monnaïus, tant que les
not can herself venture in the States of Monnaïus as much that the

habitants ne la désireront pas de tous leurs vœux.
inhabitants not her will desire -not- with all their wishes

Mais elle te fait dire de ne pas perdre courage. Tes amis
But she you made say of not -not- to lose courage Your friends

d'Autonomie	pensent	à	toi	et	aux	moyens	de	te	délivrer.	Trois
of Autonomy	think	to / of	you	and	to the / of the	means	of	you	to deliver to free	Three

d'entre	eux	l'ont	déjà	quittée	pour	Argyrocratie	dans	l'espoir	de
of between	them	it have	already	left	for	Argyrocratie	in	the hope	of

t'être	utile.
you to be	useful

Donc,	courage	et	espoir	!
Then	courage	and	hope	!

Et	l'ayant	baisé	au	front,	elle	lui	ferma	doucement	les	yeux,
And	him having	kissed	on the	face	she	him	closed	softly	the	eyes

l'endormant	de	sa	voix	caressante,	l'étendant	sur	sa	couche	de	paille.
him lulling	with	her	voice	caressing	him laying down	on	his	bed	of	straw

Puis,	se	raccrochant	au	rayon	qui	l'avait	apportée,	elle	disparut,
Then	herself	hanging	on the	ray	which	her had	brought	she	disappeared

laissant	une	vague	clarté	dans	le	cachot.
leaving	a	vague	clarity light	in	the	dungeon

Le départ des conjurés
The depart of the conspirators

Laissons notre malheureux prisonnier aux rêves étoilés qu'en son sommeil
(We) leave our unhappy prisoner to the dreams starry that in his sleep
Let's leave

lui a soufflés la fée Espérance, et retournons un peu à Autonomie,
him has blown the fairy Hope and return a bit to Autonomy (land)

pour voir ce que deviennent nos autres personnages, comment ils ont
for to see this that became (of) our other characters how they have

accepté la disparition de leur camarade.
accepted the disappearance of their comrade

En même temps que Solidaria était avertie par le cri de détresse de
In (the) same time that Solidaria was warned by the cry of distress of

celui qu'on enlevait, Labor était encouru avec toute son équipe. Lui
the one that one took away Labor was run in with all his team He
had run up

avait été prévenu par le carabe que Nono avait délivré de la mésange.
had been warned by the beetle that Nono had freed of the tit

Il avait assisté à son entrevue de la veille avec Monnaïus,
He had assisted at his between-seen of the evening before with Monnaïus
{The beetle} glimpse

il s'était rendu compte du danger que courait l'enfant, et
he himself was rendered account of the danger that ran the child and
himself had

s'était posté non loin de lui pour l'avertir. Mais un ennemi lui
himself was posted not far from him for to warn him But an enemy him
himself had

ayant fait la chasse, il avait dû fuir, puis se cacher pour
having made the hunt he had had to flee then himself hide for

échapper à la poursuite ; c'est en se rendant à Autonomie qu'il
to escape at the pursuit ; it is in himself giving over to Autonomy that he
going

avait assisté à l'enlèvement, et qu'il avait couru avertir Labor.
had assisted at the kidnapping and that he had run to inform Labor

La fureur des enfants fut grande contre Monnaïus. Ils l'auraient
The fury of the children was great against Monnaïus. They him would have

certainement mis en pièce, s'il leur était tombé entre les mains. Mais
certainly put in piece if he them was fallen between the hands. But
ripped to pieces had

Monnaïus était maintenant derrière le mur de son château-fort à
Monnaïus was now behind the wall of his fortified castle at

l'abri de leur colère.
the shelter of their anger

Le manque de confiance de Nono fut généralement blâmé; mais comme
The lacks of confidence of Nono was generally blamed but like

il en était la première victime et dans le malheur, on laissa les
he of it was the first victim and in the misfortune one left the

récriminations de côté afin d'aviser à ce qu'il était possible de faire
recriminations of side so of to notify to this that it was possible of to do
to the for to inform about what

pour le tirer des griffes du roi d'Argyrocratie.
for him to pull from the claws of the king of Argyrocratie

Solidaria, qui était revenue de sa poursuite inutile, présidait à la
Solidaria who was come back from her pursuit useless presided at the
had

discussion qui commença par être tumultueuse, chacun apportant son
discussion which started by to be tumultuous each bringing their

projet, émettant ses idées les plus spontanées ; les plus affirmatives
project emitting their ideas the most spontaneous ; the most affirmative

n'étant pas toujours les plus pratiques.
not is -not- always the most practical

Hans, Mab, Biquette, Sacha et Riri étaient inconsolables. Hans surtout,
Hans Mab Biquette Sacha and Riri were inconsolable Hans especially

trépignait d'impatience, et ne parlait rien moins que de marcher en
stamped of impatience and not spoke nothing less than of walk in

masse sur Argyrocratie.
mass on Argyrocratie

Mais il ne fut pas difficile de lui démontrer que la colonie était
But it not was -not- difficult of him to demonstrate that the colony was

trop faible pour pouvoir s'attaquer aux forces formidables des
too weak for to be able themselves attack -to- the forces formidable of the

Argyrocratiens, tant que l'on ne se serait pas
Argyrocratiens as much as -it- one not himself would be -not-
would have

créé des intelligences parmi eux.
created of the intelligences among them
gathered information from

En désespoir de cause, Hans proposa de partir seul pour Argyrocratie, de
In despair of cause Hans proposed of to leave alone for Argyrocratie of

se mettre à la recherche de Nono, et là, une fois qu'il
himself to put to the search of Nono and there one time that he

l'aurait trouvé, on verrait ce qu'il serait possible de faire pour
him would have found one would see this that he would be possible of to do for

revenir à Autonomie.
to return to Autonomy

Solidaria convint qu'il y aurait quelque chance de réussite. Si elle
Solidaria agreed that it there would have some chance of success If she
that there was

était impuissante au pays de Monnaïus, elle pouvait cependant, d'une
was powerless at the country of Monnaïus she could however of a
in the in a

façon indirecte, aider aux efforts de ceux qui ont confiance en elle. Sa
way indirect help at the efforts of those who have confidence in her Her

seule crainte était que Hans échouât dans son entreprise, se fit
alone fear was that Hans failed in his mission himself made

découvrir par les suppôts de Monnaïus, et que l'on eût à déplorer la
discover by the minions of Monnaïus and that -it- one had to deplore the

perte de deux membres de la colonie, au lieu d'un.
loss of two members of the colony at the place of one

Mais Hans déclara que la colonie se devait à elle-même de travailler
But Hans declared that the colony itself owed to her-self of to work

à la délivrance d'un de ses membres. Quoi qu'il pût arriver, il était
at the deliverance of one of its members What that he could arrive he was
Whatever him happen

résolu à tout sacrifier pour venir en aide à son ami.
decided to all sacrifice for to come in aide to his friend

Mab ajouta qu'elle-même était décidée à accompagner Hans dans son
Mab added that she herself was determined to accompany Hans in his

entreprise, deux volontés étant plus efficaces qu'une. Il n'y eut donc
mission two wills being more effective than one It not there had then

plus qu'à chercher les moyens de faciliter la besogne aux deux
more than to search the means of to facilitate the task to the two
of the

hardis volontaires.
bold volunteers

Après une laborieuse discussion où l'on proposa et rejeta une foule
After a laborious discussion where -it- one proposed and rejected a crowd

de projets, on s'arrêta à cette décision. Hans et Mab se
of projects one himself halted to this decision Hans and Mab themselves
stopped

déguiseraient en musiciens ambulants. Il y en avait un grand nombre
disguised in musicians traveling It there in had a large number
There were of them

qui parcouraient les villages d'Argyrocratie, gagnant leur vie en jouant de
who roamed the villages of Argyrocratie earning their life in playing -of-
bread

leurs instruments.
their instruments

Hans et Mab auraient plus de chances de passer inaperçus, de
Hans and Mab would have more -of- chances of to pass unnoticed of

se glisser parmi le menu peuple au milieu duquel Nono avait
themselves slip among the lesser people at the middle of the which Nono had

dû être abandonné, et plus de facilités à se renseigner sur
had to be abandoned and more of facilities to themselves give information on
capabilities

son sort.
his fate

Hans fut muni d'une clarinette, et Mab d'un tambourin. Au cas
Hans was provided with a clarinet and Mab with a tambourine At the case

où Nono serait retenu prisonnier quelque part, Labor leur remit
where Nono would be retained prisoner some side / somewhere Labor them handed over

une petite lime pouvant aisément se cacher, mais capable de scier les
a little file {tool} being able easily itself to hide but capable of to saw the

chaînes les plus fortes, les barreaux les plus épais. Électricia leur
chains the most strong the bars the most thick Electricia them

remit en outre un talisman leur permettant de communiquer avec
handed over in besides a talisman them permitting of to communicate with

Autonomie, d'y envoyer des nouvelles et d'en recevoir. Solidaria
Autonomy from there to send -of the- news and from of it to receive Solidaria

leur souffla sa force. Mais sachant quelle force est l'or chez les
them breathed her force But knowing what force is the gold with the

Argyrocratiens, elle leur remit une bourse pouvant leur fournir
Argyrocratiens she them handed over a purse being able (to) them provide

toute la monnaie dont ils auraient besoin sans que celle-ci
all the money of which they would have need without that this one here

s'épuisât jamais.
itself exhausted ever

Maintenant, que tout était arrêté, on avait le temps d'agir. Pour
Now that all was stopped one had the time of to act For

dépister les espions de Monnaïus, s'il y en avait dans les
to lead off track the spies of Monnaïus if it there of them had in the / if there were any

environs, il fut décidé que les deux volontaires ne partiraient que
surroundings it was decided that the two volunteers not would leave than

lorsque tout serait prêt, sous prétexte d'herborisation. Ils retrouveraient
when all would be ready under pretext of botanizing They would find back

Solidaria, à un point de la frontière qu'elle leur désigna. Là, elle
Solidaria at one point of the border that she them designated There she

se chargeait de les faire pénétrer en Argyrocratie sans qu'ils
herself charged of them to make enter in Argyrocratie without that they

eussent crainte d'être découverts.
had fear of to be discovered

Au jour fixé, Hans et Mab furent donc réveillés de bonne heure.
At the day set Hans and Mab were then woken up of good hour early

Munis de tout ce que la prévoyance de leurs amis s'ingéniait à
Provided of all this that the foresight of their friends itself contrived to

leur fournir sans trop les charger, ils firent leurs adieux à tous
them provide without too (much) them load they made their farewells to all burden

et descendirent le perron du palais.
and descended the stone porch of the palace

Mais au moment où ils allaient quitter l'esplanade, un joli petit
But at the moment where they went to leave the esplanade a pretty little

cochon, tout rose, accourut de toute la vitesse de ses petites pattes,
pig all pink ran with all the speed of his small paws

agitant sa queue en tire-bouchon, poussant de petits grognements qui
stirring its tail in corkscrew pushing -of- small grunts which uttering

avaient l'air d'être des reproches.
had the air of to be of the reproaches

Ce petit cochon était le favori du groupe dont faisait partie Nono
This little pig was the favorite of the group of which made part Nono was

; lui-même l'avait en grande prédilection, lui ayant appris à danser et
; him self he had in large predilection him having learned to dance and

à faire quelques tours.
to to make some turns

Mab l'embrassa sur son joli groin rose, lui disant :
Mab him kissed on his pretty snout pink him saying :

— Nous t'avions oublié, mon pauvre Penmoch, nous allions partir sans
— We you had forgotten my poor Penmoch we went to leave without

te dire adieu.
you to say farewell

Penmoch continuait à secouer son tire-bouchon et à grogner.
Penmoch continued to shake his corkscrew and to grunt

Hans le flatta de la main, en lui disant :
Hans him petted with the hand while him saying :

— Là, là, c'est bien. Vous êtes un joli cochon qui pensez à vos
— There there it is well You are a pretty pig who thinks to/of your

amis, mais il nous faut partir. Nous sommes pressés. Et les deux
friends but it us is necessary/we must leave We are hurried/in a hurry And the two

voyageurs se remirent en route après une dernière caresse. Penmoch
travelers themselves handed in road after a last caress Penmoch

leur emboîta le pas.
them joined the step

— Mais tu nous gênerais, nous ne pouvons pas t'emmener, répéta
— But you us embarras we not can -not- take you repeated

Hans, lorsqu'il le vit trottinant derrière eux. Et il voulut le renvoyer.
Hans when he him saw trotting behind them And he wanted him return

Penmoch protesta en grognant plus fort, et continua à suivre les deux
Penmoch protested in grunting more strong and continued to follow the two

émigrants.
emigrants

— Nous ne pouvons cependant pas l'emmener, fit Hans.
— We not can however -not- take him made/said Hans

Mab réfléchissait.
Mab thought

— Mais qu'est-ce qu'il a donc, fit-elle tout d'un coup en se
— But what is it that he has then she asked all of a strike/sudden in herself

baissant ; et elle tira un petit paquet qui pendait à son cou.
lowering ; and she pulled a little package which hung at his neck

Elle l'ouvrit, c'était un petit tablier brodé et un petit tricorne
She it opened it was a little sign embroidered and a little tricorn

galonné que Nono lui mettait lorsqu'il lui faisait faire des tours.
gallooned that Nono him put when he him made to make of the turns

— Je crois qu'il sait où nous allons, fit-elle gravement.
— I believe that he knows where we go made she/said she seriously

Emmenons-le,   il   pourra   nous   être   utile.
taking him along   he   will be able   us   to be   useful

Et   le   cochon,   se   voyant   accepté,   gambada   joyeusement   à   côté
And   the   pig   himself   seeing   accepted   gamboled   joyfully   at   (the) side

d'eux.
of them

Après   avoir   quitté   les   jardins   d'Autonomie,   Hans,   Mab   et   Penmoch
After   to have   left   the   gardens   of Autonomy   Hans   Mab   and   Penmoch

s'engagèrent,   dans   les   bois   que   quelques   jours   auparavant   ils   avaient
committed themselves   in   the   woods   that   some   days   before   they   had

parcourus   si   gaiement,   et   où   Nono   avait   fait   la   si   malencontreuse
traveled   so   merrily   and   where   Nono   had   made   the   so   unfortunate

rencontre   de   Monnaïus.
encounter   with   Monnaïus

Lorsqu'ils   eurent   fait   une   partie   du   chemin,   se   sentant   fatigués,
When they   had   made   a   part   of the   way   themselves   feeling   weary

ils   s'arrêtèrent   dans   une   clairière,   s'assirent   à   l'ombre   d'un
they   themselves halted   in   a   clearing   themselves sat   at   the shade   of a
        stopped

mûrier,   tirèrent   quelques   provisions   de   leur   bissac,   et   se
mulberry tree   pulled   some   supplies   from   their   sack   and   themselves

mirent   en   devoir   de   déjeuner   avec   appétit.   En   route   ils   avaient   fait
set   in   duty   of   to lunch   with   appetite   On   (the) road   they   had   made

provision   de   glands   pour   Penmoch.
provision   of   acorns   for   Penmoch

Pour   compléter   son   déjeuner,   les   châtaignes   abondaient   sur   le   sol.
For   to complete   his   lunch   the   chestnuts   abounded   on   the   ground

Tout   en   mangeant,   ils   causèrent   ;   et   de   quoi   pouvaient-ils   causer,   si
All   while   eating   they   chatted   ;   and   of   what   could they   talk   if

ce   n'est   de   ce   qui   les   occupait   le   plus   :   leur   cher   Nono   et   les
this   not is   of   this   who   them   occupied   the   most   :   their   dear   Nono   and   the

moyens   de   le   retrouver.
means   of   him   find back

Dans les branches du mûrier, une colonie de vers à soie, qu'ils
In the branches of the mulberry tree a colony of worms to silk that they
silk worms

n'avaient pas aperçue, les écoutait attentivement.
not had -not- perceived them listened to closely

Cette colonie était la progéniture du bombyx auquel Nono avait
This colony was the offspring of the moth to the which Nono had
to which

rendu la volée : une femelle prête à pondre. À ses petits qu'elle
rendered the flight : a female ready to lay (eggs) To her small (ones) that she
given freedom

ne devait jamais voir, comme elle leur transmettait l'instinct de tisser
not must ever see like she them transmitted the instinct of to weave
just as

un cocon, elle leur transmit sa reconnaissance envers son libérateur,
a cocoon she them transmitted her gratitude towards her liberator

avec la charge de s'acquitter pour elle.
with the charge of themselves to acquit for her
make up

Aussi, lorsqu'ils eurent compris qu'il s'agissait de celui qu'ils avaient
Also when they had understood that it itself dealt of the one that they had
concerned

charge de remercier, ils tinrent conseil sur ce qu'ils pouvaient faire
charge of to thank they held counsel on this that they could do

pour venir en aide à sa délivrance. Ils eurent bientôt trouvé, et
for to come in aide to his deliverance They had soon found and

se mirent immédiatement au travail.
themselves put immediately to the work

Hans, qui s'était couché sur le dos en attendant de se remettre
Hans who himself was laid down on the back in awaiting of himself to set again
himself had

en route, les yeux perdus en l'air, fixant, sans le voir, le
on (the) road the eyes lost in the air focusing on without it to see the

feuillage du mûrier qui le couvrait de son ombre, songeait à son
foliage of the mulberry tree who him covered with its shade thought to his
of

ami, lorsque, tout d'un coup, d'une des branches, il vit descendre un
friend when all of a strike from one of the branches he saw go down a
sudden

fil léger, et, après ce fil, glisser, l'un derrière l'autre, une infinité
wire light and after this wire slip the one behind the other an infinity

de vers à soie, qu'il reconnut à leur corps blanchâtre, à leur forme
of worms to silk that he recognized at their body whitish at their shape
      silk worms

annelée. Et il les regardait légèrement intrigué, descendre jusqu'à
corrugated And he them watched (s)lightly intrigued go down up to

terre, se mettre en colonne, et se diriger vers lui.
earth themselves to put in column and themselves to direct towards him
the ground

Ne sachant ce que ça voulait dire, il se mit sur le ventre,
Not knowing this what that wanted to say he himself put on the belly

désignant les vers à Mab qui se rapprocha de lui.
designating the worms to Mab who herself approached of him

Lorsqu'ils furent tout près, un des vers se détacha des autres,
When they were all near one of the worms itself detached from the others

vint presque sous le nez des deux observateurs, et là, dressant la
came almost under the nose of the two observers and there raising the

moitié de son corps, il leur fît entendre ceci :
half of its body he them made hear this :

— Soyez sans crainte, nous sommes des amis. Nous avons une dette
— Be without fear we are of the friends We have a debt

de reconnaissance à payer à celui que vous voulez délivrer des
of gratitude to pay to the one that you want to deliver from the
      to free

mains de Monnaïus.
hands of Monnaïus

De notre soie la plus solide et la plus légère, nous avons tissé une
From our silk the most solid and the most light we have woven a

sphère que vous n'aurez qu'à déplier, pour qu'elle se gonfle
sphere that you won't have than to unfold for that she itself inflates

d'elle-même, et vous emporte dans les airs, vous ramenant ici.
by itself and you carries in the air you bringing back here

Et sur un signe de lui, douze gros vers apportèrent une pièce de soie
And on a sign of him twelve big worms brought a piece of silk

roulée, grosse comme un cigare.
rolled big like a cigar

Mais elle était si fine, si fine, que Hans, sur l'invitation du ver,
But she was so fine so fine that Hans on the invitation of the worm

l'ayant déroulée, elle était semblable à une grande tente. Mais comme
it having unrolled she was similar to a large tent But like

elle commençait à se gonfler, sur l'indication du ver, il se
she began to itself inflate on the indication of the worm he himself

dépêcha de la rouler à nouveau et de la mettre dans sa poche.
despatched of her to roll to new and of her to put in his pocket
                                  again

Hans remercia les vers à soie de leur cadeau, leur promit d'instruire
Hans thanked the worms to silk of their gift them promised of to instruct
                the silk worms for   of to inform

leur ami de leur assistance, s'il était assez heureux pour le rejoindre.
their friend of their assistance if he was enough happy for him to rejoin

Et s'étant séparés, les vers remontèrent à leur mûrier. Hans,
And himself being separated the worms remounted to their mulberry tree Hans
   having

Mab et Penmoch se remirent en route.
Mab and Penmoch themselves handed in road

Ce ne fut que le soir qu'ils approchèrent de la frontière. Sur
This not was that the evening that they approached of the border On

chaque pic, sur chaque colline se dressaient de solides châteaux
each peak on each hill himself rose of solid castles

crénelés qui défendaient l'entrée d'Argyrocratie. Sur la route des postes
crenellated who defended the entry of Argyrocratie On the road of the posts

de soldats surveillaient ceux qui passaient. Il ne fallait pas songer
of soldiers surveilled those who passed He not was necessary -not- to think

à y pénétrer.
to there enter

Mais Solidaria connaissait une grotte percée dans une des
But Solidaria knew a cave pierced in one of the

montagnes à pic qui séparaient Autonomie d'Argyrocratie. C'est dans
mountains at peak which separated Autonomy (land) from Argyrocratie It is in
mountain peaks

cette grotte, à laquelle on arrivait par un sentier à peine tracé dans
this cave at the which one arrived by a path at pain traced in
                                                  barely visible

les bois, qu'elle leur avait donné rendez-vous, et où nos trois
the woods that she them had given appointment and where our three

voyageurs la trouvèrent, les attendant.
travelers her found them awaiting

Solidaria leur donna le secret d'ouvrir un souterrain qu'elle seule
Solidaria them gave the secret of to open an underground that she alone

connaissait, et qui, de cette grotte, conduisait jusque dans le pays
knew and which from this cave led until in the country

d'Argyrocratie, en arrière de la ligne des forts et des postes de
of Argyrocratie in (the) back of the line of the forts and of the posts of

soldats.
soldiers

Mais comme il faisait nuit, elle les engagea à attendre jusqu'au
But like it made night she them committed to await up to the
              was

lendemain pour y pénétrer. Hans et Mab remercièrent Solidaria, qui
following day for there to enter Hans and Mab thanked Solidaria who

les engagea encore une fois à réfléchir. Une fois de l'autre côté, la
them commited still one time to reflect One time of the other side the
                                                      on

grotte se refermerait sur eux, et la sphère des vers à soie, ne
cave itself would close on them and the sphere of the worms at silk not

les ramènerait qu'à condition qu'ils eussent fait tous leurs efforts
them would bring than at (the) condition that they had made all their efforts

et réussi à retrouver leur camarade.
and succeeded to find back their comrade

Et comme ils restaient inébranlables, elle leur souhaita bonne chance
And like they remained unshakeable she them wished good fortune

et les embrassa avant de les quitter. Puis ils firent un repas du
and them embraced before of them to leave Then they made a meal of the

reste de leurs provisions sans oublier Penmoch, s'arrangèrent
rest of their supplies without to forget Penmoch arranged for themselves

ensuite un lit de feuilles sèches et de mousse et s'endormirent
subsequently a bed of leaves dry and of moss and themselves slept
fell asleep

enfin, un peu anxieux, en songeant au lendemain.
finally a bit anxious while dreaming to the following day
of the

À l'aventure
At the adventure

Le lendemain, lorsqu'ils s'éveillèrent, il faisait grand jour. Disant un
The following day when they -themselves- awoke it made large day Saying a
was broad daylight

dernier adieu au pays d'Autonomie, Hans fit jouer le ressort que
last farewell to the country of Autonomy Hans made play the contraption that

lui avait indiqué Solidaria, puis, bravement, ils s'engagèrent tous
him had indicated Solidaria then bravely they committed themselves all

trois dans le couloir qui s'ouvrit devant eux, sorte de boyau
three in the corridor which itself opened in front of them kind of intestine

sombre qui leur souffla un vent frais et humide au visage. Derrière
dark which them breathed a wind fresh and moist at the face Behind
in the

eux, la pierre qui le fermait s'était replacée d'elle-même, leur
them the stone which it closed itself was replaced of she-same them
served to close it itself had moved back all by itself

ôtant tout espoir de retour.
removing all hope of to return

À l'aide du talisman d'Électricia, qui pouvait aussi leur fournir de la
To the help of the talisman of Electricia who could also them provide of the
With

lumière, ils s'éclairèrent sur leur route. Mais rien ne vint les
light they themselves lit up -on- their road But nothing not came them

entraver ; après deux heures de marche, ils débouchèrent dans le ravin
hamper ; after two hours of march they came out in the ravine

que leur avait indiqué Solidaria. S'étant retournés pour voir encore
that them had indicated Solidaria Themselves being returned for to see still
Having

une fois le souterrain, l'entrée avait disparu. Plus rien n'en décelait
one time the underground the entry had disappeared More nothing not of it betrayed
tunnel Nothing of it

la trace.
the trace

Grimpant une pente douce, nos trois voyageurs se trouvèrent sur
Climbing a slope soft our three travelers themselves found on

la route. Ils étaient dans le pays de leur ennemi.
the road They were in the country of their enemy

Ils marchèrent droit devant eux, et ne tardèrent pas à voir pointer
They marched straight in front of them and not delayed -not- to see point

les toits des premières maisons d'un village.
the roofs of the first houses of a village

Ils hâtèrent le pas. Midi approchait. Le village était encore loin, leur
They hastened the step Noon approached The village was still far their

déjeuner du matin avait été des plus sommaires, et leurs provisions
lunch of the morning had been of the most summary and their supplies

étaient épuisées.
were exhausted

Ils l'atteignirent enfin. C'était un hameau misérable, ne se composant
They it reached finally It was a hamlet miserable not itself composing

guère que d'une dizaine de maisons qui bordaient la route.
hardly than of a ten-some of houses which lined the road

Pour rester dans leur rôle de musiciens ambulants, avant de penser à
For to stay in their role of musicians traveling before of to think to

se restaurer, ils s'arrêtèrent au milieu de la route, et
themselves restore they themselves halted at the middle of the road and
feed stopped

commencèrent à jouer un des airs qui se jouent en
began to play one of the tunes which themselves play in
are played

Argyrocratie, et que Solidaria leur avait appris avant de partir, Hans en
Argyrocratie and that Solidaria them had taught before of to leave Hans in

soufflant dans sa clarinette, Mab en agitant son tambour de basque et
blowing in his clarinet Mab in stirring her drum of basque and

en dansant.
in dancing

Au bruit de la musique, Penmoch se dressa gravement debout sur
At the noise of the music Penmoch himself raised seriously upright on

ses deux pattes de derrière, tenant, avec ses deux pattes de devant, une
his two paws of behind holding with his two paws of in front a

robe imaginaire, se mit à danser aussi.
dress imaginary himself put to dance also

Quoiqu'ils l'eûssent vu déjà danser et que leurs idées ne fussent pas
Though they him had seen already dance and that their ideas not were -not-

précisément tournées à la gaîté, Hans et Mab ne purent s'empêcher
exactly turned to the gaiety Hans and Mab not could themselves hinder
stop

de rire. Mab s'arrêta pour lui mettre son tablier, et le coiffer
of to laugh Mab himself halted for him to put his sign and him to cap
stopped

de son chapeau.
with his hat

Puis, Hans ressouffla dans sa clarinette, Mab reprit sa danse, et
Then Hans blew again in his clarinet Mab continued her dance and

Penmoch l'imita en poussant un petit grognement de satisfaction.
Penmoch her imitated in uttering a little grunt of satisfaction

La musique avait attiré quelques gamins qu'amusèrent l'air grave et
The music had attracted some kids that amused the tune serious and
who amused

la danse de Penmoch, mais ce fut tout ; à peine deux ou trois têtes
the dance of Penmoch but this was all ; at pain two or three heads

de femmes se firent-elles voir dans l'entre-bâillement des portes.
of women themselves did they see in the between-gaping of the doors
the opening

Afin d'attirer l'attention de Nono au cas où il se trouverait par
So of to attract the attention of Nono at the case where he himself would find by
in

là, Hans joua un des airs préférés d'Autonomie, l'encadrant d'un
there Hans played one of the tunes favorite of Autonomy it framing with a

motif d'Argyrocratie afin de ne pas trop se déceler.
motive of Argyrocratie so of not -not- too (much) himself reveal
musical passage

Mais leurs regards interrogateurs ne virent rien de particulier. Pendant
But their looks interrogators not saw nothing -of- particular During
questioning

que Hans continuait à jouer de la clarinette et que Penmoch dansait
that Hans continued to play -of- the clarinet and that Penmoch danced

et faisait des grâces aux petits Argyrocratiens émerveillée de voir
and made of the graces to the small Argyrocratiens amazed of to see
charms

danser un cochon, Mab alla faire la quête aux portes, tendant son
dance a pig Mab went to make the quest at the doors extending her

tambourin ; mais elle revint sans rien avoir récolté.
tambourine ; but she returned without nothing to have harvested

Nos deux artistes, que la faim talonnait, s'adressèrent à une vieille
Our two artists, that the hunger bugged themselves addressed to an old

Argyrocratienne, lui demandant de leur vendre un peu de pain. Mais
Argyrocratienne, her asking of them to sell a bit of bread But

celle-ci leur demanda à voir leur argent auparavant.
this one here them asked to see their silver before

Pour ne pas éveiller la défiance, ils ne tirèrent de leur bourse que
For not -not- to wake up the distrust they not pulled from their purse than

quelque petite monnaie qu'ils lui mirent dans la main. La vieille
some small money that they him put in the hand The old (woman)
change

leur coupa, à Hans et Mab, un morceau de pain. Hans réclama pour
them cut to Hans and Mab a piece of bread Hans demanded for

Penmoch. — La vieille parut scandalisée, mais comme elle ne leur
Penmoch — The old (woman) appeared scandalized but as she not them
shocked

en avait pas donné pour la moitié de leur argent, elle en coupa un
of it had -not- given for the half of their silver she of it cut an

autre morceau en rechignant et leur ferma la porte sur le nez.
other piece in grudging and them closed the door on the nose
reluctance

Les trois voyageurs s'éloignèrent du village en grignotant leur
The three travelers themselves moved away from the village in munching their
departed

pain, se proposant de compléter leur déjeuner plus loin.
bread themselves proposing of to complete their lunch more far
farther

Ils marchèrent ainsi quelque temps, croisant quelques rares passants sur
They marched thus some time, crossing some rare passersby on

la route, apercevant parfois quelque ferme isolée, au loin, au
the road, seeing sometimes some farm isolated, at the distance, at the

milieu des champs.
middle of the fields

À la fin ils se décidèrent à se détourner de leur chemin
At the end they themselves decided to themselves divert of their way

pour aller demander à une de ces fermes qu'on voulût bien leur
for to go ask at one of these farms that one wanted well them
whether they

vendre quelque chose à manger.
to sell some thing to eat

On leur donna du pain, du lait et du beurre. Ils demandèrent
One them gave of the bread, of the milk and of the butter. They asked

que l'on voulût bien faire cuire quelques pommes de terre pour
that -it- one wanted well to make cook some apples of earth for
potatoes

Penmoch. Le fermier leur demanda à quoi ils pensaient de traîner
Penmoch. The farmer them asked for what they thought of to trail

ainsi, derrière eux, un cochon qui ne leur serait qu'un embarras
thus, behind them, a pig who not them would be than an embarrassment

et proposa de le leur acheter.
and proposed of it (from) them to buy

Mais Hans lui dit que Penmoch n'était pas un cochon ordinaire, et
But Hans him said that Penmoch not was -not- a pig ordinary, and

qu'il ne voulait s'en défaire pour rien au monde.
that he not wanted himself of it undo for nothing at the world
get rid of in the

Et se tournant vers Penmoch.
And himself turning towards Penmoch

— Montre au monsieur comment tu es un petit cochon bien élevé.
— Show to the gentleman how you are a little pig well raised

Et Penmoch se mit debout, et fit une révérence au fermier.
And Penmoch himself put upright, and made a reverence to the farmer

— Danse-lui maintenant une valse.
— Dance him now a waltz

Et Penmoch de tourner, d'une façon gauche qui ne le rendait
And Penmoch of to turn of a way left which not him rendered
in a clumsy

que plus comique.
(other) than more comical

Le fermier rit de bon cœur, et en considération des talents de
The farmer laughed of good heart and in consideration of the talents of

Penmoch ne voulut rien accepter pour sa nourriture.
Penmoch not wanted nothing to accept for his food

Hans demanda s'ils étaient loin de quelque ville ou village.
Hans asked if they were far from some city or village

Il lui fut répondu que, en suivant la route, le village le plus proche
It him was answered that in following the road the village the most close
next

était bien encore à quelques heures de marche, et qu'ils n'y
was well still at some hours of march and that they not there

arriveraient guère avant la nuit. Mais par contre, on lui fit espérer
would arrive hardly before the night But by against one him made hope
on the other side

qu'ils pourraient y récolter quelque argent. Les habitants, pour la
that they would be able there to harvest some silver The inhabitants for the
to pick up

plupart, étaient de gros fermiers qui employaient les habitants plus
largest part were -of- big farmers who employed the inhabitants most

misérables des villages environnants. Leur éloignement des grands
wretched of the villages surrounding Their remoteness from the great

centres rendant assez rares les distractions, ils accueillaient assez
centers rendering enough rare the distractions they welcomed enough
making quite rather

généreusement les chanteurs, bateleurs et acteurs ambulants de toute
generously the singers jugglers and actors traveling of all

sorte qui passaient chez eux.
kind which passed by them

Hans et Mab demandèrent encore au fermier s'il n'avait pas vu
Hans and Mab asked still at the farmer if he did not have -not- seen

passer un garçon habillé de telle et telle façon, et ils lui détaillèrent
pass a boy dressed of such and such way and they him detailed

ce qui pouvait faire reconnaître leur camarade Nono ; — mais le
this which could make recognize their comrade Nono ; — but the

fermier ne se souvenait pas d'avoir vu passer personne qui se
farmer not himself remembered -not- of to have seen pass anyone who himself

rapprochât de ce signalement. Et Hans, Mab et Penmoch se
approached of this physical description And Hans Mab and Penmoch themselves
came close

remirent en route, fort anxieux de savoir comment ils retrouveraient
set again on (the) road very anxious of to know how they would find back

les traces de leur infortuné camarade. Peut-être en auraient-ils des
the traces of their unfortunate comrade Maybe of him would they have -of the-

nouvelles dans le bourg où ils se rendaient ?
news in the borough where they themselves rendered ?
moved towards

Mais leur espérance devait être trompée, ce n'était pas la route que
But their hope had to be mistaken this not was -not- the road that

Nono avait suivie, et ils devaient encore faire pas mal de chemin,
Nono had followed and they must still make not bad of way
little

avant d'attraper la bonne piste.
before of to catch the good trail
right

Ce ne fut, en effet, que très peu avant la tombée de la nuit
It not was in fact (other) than very little before the fall of the night

qu'ils atteignirent le bourg en question. Arrivés sur une grande place
that they reached the borough in question Arrived on a large square

où les habitants, en plus grand nombre, semblaient se promener
where the inhabitants in more large number appeared themselves to walk

de préférence, ils se mirent sous un hêtre énorme qui
of preference they themselves put under a beech huge which

ombrageait la place, accordèrent leurs instruments, — lorsqu'elle ne
shaded the place tuned up their instruments — when she not

dansait pas, Mab avait une guitare, — et ils préludèrent aux premières
danced -not- Mab had a guitar — and they preluded to the first

mesures de l'hymne des Argyrocratiens.
measures of the anthem of the Argyrocratiens

Cet hymne qui avait le don d'exalter les Argyrocratiens jusqu'à la
This anthem who had the gift of to exalt the Argyrocratiens up to the

démence, vantait les vertus d'Argyrocratie, chantait les louanges
dementia boasted the virtues of Argyrocratie sung the praises
senility

d'Argyrocratie, exaltait la force et le courage des Argyrocratiens,
of Argyrocratie exalted the force and the courage of the Argyrocratiens

insultant et menaçant de mort non seulement les ennemis d'Argyrocratie,
insulting and threatening of death not only the enemies of Argyrocratie

mais aussi tous les voisins d'Argyrocratie.
But also all the neighbors of Argyrocratie

Les promeneurs n'en eurent pas plutôt entendu les premières notes
The walkers not of it had -not- rather heard the first notes

qu'ils vinrent aussitôt faire le cercle autour des chanteurs,
(than) that they came immediately to make the circle around of the singers

demandant avec des cris féroces que ceux-ci le recommençassent encore,
asking with of the cries ferocious that these it began again

et en accompagnant les musiciens de leurs voix les plus discordantes.
and in accompanying the musicians with their voices the most discordant

Et lorsque Mab fit la quête, elle récolta une ample moisson de gros
And when Mab made the quest she reaped an ample harvest of fat
went round for money

sous. Alors, pour continuer leur rôle, Mab fit la toilette de Penmoch ;
nickels Then for to continue their role Mab made the dress of Penmoch ;

puis, prenant son tambourin, elle dansa avec lui, pendant que Hans jouait
then taking her tambourine she danced with him during that Hans played

de la clarinette.
of the clarinet

Penmoch eut encore plus de succès que l'hymne, lorsqu'il fit la quête
Penmoch had still more of success that the anthem when he made the quest
went round for money

lui-même.
him self

Tout en jouant et en dansant, Hans et Mab regardaient si, parmi la
All in playing and in dancing Hans and Mab watched if among the

foule, ils n'apercevaient pas les traits de leur ami ; mais rien que
crowd they not perceived -not- the traits of their friend ; but nothing than

des visages indifférents. Dans le dernier morceau qu'ils jouèrent, ils
of the faces indifferent In the last piece that they played they

intercalèrent un des chants d'Autonomie, le plus susceptible d'attirer
inserted one of the chants of Autonomy the most apt of to attract

l'attention de leur ami. Mais le concert fini, emballèrent lentement
the attention of their friend But the concert finished packed up slowly

leurs instruments, sans que rien leur décelât que leur appel eût été
their instruments without that nothing them revealed that their call had been

entendu.
heard

Cependant un des habitants, qu'à sa mine cossue on pouvait
However one of the inhabitants that at his looks plush one could
of who by

reconnaître pour un des riches propriétaires de l'endroit, vint les
recognize for one of the rich owners of the place came them

trouver et leur promit une pièce d'or s'ils voulaient venir chez lui.
to find and them promised a piece of gold if they wanted to come with him

Il régalait ce soir là des amis, et il voulait réserver pour ses
He regaled this evening there of the friends and he wanted to book for his
some

invités cette distraction surgie inopinément.
guests this distraction emerged unexpectedly

Les artistes acceptèrent, quoiqu'ils eussent préféré courir le village. Mais
The artists accepted though they had prefered to run the village But

refuser de gagner une pièce d'or aurait pu faire naître des
to refuse of to win a piece of gold would have been able to make be born -of the-

soupçons. Il fallait qu'ils accomplissent leur métier en conscience.
suspicions It was necessary that they accomplished their trade in consciousness
acted out serious

Ils suivirent donc le propriétaire qui leur promit en route un bon
They followed then the owner who them promised on (the) road a good

souper, pour ne pas les lâcher, de peur qu'un concurrent ne vînt
supper for not -not- them to release of fear that a competitor not came

les lui enlever en leur offrant davantage.
them (of) him to take away in them offering more

Arrivés chez lui, notre homme les fit conduire à la cuisine et servir
Arrived with him our man them made to lead to the kitchen and serve

à manger. Une grande terrine de son et de pommes de terre fut mise
to eat A large terrine of bran and of apples of earth was put
                                                    potatoes

dans un coin pour Penmoch, car Hans et Mab, ne voulurent pas
in a corner for Penmoch because Hans and Mab not wanted -not-

que leur ami fût mené à l'écurie.
that their friend was led to the stable

Puis les invités du propriétaire étant arrivés, un domestique mena les
Then the guests of the owner being arrived a servant led the
                                    having

artistes dans une grande salle au milieu de laquelle se dressait une
artists in a large room at the middle of which itself drew up a

table couverte de cristaux et d'argenterie, attendant les convives.
table covered with crystals and of silverware awaiting the guests

Le domestique les installa sur une estrade, abritée par un rideau. Ils
The servant them settled on a dais sheltered by a curtain They

devaient, pendant le repas, jouer leurs airs variés pour l'amusement du
must during the meal play their tunes varied for the amusement of the

propriétaire et de ses invités.
owner and of his guests

Ils ne tardèrent pas à les voir entrer. La femme du propriétaire
They not delayed -not- to them see enter The woman of the owner

ouvrait la marche, donnant le bras à un des invités, que les enfants,
opened the march giving the arm to one of the guests that the children

au cours de la soirée, entendirent nommer M. le Bailli. Les autres
at the course of the evening heard call Mr. the Bailiff The others

invités venaient ensuite processionnellement deux à deux ; le
guests came subsequently in procession two to two ; the

propriétaire fermant la marche. Et chacun se plaça à l'endroit que
owner closing the march And each himself placed at the place that

lui indiquait la maîtresse du lieu.
him indicated the mistress of the place

Ces gens avaient en même temps l'air si grotesque et se
These people had in (the) same time the air so grotesque and themselves

prenaient si au sérieux, que nos deux artistes, cachés par le rideau,
taking so -at the- serious that our two artists hidden by the curtain

ne se gênaient nullement de pouffer à les regarder. Penmoch
not themselves bothered by no means of to snigger at them to look at Penmoch
while looking at them

lui-même agitait son tire-bouchon, poussant quelques petits grognements,
him self moved his corkscrew pushing some small grunts
curly tail uttering

couverts par la musique heureusement.
covered by the music fortunately

Que c'était loin de la liberté et de la bonne camaraderie
That it was far from the freedom and from the good camaraderie
How

d'Autonomie ! comme on sentait que la franchise en était absente !
of Autonomy ! like one felt that the liberty of it was absent !

On servit à manger. Nos deux Autonomiens n'en revenaient pas
One served to eat Our two (kids from) Autonomy not of it came back -not-
were very surprised

de la quantité de nourriture qu'ils virent absorber sous des formes
of the quantity of food that they saw absorb under of the forms

diverses, sans compter la multitude de domestiques qui étaient employés
various without to count the multitude of servants who were employed

à les servir.
to them serve

Et leur conversation ! Après un tas de banalités, ils parlèrent de leurs
And their conversation ! After a heap of small talk they spoke of their

amis, de leurs voisins. Et comme ils en parlaient ! oh ! ils ne
friends of their neighbors And how they of them spoke ! Oh ! they not

disaient pas de méchancetés, mais c'étaient des sourires, des phrases
said -not- of wickednesses but there were of the smiles of the sentences

coupées, des sous-entendus. Les deux artistes pensèrent qu'ils n'avaient
cut of the under-heards The two artists thought that they not had
implied meanings

devant eux que la crème du bourg ; les autres devaient être
in front of them (other) than the crème of the borough ; the others must be

de bien drôles de gens.
-of- well funny -of- people

Lorsque le repas, qui dura fort longtemps, fut terminé, les convives
When the meal which lasted very long time was finished the guests
long
long

passèrent dans un grand salon, et nos deux artistes y furent conduits
passed in a large salon and our two artists there were led

pour y montrer les talents de Penmoch.
for there to show the talents of Penmoch

Comme ils écoutaient de toutes leurs oreilles, dans l'espoir d'entendre
As they listened to of all their ears in the hope of to hear

quelque chose qui les mît sur les traces de leur ami, ils furent
some thing who them would put on the traces of their friend they were

bientôt édifiés sur la politesse dont les Argyrocratiens s'étaient
soon edified on the politeness of which the Argyrocratiens themselves were
had

tant vantés à table.
so much boasted at table

D'autres personnages étaient arrivés. Dans quelques-uns, dont on
-of- others characters were arrived In some of which one
had

prononça les noms, Hans et Mab reconnurent plusieurs de ceux dont
pronounced the names Hans and Mab recognized several of those of which

on avait parlé à table. Ceux qui avaient eu le plus de sourires ou
one had spoken at (the) table Those who had had the most of smiles or

de sous-entendus à leur égard, n'étaient pas les moins empressés envers
of under-heards to their respect not were -not- the least rushed towards
implied meanings

eux, ni les derniers à leur débiter les plus grandes flatteries.
them nor the last to them reel off the most great flatteries
                                              greatest

Mab et Penmoch dansèrent leurs plus jolis pas. Penmoch fit des
Mab and Penmoch danced their most pretty steps Penmoch made of the

mines et des révérences. Puis la maîtresse du lieu, qui se
gestures and of the bows Then the mistress of the place who herself

rappelait les ânes et les chiens savants, demanda à Hans si Penmoch
reminded the donkeys and the dogs scientists asked to Hans if Penmoch

serait capable de désigner la personne la plus aimable de la société,
would be capable of to designate the person the most pleasant of the society
                    to choose

espérant secrètement que, par déférence, ce serait elle.
hoping secretly that by deference this would be her
       stealthily

— M. Penmoch, fit Hans, vous entendez la haute opinion que l'on
— Mr Penmoch made Hans you hear the high opinion that -it- one
             said

a de vous. Montrez que vous en êtes digne, et indiquez-nous
has of you Show that you of it are worthy and indicate us

au plus vite la personne la plus aimable de cette société.
at the most quick the person the most pleasant of this society
as soon as possible

Le cochon se dressa sur les deux pattes, fit le tour du salon
The pig himself raised on the two paws made the turn of the salon

en reniflant chaque personne, puis revint en faisant : rrouan !... rrouan...
in snuffling each person Then returned in making : rrouan !... rrouan

— Eh bien ! M. Penmoch, ne m'avez-vous pas compris ? fit Hans.
— Eh well ! Mr Penmoch not me have you -not- understood ? made Hans

Penmoch secoue la tête de haut en bas, en signe d'affirmative.
Penmoch shakes the head of high in low in sign of affirmative

— Eh bien ! alors, pourquoi ne me désignez-vous pas les personnes
— Eh well ! then why not me you designate -not- the people

aimables qui sont dans la société ?
friendly who are in the society ?

Le cochon secoua la tête en signe de dénégation.
The pig shook the head in sign of denial

— Vous ne voulez plus travailler ? fit Hans qui avait bien compris
— You not want more work ? made Hans who had well understood

que Penmoch n'avait pas trouvé de personne aimable, mais préféra
that Penmoch did not have -not- found of/any person pleasant but preferred

ne pas traduire la réponse.
not -not- to translate the response

Les invités firent semblant de s'extasier devant la gentillesse de l'artiste
The guests made seeming of rhapsodize in front of the kindness of the artist

à quatre pattes, mais ils riaient jaune ; la maîtresse de la maison
at four paws but they laughed yellow/forcedly ; the mistress of the house

surtout. Et les trois artistes prirent congé au milieu d'un froid.
especially And the three artists took leave at the/in the middle of a cold (atmosphere)

Lorsqu'ils furent sur la route pour se rendre à l'auberge qu'on
When they were on the road for themselves to render to the inn that one

leur avait indiquée, Hans s'adressant à son cochon, lui dit :
them had indicated Hans himself addressing to his pig him said :

— Heureusement, M. Penmoch, que notre amie Solidaria nous a garni
— Fortunately Mr Penmoch that our friend Solidaria us has furnished

notre bourse avant de partir ; autrement votre intransigeance risquerait
our wallet before of to leave ; otherwise your intransigence risked

fort de nous faire mourir de faim.
strong of us to make to die of hunger

Penmoch fit : rrouan, rrouan, et se mit à danser un cavalier seul
Penmoch made : rrouan rrouan and himself put to dance a knight alone

au milieu de la route, comme satisfait d'avoir dit leur fait aux
at the middle of the road like satisfied of to have said their fact to the

Argyrocratiens.
Argyrocratiens

Recherches infructueuses
Fruitless research

Réveillée de bonne heure le lendemain matin, les artistes descendirent
Woken up of good hour the following day morning the artists descended
early the morning of the following day

sous prétexte de prendre l'air, et de faire le tour du village ;
under pretext of to take the air, and of to make the turn of the village ;

mais en réalité pour interroger les domestiques et servantes de l'auberge,
but in reality for to question the domestics and servants of the inn

ayant imaginé de dire qu'un camarade de leur troupe les avait perdus,
having imagined of to say that a comrade of their band them had lost

ce qui leur permettait de questionner et de donner son
this which them allowed of to question and of to give his

signalement, en s'informant si on l'avait vu.
physical description in themselves informing if one him had seen
inquiring

Mais le village était placé sur une route peu fréquentée, et
But the village was placed on a road little frequented, and

quoi qu'il fût plus facile, à cause de leur rareté, de remarquer les
what that it was more easy, at cause of their scarcity, of to notice the
even though that it be-

voyageurs qui le traversaient, personne ne put leur donner aucun
travelers who it crossed, no one -not- could them give any

renseignement.
piece of information

S'étant fait servir à déjeuner, ainsi qu'à Penmoch, ils firent leurs
Themselves being made serve at lunch as well as to Penmoch they made their
Having

préparatifs de départ, sans que personne essayât de les retenir.
preparations of departure, without that anyone tried of them to retain

L'intérêt qu'ils avaient excité était passé. Chacun regrettait de ne pas
The Interest that they had excited was passed. Each regretted of not -not-
had

avoir eu l'idée du gros richard, mais ne se souciait plus de
to have had the idea of the big rich person but not himself cared (any)more of

les entendre après lui.
them to hear after him

Munis de leurs instruments, Penmoch trottinant à côté d'eux, ils
Provided with their instruments Penmoch trotting at (the) side of them they

se remirent en route.
themselves set again in road

Au premier village, ils n'eurent aucun succès, ne récoltèrent pas un
At the first village they had not any success not reaped -not- a

liard ; ce qui, du reste, les préoccupait peu ; mais non plus
farthing ; this which of the rest them concerned little ; but not more
                         for the   either

aucun indice qui les mît sur les traces de celui qu'ils cherchaient.
any sign which them put on the traces of the one that they were looking for

Au suivant, les gamins du village les poursuivirent à coups de
At the following the kids of the village them pursued at blows of
                                                                   with

pierres, parce qu'ils leur arrachèrent des mains une malheureuse
stones because that they them tore from the hands an unhappy

hirondelle blessée, qu'ils voulaient plumer toute vive. Vu le nombre
swallow wounded that they wanted to pluck all live Seen the number

des gamins, ils auraient été fort maltraités, et la fuite ne leur
of the kids they would have been very mistreated and the flight not them

aurait pas été facile, si Solidaria, qui les protégeait de loin,
would have -not- been easy if Solidaria who them protected from (a) far

n'eut fait passer, dans leurs jambes, toute la force de la communauté,
was not made pass in their legs all the force of the community

ce qui leur donna une vélocité telle que, en moins de rien, ils
this which them gave a velocity such that in less of nothing they

étaient à une si grande distance qu'ils n'entendirent plus les
were at a so great distance that they not heard (any)more the

hurlements des petits Argyrocratiens. Ils se retournèrent : les
howls of the small Argyrocratians They themselves turned : the

méchants gamins ne leur apparaissaient plus sur la route que comme
naughty kids not them appeared (any)more on the road than like
seemed

un amas de fourmis.
a mass of ants

Hans et Mab, étonnés, se doutèrent bien que c'était leur amie
Hans and Mab astonished themselves doubted well that it was their friend
suspected

Solidaria qui était venue à leur secours. En leur cœur, ils lui
Solidaria who was come to their aide In their heart they her
had

adressèrent un chaleureux remerciement. Penmoch, à côté d'eux, agitait
addressed a warm thanks Penmoch at (the) side of them moved
wagged

joyeusement sa queue qui se contournait de gauche à droite, et
joyfully his tail which itself turned from left to right and

de droite à gauche. En son groin, il tenait un large morceau d'étoffe
from right to left In his snout he kept a wide piece of cloth

arraché au fond de culotte d'un des petits bandits.
ripped at the back of underwear from one of the small bandits

Un ruisseau faisait entendre ses glouglous joyeux, en un pré au bord
A stream made hear its gurgles happy in a meadow at the side

de la route ; ils s'y dirigèrent. Il s'agissait de panser la
of the road ; they themselves there headed It itself dealt of bandage the
concerned

malheureuse bestiole qu'ils avaient arrachée à la cruauté des petits
unhappy small animal that they had torn away to the cruelty of the small
from

Argyrocratiens et que Hans tenait haletante dans sa main.
Argyrocratians and that Hans kept breathing heavily in his hand

— Pauvre petite chose ! fit Mab, en lavant les plaies de la bête.
— Poor little thing ! made Mab in washing the wounds of the animal
said

Puis, tirant de leur bissac une petite boîte d'un onguent merveilleux
Then pulling from their satchel a little box with an ointment wonderful

que leur avait remise Solidaria, ils en oignirent les plaies de la
that them had handed over Solidaria they of it anointed the wounds of the
smeared

blessée.
wounded

L'hirondelle guérie comme par enchantement, s'échappa des mains de
The swallow healed like by enchantment itself escaped from the hands of

Mab, faisant entendre un gazouillis joyeux, restant à voltiger autour de
Mab, making hear a chirps happy remaining to flutter around of

ses sauveurs qui, sollicités par l'appétit et le charme de l'endroit,
its saviors who solicited by the appetite and the charm of the place
attracted

s'étaient mis à déjeuner, ayant eu la précaution de faire garnir
themselves were put to lunch having had the precaution of to make fill up
had

leur bissac avant de quitter le bourg où ils avaient passé la nuit.
their satchel before of to leave the borough where they had passed the night

Et, lorsqu'ils se remirent en route, l'hirondelle les suivit.
And when they themselves set again on (the) road the swallow them followed

Et ils marchèrent ainsi de compagnie, l'hirondelle ayant fini par
And they marched thus of company the swallow having finished by
as

faire connaissance avec Penmoch, qu'elle taquinait parfois.
to make acquaintance with Penmoch that she teased sometimes

Ils marchèrent ainsi, des jours, sans rien découvrir de leur ami.
They marched thus -of the- days without nothing to discover of their friend

Un matin qu'ils déjeunaient près d'une source, ils virent venir sur la
One morning that they lunched near of a source they saw come on the

route deux archers à cheval, conduisant, enchaîné, un jeune gamin de
road two archers at horse leading chained a young kid of

leur âge.
their age

Les deux soldats, ayant aperçu la source, y dirigèrent leurs chevaux
The two soldiers having perceived the source there headed their horses

pour les y faire boire, après avoir permis au petit garçon de
for them there to make drink after to have permitted to the little boy of

s'y désaltérer.
himself there to quench (the thirst)

Puis ayant aperçu nos trois voyageurs, l'un d'eux, d'un ton bourru,
Then having perceived our three travelers, the one of them of a tone surly

leur demanda qui ils étaient ? ce qu'ils faisaient ? où ils allaient
them asked who they were ? this what they did ? where they went

? où ils avaient volé le cochon qu'il traînaient avec eux ?
? where they had stolen the pig that it dragged with them ?

Mais Solidaria avait avisé à cela. Hans sortit de sa poche un papier
But Solidaria had conceived for that Hans got out of his pocket a paper

qui leur donnait, au nom de Monnaïus, le droit de circuler sur
which them gave, at the / in the name of Monnaïus, the right of to go around on

les routes ; puis il fit remarquer à l'archer que le cochon était son
the roads ; then he made notice to the archer that the pig was his

ami, qu'il ne l'avait pas volé.
friend, that he not him had -not- stolen

— N'est-ce pas, mon vieux Penmoch ? fit-il en le caressant ; fais
— Not is this -not- my old Penmoch ? made he / said he in him caressing ; make

voir à M. l'archer que nous sommes deux bons camarades.
to see to Mr the archer that we are two good comrades.

Penmoch se serra contre les jambes de Hans, et fit entendre un
Penmoch himself pressed against the legs of Hans, and made hear a

rrouan !... rrouan furieux à l'adresse de l'archer, lui montrant les dents
rrouan !... rrouan furious to the address of the archer, him showing the teeth

d'une façon terrible.
of a / in a way terrible.

Cela fit rire les deux archers qui devinrent plus sociables.
That made laugh the two archers who became more sociable.

Mab en profita pour demander au petit garçon ce qu'il avait
Mab of it took advantage for to ask to the little boy this that he had

fait pour qu'on le conduisit ainsi enchaîné comme un criminel ?
done for that they him led thus chained like a criminal ?

Tout en pleurant, le malheureux leur raconta que ses parent étant morts,
All in weeping, the unhappy (one) them told that his parents being dead,

personne n'avait voulu le recueillir. Alors, il avait couru de village
no one did not have wanted him to collect Then he had run from village
to take care of

en village, travaillant quand on voulait l'employer, vivant d'aumônes, un
in village working when one wanted to employ him living of alms a

peu de maraude, couchant à la belle étoile, lorsqu'on refusait ses
bit of marauding laying down to the beautiful star when one refused his

services. Les archers venaient de l'arrêter parce qu'il n'avait
services The archers came of him to arrest because that he did not have

pu justifier d'aucun gîte.
been able to justify any home

Ils l'emmenaient au prévôt de la prochaine ville qui, probablement,
They him took to the provost of the next city who probably

l'enverrait en prison.
would send him in prison

Émus de pitié, Hans et Mab demandèrent la permission de donner à
Moved by pity Hans and Mab asked the permission of to give to

ce pauvre garçon le reste de leurs provisions. Les deux archers
this poor boy the rest of their supplies The two archers

grommelèrent bien un peu, mais ils accordèrent la permission demandée,
grumbled well a bit but they granted the permission asked

et repartirent emmenant leur prisonnier. Penmoch, allant derrière eux en
and departed leading their prisoner Penmoch going behind them in

tapinois, mordit la jambe du cheval de l'un d'eux, évitant la ruade
stealthily bit the leg of the horse of the one of them avoiding the kick

de l'animal, qui manqua jeter le cavalier sur la route.
of the animal which failed to throw the knight on the road
almost threw

Celui-ci s'étant retourné pour voir ce qui arrivait à son cheval,
That one himself being returned for to see this which arrived to his horse
himself having happened

vois Penmoch, à dix pas en arrière, broutait tranquillement une touffe de
sees Penmoch at ten steps in back grazing quietly a tuft of

gazon.
lawn
grass

Un autre jour, ce fut un pauvre vieux qu'ils virent ainsi emmener.
An other day it was a poor old (man) that they saw thus to take along being taken

Il leur raconta qu'il avait travaillé tant qu'il avait pu, mais il
He them told that he had worked as much as he had been able but he

gagnait peu et les chômages et les maladies, du reste, lui
earned little and the unemployment periods and the diseases of the rest him

permettaient à peine de vivre et d'élever sa famille ; il avait vieilli,
permitted at pain of to live and of to raise his family ; he had aged
barely to sustain

vivant au jour le jour.
living to the day the day
day by day

Maintenant, il était trop faible pour travailler ; sa femme était morte
Now he was too weak for to work ; his woman was dead

d'épuisement, sa fille était disparue un beau jour, son fils enrôlé de
of exhaustion his daughter was missing one beautiful day his son enlisted by

force comme soldat de Monnaïus. Il était sans ressources, on
force as soldier of Monnaïus He was without resources one

l'emmenait en prison.
took him in prison

Hans et Mab, navrés de ne pouvoir rien faire pour déliver le
Hans and Mab sorry of not to be able nothing to do for to free the

malheureux, ce qui ne lui aurait pas été d'un grand secours
unfortunate one this which not him would have -not- been of a large help

du reste, lui remirent en pleurant quelques pièces de monnaie, fort
of the rest him handed while weeping some pieces of money very
for the

peu pour ne pas éveiller la défiance des archers, et c'est en
little for not -not- to wake up the distrust of the archers and it is in

devisant sur le mauvais sort des pauvres gens, et la cruauté des
chatting about the bad fate of the poor people and the cruelty of the

Argyrocratiens, qu'ils continuèrent leur route.
Argyrocratians that they continued their road

Mais au milieu de ces incidents, toujours aucune nouvelle de leur ami.
But at the middle of these incidents always not any new(s) of their friend

Un soir, à l'orée d'un bois qu'ils venaient de traverser, leur
One evening at the edge of a woods that they came of to cross their

attention fut attirée par la vue d'un jeune homme qui, couché sur le
attention was attracted by the sight of a young man who laid down on the

sol, semblait épuisé, hors d'état de marcher.
ground seemed exhausted out of state of to walk
uncapable

Ils s'approchèrent de lui. Hans tira de son bissac une fiole. Il
They themselves approached of him Hans drew from his satchel a flask He

fit boire quelques gouttes de la liqueur qu'elle contenait à l'inconnu
made drink some drops of the liqueur that she contained to the unknown
that it

que cela ranima et qui put leur raconter que, traqué par les
that that reanimated and who could them tell that hunted by the

archers, il se cachait dans ce bois ; depuis deux jours n'ayant
archers he himself hid in this woods ; since two days not having

pu trouver à manger, il avait voulu essayer de gagner le prochain
been able to find to eat he had wanted to try of to reach the next

village, mais il venait de tomber là à bout de forces.
village but he came of to fall there at (the) end of (his) forces

Aussitôt nos voyageurs lui vidèrent leur bissac sur les genoux, et,
Immediately our travelers (for) him emptied their satchel on the knees and

tout en se restaurant, il leur raconta que l'on avait voulu le
all of it himself restoring he them told that it one had wanted him

faire soldat de Monnaïus, qu'il n'avait pas voulu se laisser
to make soldier of Monnaïus that he did not have -not- wanted himself to let

enrôler, et qu'il avait quitté son village, cherchant du travail sur sa
enroll and that he had left his village searching -of-the- work on his
enlist

route. Il y avait trois jours, il était arrivé en ce pays, exténué de
road It there had three days he was arrived in this country weakened of
It had been had

fatigue, personne n'ayant voulu l'employer, il était entré en une
exhaustion no one -not- having wanted to employ him he was entered in a
had

villa dont le propriétaire était à table devant un succulent dîner.
villa of which the owner was at (the) table in front of a succulent dinner

Il lui avait demandé un morceau de pain, mais l'autre lui avait
He him had asked a piece of bread But the other (one) him had

répondu que c'était honteux à son âge de demander l'aumône, qu'il
answered that it was shameful at his age of to ask the alms that he

ferait mieux de chercher du travail, et avait appelé sa bonne pour
would do better of to seek of the work and had called his goodwife for servant girl

lui fermer la porte au nez.
him to close the door at the nose

Rendu furieux par l'injustice de ce mauvais riche, il l'avait battu,
Rendered furious by the injustice of this bad rich he him had beaten

emportant ce qu'il avait pu ramasser de victuailles sur la table,
carrying this that he had been able to pick up from (the) victuals on the table the food

et était venu se cacher dans ce bois, dont il n'avait plus
and was come himself hide in this woods of which he did not have more had

osé sortir, ayant vu les archers qui étaient à sa recherche.
dared to go out having seen the archers who were at his search

Hans lui remit une poignée de monnaie pour lui permettre de
Hans him handed over a fist of money for him to allow of

gagner un endroit où il ne serait pas connu. Puis, comme partout
to reach a place where he not would be -not- known Then like everywhere

où il passait, il lui demanda s'il n'aurait pas rencontré Nono
where he passed he him asked if he would not -not- (have) encountered Nono

dont il lui donna le signalement. Mais l'autre n'avait rencontré
of which he him gave the physical description But the other not had encountered

personne qui lui ressemblât.
anyone who him resembled

Et nos quatre voyageurs (ils étaient quatre maintenant que l'hirondelle
And our four travelers they were four now as the swallow

les suivait), se remirent en marche tristement.
them followed themselves set again in march sadly

Un jour encore, comme ils s'approchaient d'un village, près d'un
One day still as they themselves approached of a village near of an

enclos ils virent un rassemblement qui s'était formé.
enclosure they saw a rally which itself was formed
itself had

Ils s'approchèrent, curieux de voir quelle en était la cause, et
They themselves approached curious of to see what of it was the cause and

au pied d'un arbre ils virent étendu, le corps d'un enfant d'une
at the foot of a tree they saw stretched out the body of a child of a

douzaine d'années. La figure blanche comme de la cire, les yeux grands
dozen of years The figure white like of the wax the eyes large
wide

ouverts, mais sans regard, une blessure sanguinolente sur le côté de
open but without look a wound bloodstained on the side of

la tête tout indiquait qu'il était mort et quelle était la cause du
the head all stated that he was dead and which was the cause of the

trépas.
death

Un archer interrogeait un gros paysan dont la mine vermeille annonçait
An archer questioned a fat peasant of which the looks vermilion indicated
reddish

la florissante santé, ainsi qu'une certaine aisance. Le rustre expliquait
the flourishing health as well as a certain ease The rustic explained

que, furieux de voir piller son poirier dont les plus beaux fruits
that furious of to see loot his pear tree of which the most beautiful fruits

disparaissaient au fur et à mesure qu'ils mûrissaient, il s'était
disappeared at the forum and to measure that they ripened he himself was
himself had

embusqué pour surprendre les voleurs. Il avait vu le jeune garçon
ambushed for to surprise the thieves He had seen the young boy

l'escalader ; mais lorsqu'il avait voulu courir après, le garçon s'était
it climb ; but when he had wanted to run after the boy himself was
himself had

sauvé ; alors il l'avait atteint d'une grosse pierre qui l'avait jeté à
saved ; then he him had reached with a big stone which him had thrown to

terre.
earth

Il	terminait	son	récit	lorsqu'une	femme	échevelée,	toute	en	larmes,	fendit
He	ended	his	story	when a	woman	disheveled	all	in	tears	split

la	foule	et	vint	tomber	à	genoux	devant	le	petit	cadavre	qu'elle
the	crowd	and	came	to fall	at (the)	knees	in front of	the	little	corpse	that she

embrassait éperdument.
kissed madly

Fou	de	douleur,	le	père	la	suivait	et	lorsqu'il	vit	le	meurtrier	de
Insane	of	pain	the	father	her	followed	and	when he	saw	the	murderer	of

son	enfant,	il	voulut	se	précipiter	dessus	et	le	frapper	;	mais
his	child	he	wanted	himself	to rush at	on top	and	him	to hit	;	but

d'autres	archers	qui	étaient	venus	joindre	le	premier	se	saisirent
of other other	archers	who	were had	come	to join	the	first	themselves	seized

de	lui,	lui	disant	de	se	tenir	tranquille,	s'il	ne	voulait	pas
of	him	him	saying	of	himself	to keep	quiet	if he	not	wanted	-not-

aggraver	son	cas	;	que	le	paysan	était	dans	son	droit,	en	défendant
to aggravate	his	case	;	that	the	peasant	was	in	his	right	in	defending

sa	propriété,	et	ils	l'emmenèrent	chez	le	prévôt,	lui	disant	qu'il
his	property	and	they	him took along	with	the	provost	him	saying	that he

aurait	à	répondre	des	dégâts	causés	par	son	fils	dans	le	verger.
would have	to	answer	of the	damages	caused	by	his	son	in	the	orchard

Pénétrés	d'horreur,	Hans,	Mab	et	Penmoch	traversèrent	le	village	sans
Penetrated	by horror	Hans	Mab	and	Penmoch	crossed	the	village	without

s'y	arrêter.	L'hirondelle	elle-même	fit	un	long	détour	pour
themselves there	stop	The swallow	she herself	made	a	long	detour	for

éviter	d'y	passer.
to avoid	by there	to pass

Premières traces
First traces

Cependant	le	voyage	durait	depuis	quelque	temps,	et	nos	amis	se
However	the	journey	lasted	since already	some	time	and	our	friends	themselves

désolaient	de	n'avoir	rien	pu	découvrir,	faisant	les	plus	tristes
desolated	of	not to have	nothing anything	been able	to discover	made	the	most	sad saddest

conjectures	sur	la	sort	de	leur	ami.	Ils	se	dirigeaient	vers	la
conjectures	on	the	fate	of	their	friend	They	themselves	headed	towards	the

capitale,	partout	on	leur	disait	que	c'était	là	que	se	rendaient
capital	everywhere	one	them	said	that	it was	there	that	themselves	rendered went

les	étrangers.
the	foreigners

Enfin	un	jour	ils	arrivèrent	au	village	où	Nono	avait	fait	ses
Finally	one	day	they	arrived	at the	village	where	Nono	had	made	his

débuts	de	musicien.
beginnings	of	musician as a musician

Lorsque,	selon	leur	habitude,	ils	eurent	donné	leur	concert,	en	y
When	according to	their	habit	they	had	given	their	concert	in	there

mêlant	des	airs	d'Autonomie,	la	bonne	femme	qui	avait	été
mixing	-of- the	tunes	of Autonomy	the	good	woman	who	had	been

secourable	à	Nono,	et	qui	reconnut	un	des	airs	de	l'accordéon
helpful	to	Nono	and	who	recognized	one	of the	tunes	of	the accordion

merveilleux	s'informa	auprès	de	Hans	si,	lui	aussi,	ne	venait	pas
wonderful	herself inquired	close with	of	Hans	if	he	also	not	came	-not-

d'Autonomie	?
from Autonomy	?

Hans,	qui	ignorait	dans	quel	but	lui	était	faite	cette	question,
Hans	who	did not know	in	what	goal intention	him	was	made	this	question

l'interrogea sur ce qui pouvait lui avoir fait penser cela ?
her questioned on this which could her have made think that ?

La femme leur expliqua qu'il y avait quelque temps déjà, un
The woman them explained that it there had some time already (that) a
that it had been

enfant de leur âge était passé, jouant des airs comme eux
child of their age was passed playing -of-the- tunes like they
had

venaient d'en jouer, airs que l'on n'entendait nulle part ailleurs.
came of them to play tunes that -it- one not heard no side elsewhere
just played no where else

Et au signalement qu'elle leur donna du jeune garçon, Mab et
And at the physical description that she them gave of the young boy Mab and

Hans reconnurent leur ami. Leur cœur battit d'allégresse, ils avaient
Hans recognized their friend Their heart beat of joy they had

donc enfin un fil conducteur. Et la femme ayant ajouté qu'elle avait
then finally a thread conductor And the woman having added that she had
to lead them

encouragé le jeune voyageur à se rendre à Monnaïa, ils se
encouraged the young traveller to himself render to Monnaia they themselves

remirent en route immédiatement.
set again in road immediately

Dans les villages, sur la route, la musique de leur ami avait laissé
In the villages on the road the music of their friend had left

quelques souvenirs ; ils purent ainsi suivre ses traces sans trop
some memories ; they could thus follow his traces without too (much)

de difficultés.
-of- difficulties

Un après-midi, vers le soir, ils arrivèrent à la ferme où Nono,
An afternoon towards the evening they arrived at the farm where Nono

moyennant sa musique, avait trouvé l'hospitalité. Pour rester dans leur
through his music had found the hospitality For to stay in their

rôle, nos artistes proposèrent leur musique et les gentillesses de Penmoch
role our artists proposed their music and the nicenesses of Penmoch

en échange d'un morceau de pain, et d'une place dans le foin.
in exchange of a piece of bread and of a place in the hay
for a for a

Mais le fermier, occupé à réparer un poulailler dans sa cour, et fort
But the farmer occupied to repair a chicken coop in his court and very

peu sensible tous les jours, surtout en voyant trois écuelles de soupe à
bit sensitive all the days especially in seeing three bowls of soup to

donner, exigea d'être payé, espérant bien avoir la musique par-dessus
give demanded of to be paid hoping well to have the music on top of

le marché.
the deal

Hans sortit quelque menue monnaie de sa bourse et la donna au
Hans got out some small money from his wallet and it gave to the
change

fermier qui s'en contenta, et les fit entrer dans la salle
farmer who himself with it satisfied and them made enter in the room

commune, où ils s'installèrent dans un coin avec Penmoch.
common where they themselves installed in a corner with Penmoch

La grosse servante s'occupait de préparer la soupe, le vieux
The big servant girl herself occupied of to prepare the soup the old

grand-père était toujours sous le manteau de la cheminée, le fils et
grandfather was always under the mantel of the fireplace the son and
still
by

sa famille au dehors s'occupaient de divers travaux, un des
his family at the outside themselves occupied with diverse works one of the

valets de la ferme était en train de réparer le manche d'une bêche.
servants of the farm was in process of to repair the handle of a spade
farmhands

Le valet et la servante causaient, sans s'occuper des
The servant and the servant girl chatted without themselves to occupy of the
farmhand

musiciens, ni de l'aïeul que l'âge rendait sourd. Le valet se
musicians nor of the grandfather that the age rendered deaf The servant himself
farmhand

plaignait de la dureté des maîtres qui l'accablaient de travaux et
complained of the severity of the masters who him overwhelmed with works and

refusaient de lui accorder une légère augmentation.
refused of him to grant a slight increase

— Dame, faut être juste aussi, disait la servante, le maître a
— Lady, (it) is necessary to be fair also, said the servant girl the master has

des frais. Pense donc qu'il te donne déjà trente écus par an.
-of the- costs Think then that he you gives already thirty ecus per year
{silver coins}

À ce prix-là, les valets de ferme ne lui manqueront pas.
At this price there the servants of farm not him lack -not-
farmhands

Il en passe tous les jours qui ne demanderaient pas mieux que de
It of them pass all the days who not ask -not- better than of
There of them come by more

se louer, même pour moins.
themselves to rent even for less
to hire

— Oui, mais lui feraient-ils la besogne que je lui fais ?
— Yes but (for) him would they do the job that I (for) him do ?

— Oh ! pour ce qui est de ça, tu ne dors pas sur la besogne,
— Oh ! for this which is of that you (do) not sleep -not- on the job
for that matter

et tu n'es pas embarrassé à n'importe quels travaux de la ferme.
and you not are -not- embarrassed to not matters what works of the farm
always will do

C'est bien pour cela que le maître tient à toi. — Mais deux écus
It is well for that that the master holds to you — But two ecus
cares about you {silver coins}

de plus, c'est une somme, sais-tu ?
-of- more it is a sum you know ?

— Deux écus, qu'est-ce que c'est pour lui ! Mais il est avare. Il
— Two ecu's hat is it that it is for him ! But he is (a) miser He
{silver coins} that's nothing

préfère entasser ses pièces d'or, sans compter le champ qu'il vient
prefers to pile up his pieces of gold without to count the field that he comes

de prendre à ce pauvre diable de Jean Bidou qui n'a pas pu
of to take to this poor devil of Jean Bidou who not has -not- been able
from

lui rembourser les pistoles qu'il lui avait prêtées, et qui en vaut
him to refund the pistoles that he him had loaned and which of it is worth
{coins}

le double. Et le pré qui jouxte sa roseraie,
the double And the meadow which adjoins his rosary

est-ce qu'il n'y a pas de mon travail dans la valeur qu'il a
is it that he not there has -not- of my work in the worth that it has
isn't there

acquise ?
acquired ?

— Oui, te voilà revenu aux billevesées qui te trottent par la
— Yes you see there come back to the nonsense which you trot through the

tête depuis que cet « innocent » qui prétendait venir d'un pays
head since that this innocent who claimed to come from a country
innocent kid

au nom si baroque, que l'on ne connaît seulement pas, est passé par
at the name so baroque that it one not knows only -not- is passed by

ici.
here

Hans et Mab dressèrent l'oreille. Penmoch fit entendre un léger
Hans and Mab pricked up the ear Penmoch made hear a light

grognement.
grunt

— Innocent ! innocent ! reprit le valet, pas si innocent que cela, il
— Innocent ! innocent ! continued the servant -not- so innocent than that it

m'est avis. Il y avait du vrai dans ce qu'il nous a dit. Je
(to) me is (the) opinion It there had of the true in this that he us has said I
There was truth

n'ai reçu aucune instruction, vois-tu, je ne sais pas lire, — Hans
not have received any instruction see you I not know -not- to read — Hans

et Mab se regardèrent, semblant se demander, comment il
and Mab each other looked at seeming themselves to ask how it

était possible qu'un homme ne sût pas lire — Mais j'ai ma
was possible that a man not knew -not- to read — But I have my

jugeotte qui me dit qui si le maître n'avait pas de pauvres
savvy which me says which if the master did not have -not- -of- poor
that

diables comme toi et moi pour faire son travail, s'il était seul, avec
devils like you and me for to make his work if he was alone with

sa famille, il ne pourrait pas cultiver toute la terre qu'il a. Tout
his family he not could -not- cultivate all the earth that he has All

l'argent que cette terre en plus lui rapporte est donc du travail de
the money that this earth in more him brings back is then from the work of

toi, moi, Pierre, Claude, et de tous ceux qu'il embauche quand il
you me Pierre Claude and of all those that he hires when he

en a besoin. Et voilà !
of them has need And see there !

— Heu ! heu ! mon pauvre ami, le maître te l'a expliqué pourtant ;
— Hey ! hey ! my poor friend the master you it has explained however ;

si on partageait les terres entre tout le monde, il y en a qui
if one shared the lands between all the world it there of it has who
everybody there would be those

ne voudraient rien faire et vendraient leur part, et ça reviendrait
not would like nothing to do and would sell their part and it would return to

comme ça est maintenant. Tu vois donc bien que t'as tort d'avoir
how it is now You see then well that you have wrong of to have
you are

des idées semblables, puisque c'est pas possible.
-of- the ideas similar since it is not possible

— Oui, tout ça, ça va bien, ce sont les maîtres qui disent cela.
— Yes all that that goes well these are the masters who say that

Mais je trime bien, et dur encore, pour le nôtre, pourquoi que je ne
But I work well and hard still for the ours why that I not

travaillerais pas aussi bien pour moi ? Non, vois-tu, la Jeanne,
would work -not- as well for myself ? No see you -the- Jeanne

il y a quelque chose là qui me dit que tout n'est pas comme
it there has some thing there which me says that all not is -not- like
there is

ça devrait être.
it should be

Et je regrette beaucoup de ne pas avoir demandé au p'tiot où
And I regret a lot of not -not- to have asked to the little dude where

se trouvait ce joli pays dont il nous a parlé. Je crois qu'il
itself found this pretty country of which he us has spoken I believe that it

existe, moi ; et je voudrais y aller.
exists me ; and I would like there to go

En ce moment, malgré sa prudence, Hans intervint dans la
In this moment, in spite of his prudence, Hans intervened in the

conversation, affirmant l'existence d'Autonomie, et demandant de plus
conversation, affirming the existence of Autonomy, and asking -of- more

amples renseignements sur le voyageur en question que lui et sa
ample information on the traveller in question that he and his
plentiful

compagne connaissaient et qu'ils avaient hâte de retrouver.
companion knew and that they had haste of to find back
were in a hurry

La servante et le valet ne purent donner que fort peu
The servant girl and the servant not could to give (other) than very few
farmhand

d'indications. Tout ce qu'ils savaient, c'est que le jeune voyageur avait
-of- indications All this that they knew it is that the young traveller had

parlé qu'il se rendait à la ville, et qu'il en avait pris la
spoken that he himself rendered to the city and that he of it had taken the

route.
road

Puis le valet questionna Hans sur le pays d'Autonomie, où il se
Then the servant questioned Hans on the country of Autonomy where it itself
farmhand

trouvait ?
found ?

Mais les deux Autonomiens ne pouvaient, sans se trahir, indiquer
But the two Autonomians not could without themselves betray indicate
(from) Autonomy

leur route, — qui s'était refermée derrière eux, du reste — ils ne
their road — which itself was closed again behind them of the rest — they not
had for the

purent que donner des indications fort vagues, des renseignements fort
could than give of the indications very vague of the information very

peu précis.
bit precise

Et ces renseignements incomplets laissèrent le valet toujours aussi
And these pieces of information incomplete left the valet always as

perplexe.
perplexed

La servante apercevant venir le fermier, engagea les enfants à ne pas
The servant girl seeing come the farmer committed the children to not -not-told

parler du pays d'Autonomie. Elle avait remarqué que, lorsqu'on parlait
speak of the country of Autonomy She had noticed that when one spoke

de ce pays et de ses mœurs, cela mettait le fermier de fort
of this country and of its mores that put the farmer of in (a) very

mauvaise humeur.
bad mood

Celui-ci entra en grommelant que le travail n'avançait pas. Et il alla
That one entered in grumbling that the work not advanced -not- And he went

fumer sa pipe près du feu.
to smoke his pipe near -of- the fire

Peu à peu, les habitants de la ferme arrivèrent l'un après l'autre.
Bit by bit the inhabitants of the farm arrived the one after the other

Puis la belle-fille, qui était en course dans le village, arriva avec ses
Then the daughter in law who was in run in the village arrived with her

deux enfants qui eurent bientôt fait connaissance avec Penmoch.
two children who had soon made acquaintance with Penmoch

On se mit à table. Les deux Autonomiens, pour leur argent, eurent
One oneself put at (the) table The two Autonomians for their silver had

une écuellée de soupe, avec une tartine de pain.
a bowlful of soup with a buttered slice of bread

Puis, le repas fini, et quand tout fut rangé, nos deux artistes firent
Then the meal finished and when all was tidied our two artists made

quelque musique pour plaire aux deux enfants. Mab dansa avec
some music for to please -to- the two children Mab danced with

Penmoch, et l'heure d'aller se coucher étant venue, on mena les
Penmoch and the time of to go oneself lay down being come one led the

trois artistes dans la grange où ils se blottirent dans la paille,
three artists in the barn where they themselves snuggled in the straw

heureux	de	voir	qu'ils	ne	perdaient	pas	les	traces	de	celui	qui	était
happy	of	to see	that they	not	lost	-not-	the	traces	of	the one	who	was

l'objet	de	leur	sollicitude.
the subject	of	their	solicitude concern

Tristes nouvelles
Sad news

Avant de prendre congé de la famille du fermier, sachant qu'ils
Before of to take leave of the family of the farmer knowing that they

auraient encore une longue route à faire avant d'arriver à la ville,
would have still a long road to make before of to arrive at the city

Hans se fit garnir son bissac de victuailles qu'il paya, et les
Hans himself made fill up his satchel with victuals that he paid and the
food stuffs

trois artistes, avec l'hirondelle qui les attendait à la porte de la
three artists with the swallow who them awaited at the door of the

ferme, reprirent leur route.
farm resumed their road

Ils marchaient d'un pas allègre, espérant, cette fois, ne pas tarder à
They moved with a step joyful hoping this time not -not- to delay to

retrouver leur camarade.
find back their comrade

Cependant, après un bout de chemin, mis en appétit par la marche, ils
However after an end of way put in appetite by the march they

s'arrêtèrent près d'une source pour déjeuner. Et, tout en déjeunant, ils
themselves halted near of a source for to lunch And all in lunching they
stopped spring while

causaient de leurs espérances, lorsque, tout d'un coup, d'un trou qu'ils
chatted of their hopes when all of a strike from a hole that they
sudden

n'avaient pas aperçu sortit une petite bête noire, au poil soyeux, qui
not had -not- perceived got out a little animal black at the fur silky who
with

tout en clignant des yeux leur dit :
all in winking of the eyes them said :

— Celui dont vous parlez m'a sauvé la vie. Je crois que je puis
— The one of which you talk me has saved the life I believe that I can

vous être utile dans vos recherches, si mon infirmité m'empêche de voir
you be useful in your researches if my infirmity prevents me of to see

clair en plein jour, en revanche, je vois très bien dans l'obscurité.
clear in full day in revenge I see very well in the darkness
                    on the contrary

Emmenez-moi. Promettez-moi seulement de ne pas me laisser dans la
Take me Promise me only of not -not- me to leave in the

ville.
city

Hans et Mab émerveillés, mais nullement étonnés — il leur était
Hans and Mab marveling but by no means astonished — -it- them was
                                                                had

déjà arrivé tant d'aventures — se consultèrent pendant que
already arrived so many -of- adventures — each other consulted during that
happened

Penmoch flairait cette petite bête dont la tête se terminait en une
Penmoch sniffed this little animal of which the head itself ended in a

espèce de groin comme le sien.
kind of snout like -the- his

— C'est une alliée qui nous est suscitée par Solidaria, affirma Mab.
— This is an ally which us is aroused by Solidaria affirmed Mab

Emmenons-la, nous nous en trouverons bien. Et, Hans faisant à la
Let's take her we ourselves of her will find good And Hans making for the

taupe une place dans son bissac, ils reprirent tous ensemble le chemin
mole a place in his satchel they resumed all together the road

de Monnaïa qu'ils atteignirent le lendemain matin.
of Monnaïa that they reached the following day morning
to   following morning

Selon une vieille coutume qui voulait que tout musicien, tout
According to an old custom which wanted that all musician all

bateleur qui entrait dans la ville, jouât un morceau de son répertoire,
tumbler who entered in the city played a piece of their repertoire
acrobat

fît danser ses bêtes savantes, Hans dut jouer aux fouines et tigres
made dance their animals trained Hans had to play to the martens and tigers

de la porte par laquelle ils entrèrent l'hymne de Monnaïa, pendant
of the gate by which they entered the anthem of Monnaïa during

que Mab et Penmoch dansèrent et firent la révérence, aux grands
that Mab and Penmoch danced and made the reverence at the great

éclats de rire de toute la garnison qui était accourue.
bursts of laughter of all the garrison who was run up
had

Mais ce n'était pas le tout d'avoir atteint la capitale ; nos jeunes
But this not was -not- -the- all of to have reached the capital ; our young

amis n'étaient pas au bout de leurs peines. Lorsqu'arriva la fin de
friends not were -not- at the end of their pains When arrived the end of

la journée, ayant parcouru un nombre incalculable de rues, ils durent
the day having traveled a number incalculable of streets they had to

s'avouer qu'il ne leur serait pas facile de retrouver les
themselves confess that it not (to) them would be -not- easy of to find back the

traces de leur ami.
traces of their friend

Toutefois, ils se félicitaient d'avoir choisi le déguisement qu'ils
However they themselves congratulated of to have chosen the disguise that they

portaient ; cela leur permettait d'aller partout, de pénétrer dans les
wore ; that them allowed of to go everywhere of to enter in the

établissements publics, jusque dans les cours des maisons, et de voir
institutions public until in the courtyards of the houses and of to see

la foule s'amasser autour d'eux.
the crowd itself gather around of them

Le soir venu, ils louèrent une mansarde dans un quartier perdu,
The evening come they rented an attic in a quarter lost
neighborhood

dans une maison où logeaient nombre de musiciens ambulants, de
in a house where lived (a) number of musicians traveling -of-

chanteurs des rues, faiseurs de tours et bateleurs de toute sorte.
singers of the streets makers of turns and acrobats of all kind(s)
acrobats

Dans leurs courses ils eurent l'occasion de constater quelle misère
In their walks they had the opportunity of to note what misery

effroyable régnait dans la capitale d'Argyrocratie ; mais dans la maison
appalling reigned in the capital of Argyrocratia ; but in the house

qu'ils habitaient, à côté d'une misère sans nom, ils purent
that they dwelt in at (the) side of a misery without name they could

constater des faits de cruauté qui leur serrèrent le cœur encore plus.
note of the facts of cruelty which them shook the heart still more

De malheureux enfants comme eux, plus jeunes même, étaient sous la
-Of- unhappy children like them more young even were under the

dépendance d'un maître qui en avait ainsi plusieurs sous son
addiction of a master who of them had like that several under his

exploitation. Ils étaient tenus de lui apporter chaque soir une certaine
exploitation They were kept by him to bring each evening a certain
forced

somme qu'il leur fixait ; en échange de quoi il leur mesurait
sum that he them fixed ; in exchange of what he them measured

parcimonieusement une pitance insuffisante.
parsimoniously a pittance inadequate
scarcely

Lorsqu'ils avaient le malheur de rentrer avec la somme incomplète,
When they had the misfortune of to come back with the sum incomplete

il les maltraitait, les battait, les faisait coucher sans souper.
he them mistreated them beat them made lay down without supper
sleep

Des femmes louaient des enfants en bas âge, jusqu'à deux, trois,
-Of the- women hired -of the- children in low age up to two three

dont un au maillot, et elles couraient ainsi la ville, quelque temps
of which one at the shirt and they ran thus the city some time

qu'il fît, pour implorer la pitié des passants ; pinçant sournoisement
that he made for to implore the pity of the passersby ; pinching slyly
said

les enfants, afin d'apitoyer davantage par leurs cris.
the children so of to pity more by their cries

Hans et Mab, dans leur chambrette, ne se parlaient de ces
Hans and Mab in their small bedroom not themselves spoke of these

horreurs qu'en frissonnant, et, comparant cette vie avec celle
horrors (other) than while shivering and comparing this life with the one

qu'ils menaient à Autonomie, ils ne pouvaient concevoir comment les
that they led at/in Autonomy (land) they not could conceive how the

Argyrocratiens pouvaient être assez stupides pour vivre dans un état
Argyrocratians could be enough stupid for to live in a state

pareil.
similar

Leurs conversations étaient interrompues parfois par leur amie l'hirondelle
Their conversations were interrupted sometimes by their friend the swallow

qui, s'étant logée sur le toit, auprès de leur mansarde, venait frapper
who itself being lodged on the roof close of their attic came to knock

au carreau, leur apportant les nouvelles qu'elle avait pu recueillir,
at the tile/window pane them bringing the news that she had been able to gather

leur demandant celles qu'ils avaient pu récolter.
them asking those that they had been able to harvest/to collect

La taupe, assise sur la table, écoutait gravement.
The mole seated on the table listened seriously

Un soir, tout émue, l'hirondelle vint leur dire qu'en passant dans un
One evening all moved the swallow came them say that while passing in a

quartier populeux son attention avait été attirée par un enfant qui
quarter populous his attention had been attracted by a child who

tenait un accordéon qui jouait, seul, les airs qu'elle leur avait entendu
kept an accordion which played alone the tunes that she them had heard

souvent jouer.
often play

Nos deux amis se rappelèrent l'accordéon dont Riri avait fait
Our two friends themselves recalled the accordion of which Riri had made

présent à Nono. Au signalement donné par l'hirondelle, ils ne
present to Nono. At the physical description given by the swallow they not

reconnurent pas leur camarade. Peut-être leur ami avait-il passé par
recognized -not- their comrade Maybe their friend had he passed by

là ? Ce ne pouvait être que son jouet.
there ? This not could be (other) than his toy

Ils se firent expliquer la situation de la rue, embrassèrent
They themselves made explain the situation of the street kissed

l'hirondelle pour sa bonne nouvelle, se promettant d'aller le
the swallow for his good new(s) themselves promising of to go the

lendemain visiter le quartier que leur avait désigné la gentille
following day visit the quarter that them had designated the kind

messagère.
messenger

En débutant, ils avaient bien pensé, afin de doubler leurs chances, à
In beginning they had well thought so of to double their chances to
the beginning

parcourir la ville chacun de son côté. Mais Mab s'était effrayée de
roam the city each by their side But Mab himself was scared of
himself had

courir seule les rues d'un si vilain pays et avait demandé à Hans de
to run alone the streets of a so ugly country and had asked to Hans of

ne pas la quitter. Comme celui-ci, de son côté, lorsqu'il avait la
not -not- her to leave Like that one from his side when he had the

présence de Mab, se sentait plus d'assurance, ils avaient résolu de
presence of Mab himself felt more of assurance they had decided of
assured

ne pas se quitter un seul instant.
not -not- each other to leave a sole moment

Le lendemain, ils partirent donc pour commencer leur enquête, guidés
The following day they left then for to begin their investigation guided

par l'hirondelle.
by the swallow

Mais ce jour-là, soit que l'enfant à la musique ne fût pas sorti,
But this day there be it that the child at the music not was -not- gone out
with

soit qu'il ne fût pas dehors aux instants où ils passèrent et
be it that he not was -not- outside at the moments where they passed and

repassèrent, ils rentrèrent le soir, harassés, sans avoir rien
passed again they returned the evening weary without to have nothing

pu découvrir.
been able to discover

Ce n'est que le cinquième jour, toujours guidés par l'hirondelle,
It not is (other) than the fifth day always guided by the swallow

qu'ils finirent par trouver sur le pas de la porte de notre ancienne
that they finished by to find on the step of the door of our ancient

connaissance le tailleur, l'enfant au milieu de cinq ou six galopins de
acquaintance the tailor the child at the middle of five or six urchins of

son âge, les régalant de musique.
his age them regaling with music

Ne sachant comment interroger le tailleur, Hans imagina de découdre son
Not knowing how to question the tailor Hans imagined of to unpick his

habit et d'entrer pour le faire raccommoder. Et pendant que le
dress and of to enter for it to make mend And during that the

tailleur s'escrimait, Hans amena la conversation sur le merveilleux
tailor himself applied Hans led the conversation on to the wonderful

accordéon, disant qu'il connaissait le pays où on en fabriquait
accordion saying that he knew the country where one of them constructed

de semblables.
-of- similar (ones)

Le tailleur dit qu'il lui avait été laissé, par un de ses ouvriers, mais
The tailor said that it him had been left by one of his workmen but

sembla vouloir détourner la conversation, chaque fois que Mab et Hans
seemed to want to divert the conversation each time that Mab and Hans

l'interrogeaient soit sur la boîte, soit sur son propriétaire.
him interrogated be it on the box be it on its owner

Un individu qui était dans la boutique du tailleur, et n'avait rien
An individual who was in the shop of the tailor and not had nothing

dit, se leva et sortit en souhaitant le bonsoir.
said himself raised and got out in wishing the good evening

Quelle que fût leur insistance, Hans et Mab ne purent rien tirer
What that was their insistence Hans and Mab not could nothing pull
Whatever

du tailleur et s'en allèrent, se promettent d'y
from the tailor and themselves of there went themselves promising of there

retourner.
to go back

Mais ils avaient à peine tourné la rue que celui qu'ils avaient
But they had at pain turned the street that the one that they had
barely

trouvé dans la boutique du tailleur les rejoignit, et les aborda en
found in the shop of the tailor them joined again and them accosted in

ces termes :
these terms :

— Je vois que vous êtes des amis du jeune Nono auquel
— I see that you are -of- the friends of the young Nono to which

appartenait la musique que vous avez reconnue entre les mains de
belonged the music that you have recognized between the hands of

l'enfant du tailleur. Mais vous perdez votre temps à questionner celui-ci,
the child of the tailor. But you lose your time to question that one

il a trop peur des exempts de Monnaïus, et, dans votre intérêt,
he has too (much) fear of the policemen of Monnaïus and in your interest

vous ferez bien de ne pas y retourner.
you will do well of not -not- there to go back

L'individu était un des trois amis de Nono. Il raconta à Hans et
The individual was one of the three friends of Nono He told to Hans and

Mab consternés l'arrestation de leur ami, sa condamnation, comment le
Mab dismayed the arrest of their friend his conviction how the

tailleur avait déposé contre lui, et tout ce qui s'en était suivi.
tailor had deposited against him and all this which itself of it was followed
witnessed

Lui-même, pendant quelque temps, avait été surveillé comme suspect.
Him-same during some time had been watched as suspect
He himself

Les enfants lui demandèrent si, depuis, il avait eu des nouvelles de
The children him asked if since he had had -of the- news of

Nono, s'il savait où ce dernier était enfermé.
Nono if he knew where this last (one) was locked up

L'homme, par chance, avait un cousin qui était geôlier, et que, malgré
The man by fortune had a cousin who was gaoler and that in spite of

sa répugnance à cause de ses fonctions, il allait voir de temps à
his repugnance at cause of his functions he went to see from time to

autre. Justement, après sa condamnation, Nono avait été transféré dans
other Exactly after his conviction Nono had been transferred in
time

un des cachots que contenait le palais royal de Monnaïus et où
one of the dungeons that contained the palace royal of Monnaïus and where

son cousin était de service. Il pouvait ainsi en avoir des nouvelles
his cousin was of service He could thus of it have -of the- news

de temps en temps. Son cousin même avait bien voulu, une fois, lui
from time in time His cousin even had well wanted one time him

remettre une lettre du prisonnier qui se portait bien, et prenait
hand over a letter of the prisoner who himself carried well and took
carried

son mal en patience.
his bad in patience
misfortune

Puis, leur ayant promis de retourner voir son cousin pour tâcher
Then them having promised of to go back to see his cousin for try

d'avoir quelques nouvelles, il les quitta ayant pris rendez-vous avec
of to have some news he them left having taken appointment with

eux à quelques jours de là, mais en leur recommandant la plus
them at some days from there but in them recommending the most

grande circonspection, et la discrétion la plus absolue.
large care and the discretion the most absolute

Aussitôt rentrés, Hans, Mab, l'Hirondelle, Penmoch et la Taupe
Immediately (having) come back Hans Mab the Swallow Penmoch and the Mole

tinrent conseil. Ils avaient le cœur bien gros de savoir
held counsel They had the heart well big of to know
were very emotional to know that

leur ami prisonnier, mais ils savaient où il était, avaient quelque
their friend prisoner But they knew where he was had some
their friend was a prisoner

espérance de lui faire parvenir de leurs nouvelles.
hope of him to make reach with their news
succeed

Il n'y avait rien dont ils ne fussent capables pour le sauver.
It not there had nothing of which they not were capable for him to save
There was nothing would be incapable

Hans s'était arrêté à ce moyen : c'était de profiter de l'avarice
Hans himself was stopped at this means : it was of to profit from the greed
had thought solution

qui animait chaque Argyrocratien, d'aller trouver le cousin de leur
which animated each Argyrocratian, of to go find the cousin of their

nouvel ami, de lui donner assez d'or — leur bourse était inépuisable
new friend, of him to give enough of gold — their wallet was inexhaustible

— pour le décider à laisser s'enfuir son prisonnier.
— for hi to decide to let himself flee his prisoner

Mab convint que le moyen n'était pas à dédaigner, mais, pourrait-on
Mab agreed that the means not was -not- to disdain but could they
solution should be considered

se lier au geôlier ? Ne les trahirait-il pas après leur avoir
themselves bind to the gaoler ? Not them would he betray -not- after them to have

arraché tout ce qu'il aurait pu ? La mauvaise foi des
ripped all this that he would have been able to ? The bad faith of the

Argyrocratiens étant tout au moins aussi grande que leur avarice. Même,
Argyrocratians being all at the least as large as their avarice. Even

lui était-il possible de faire évader un prisonnier ? Ils avaient été
him was it possible of to make escape a prisoner ? They had been

à même de voir combien les Argyrocratiens se méfiaient les uns
to even of to see how much the Argyrocratians each other mistrusted the ones
capable

des autres, ayant toujours trois espions pour en surveiller un quatrième.
of the others, having always three spies for of it to monitor a fourth

En risquant leur liberté ils risquaient aussi celle de leur ami. Il leur
In risking their freedom they risked also that of their friend It them
might risk

fallait agir avec prudence, et selon les circonstances.
was necessary to act with prudence, and according to the circumstances

L'important pour le moment était de nouer des relations avec le
The important (part) for the moment was of to tie -of the- relations with the
to connect

309

prisonnier. On verrait ensuite.
prisoner One would see subsequently

L'Hirondelle se proposa comme messagère.
The Swallow himself proposed as messenger

La Taupe se fit forte de creuser jusqu'à lui. Personne ne douta
The Mole himself made strong of to dig up to him Person not doubted

plus du succès.
(any)more of the success

La visite à la prison
The visit to the prison

Le	jour	du	rendez-vous	arrivé,	les	deux	artistes,	laissant	Penmoch	et
The	day	of the	appointment	arrived	the	two	artists	leaving	Penmoch	and

la	Taupe	à	la	maison,	se	rendirent	à	l'endroit	où	ils	devaient
the	Mole	at	the	house	themselves	rendered	to	the place	where	they	must

trouver	le	cousin	du	geôlier.
find	the	cousin	of the	gaoler.

Celui-ci	les	attendait,	tout	joyeux.	Il	avait	parlé	à	son	cousin	de	deux
That one	them	awaited	all	happy	He	had	spoken	to	his	cousin	of	two

étrangers	dont	il	avait	fait	connaissance	et	qui	désiraient	visiter	une
foreigners	of which	he	had	made	acquaintance	and	who	wanted	to visit	a

prison.	Il	était	permis	aux	geôliers,	lorsqu'ils	étaient	de	service,	de
prison.	It	was	permitted	to the	jailers	when they	were	of	service	of

recevoir	leur	famille,	car	alors	ils	ne	pouvaient	pas	sortir	de	tout
to receive	their	family	because	then otherwise	they	not	could	-not-	go out	of	all all

un	mois.
a	month

Moyennant	deux	pièces	d'or,	son	cousin	acceptait	de	les	faire	passer
By means of	two	pieces	of gold	his	cousin	accepted	of	them	to make	pass

pour	des	neveu	et	nièce,	et	de	les	promener	dans	la	partie	de
for	-cf- the	nephew	and	niece	and	of	them	to walk	in	the	part	of

la	prison	où	il	leur	était	permis	de	circuler.	Le	lendemain,
the	prison	where	it	them	was	permitted	of	to go around	The	following day

dimanche,	était	justement	un	bon	jour.
Sunday	was	exactly	a	good	day

L'Insoumis,	c'était	le	nom	de	leur	nouvel	ami,	viendrait	les	prendre
The Rebellious	it was	the	name	of	their	new	friend	would come	them	take

chez eux.
with them

Et comme c'était convenu, le lendemain, à l'heure fixée il vint les
And as it was agreed the following day to the time fixed he came the

chercher.
to seek

Comme de juste, pour aller dans la prison, on n'entrait pas par la
Like of just for to go in the prison one not entered -not- through the
    Naturally

porte d'honneur du palais, mais par la poterne d'une des tours.
door of honor of the palace But by the postern of one of the towers
                               back door

Arrivés à cette poterne, une sentinelle leur demanda où ils allaient.
Arrived at this postern a sentinel them asked where they went
           back door

Sur leur réponse qu'ils voulaient voir le porte-clefs, Tourment, la
On their response that they wanted to see the carry-keys Torment the
                                prison guard

sentinelle appela un soldat qui les conduisit près de celui qu'ils
sentinel called a soldier who them led near of the one that they

demandaient.
asked (for)

Celui-ci les embrassa comme s'il était réellement l'oncle qu'il
That one them embraced like if he was actually the uncle that he

prétendait, serra la main de son cousin, lui demandant des nouvelles
claimed tightened the hand of his cousin him asking of the news

de leurs parents et amis, puis les fit asseoir en leur offrant de
of their parents and friends Then them made sit in them offering of

se rafraîchir. Justement son service venait de finir, il avait trois
themselves to refresh Exactly his service came of to end he had three
              Right then

heures de libres devant lui.
hours of free (time) in front of him

Ce geôlier, malgré le métier répugnant qu'il faisait, était plutôt un
This gaoler in spite of the trade repugnant that he made was rather an

ignorant qu'un méchant homme. Sa double physionomie tenait plutôt du
ignorant that a mean man His double aspect kept rather of the

chien de garde que de la bête féroce.
dog of guard than of the animal fierce

À vingt ans, il avait été enrôlé parmi les soldats de Monnaïus. Là,
At twenty years he had been enlisted among the soldiers of Monnaïus There

il avait pris l'habitude d'obéir et de vivre sans s'inquiéter de
he had taken the habit of to obey and of to live without himself to worry of
to obey

rien. Chez ses parents il avait vu combien était difficile la vie de
nothing With his parents he had seen how much was difficult the life of

l'ouvrier, excédé de travail à certains moments, sans cesse hanté
the worker exceeded with work at certain moments without stop haunted
overwhelmed

par la crainte du chômage et de la misère. Aussi, son temps
by the fear of the unemployment and of the misery Also his time

fini, il avait sollicité cette place que sa bonne conduite lui avait
finished he had applied for this spot that his good behaviour him had
sought

fait avoir tout de suite.
made to have all of following
immediately

Et c'était sans se rendre compte de la triste idée qu'il donnait
And it was without himself to render account of the sad idea that it gave

de son caractère qu'il racontait cela ; avec fierté, même.
of his character that he told that ; with pride even

Mab lui demanda si ça ne le rendait pas triste de voir les
Mab him asked if that not him rendered -not- sad of to see the

prisonniers. Il devait y avoir, en la prison, des désespoirs terribles,
captives It must there to have in the prison of the hopes terrible

des crises de larmes et de sanglots !
of the crises of tears and of sobs !

Le geôlier haussa les épaules. Ceux qui se faisaient mettre en
The gaoler shrugged the shoulders Those who themselves made put in

prison n'étaient pas bien intéressants. Ils n'avaient qu'à faire comme
prison were not -not- well interesting They not had than to to make like

tout le monde, à obéir et à travailler. Les maîtres ne pouvaient
all the world to obey and to work The masters not could

ordonner que des choses justes. Et lui obéissait à ses maîtres.
order (other) than of the things righteous And he obeyed to his masters

D'un air indifférent, Hans lui demanda s'il n'y avait pas s'il n'y avait pas
With an air indifferent Hans him asked if it not there had not
if there wasn't

en ce moment, dans les cachots du palais, quelque prisonnier
in this moment in the dungeons of the palace some prisoner

intéressant, et si on pouvait le voir ?
interesting and if one could him see ?

Et le geôlier, qui était bavard, leur détailla la vie des prisonniers.
And the gaoler who was chatterbox them detailed the life of the captives

Justement Nono était dans son service, et il n'eut garde de l'oublier
Precisely Nono was in his service and he was not guard of him to forget
was careful not to forget him

dans son récit, son affaire ayant fait, à son moment, assez de bruit.
in his story his business having made at its moment enough of noise

Il promit à ses visiteurs de le leur faire voir par un petit judas
He promised to his visitors of him them to make see by a little judas
watch hole

percé dans la porte de chaque cachot.
perforated in the door of each dungeon

Puis, se levant, il prit un trousseau de clefs et les engagea à le
Then himself raising he took a bundle of keys and them engaged to him
told

suivre, s'ils voulaient visiter avec lui la prison.
follow if they wanted to visit with him the prison

Il les conduisit d'abord dans quelques cachots inoccupés, puis en
He them led of first in some dungeons unoccupied then in
initially

différentes salles plus sombres les unes que les autres, jusqu'à ce qu'ils
different rooms more dark the ones than the others up to this that they
darker

arrivèrent dans une qui était garnie d'armoires.
arrived in one which was furnished of cabinets

— C'est là-dedans, fit-il en désignant les armoires, que l'on enferme
— It is there inside made he in designating the cabinets that it one shut
said he

les instruments de torture.
the instruments of torture.

— Comment, de torture ? fit l'Insoumis, mais elle est abolie.
— How of torture ? made the Rebellious but she is abolished
it

Une centaine d'années auparavant, en effet, les Argyrocratiens avaient fait
A hundred of years before in fact the Argyrocratians had made

une révolution où l'on avait aboli la torture.
a revolution where -it- one had abolished the torture.

Mais le geôlier leur expliqua que l'ingéniosité des conseillers au
But the gaoler them explained that the ingenuity of the advisors at the

Parlement n'avait pas tardé à inventer des instruments nouveaux qui
Parliament not had -not- delayed to invent of the instruments new which

faisaient souffrir autant le prisonnier, avec l'avantage de ne pas laisser
made suffer as much the prisoner, with the advantage of not -not- to let

trace de blessure.
trace of (a) wound

Ouvrant une armoire, il leur fit d'abord voir "la prévention" qui
Opening a cupboard he them made first see the preventive measure which

enlevait le prévenu de sa famille, de son milieu et qui,
took away the information from his family, from his environment and which

compliquée de la mise au secret, le faisait passer par toutes les
complicated by the put at the secret, him made pass through all the
secrecy

phases de l'angoisse et de l'inquiétude.
phases of the anxiety and of the worry

Il y avait ensuite "l'instruction secrète", "les fausses dépositions", et
It there had subsequently the instruction secret the false depositions and
the decision

infinité d'autres instruments qui garnissaient les armoires. On parlait
(an) infinity of other instruments which decorated the cabinets One spoke
filled

d'empêcher les juges de se servir de l'instruction secrète, mais
of to prevent the judges of themselves to serve of the instruction secret but
the decision

ceux-ci n'avaient que l'embarras du choix pour terrasser le
these not had than the embarrassment of -the- choice for ground the
a mass take down

prisonnier le plus robuste, et il ouvrait les armoires
prisoner the most robust, and he opened the cabinets

les unes après les autres, leur montrant une infinité de petits
the ones after the others, them showing an infinity of small
one after the other

instruments, acérés et aigus comme des serres d'oiseaux de proie.
instruments, sharp and pointy as -of- the claws of birds of prey

Hans demanda comment les prisonniers passaient leur temps.
Hans asked how the captives passed their time

Ils étaient forcés de travailler pour le compte d'entrepreneurs qui, en
They were forced of to work for the account of entrepreneurs who, in

faisant des cadeaux aux administrateurs, aux directeurs, achètent le
making -of the- gifts to the administrators, to the directors, bought the

droit exclusif de faire travailler les prisonniers, au prix qui leur
right exclusive of to make work the captives, at the price which them

convient, bien au-dessous de ce qu'ils seraient forcés de payer à un
convened well at the under of this that they would be forced of to pay to a
below

ouvrier libre. Ce qui leur permettait de réaliser de grands bénéfices
worker free. This which them allowed -of- to realize -of- great earnings

et de vivre en grands seigneurs.
and -of- to live as great lords

Hans demanda comment il se faisait que Monnaïus tolérât ces
Hans asked how it himself made that Monnaïus tolerated these
it could be

injustices.
injustices

Mais le geôlier leur expliqua qu'il n'y avait rien de répréhensible
But the gaoler them explained that it not there had nothing -of- objectionable
that there was

dans	cela.	C'était	aux	prisonniers	à	ne	pas	se	mettre	hors
in	that	It was	to the	captives	to	not	-not-	themselves	put	outside

des	honnêtes	gens.	Ils	étaient	en	prison	pour	leur	punition.
of the	honest	people	They	were	in	prison	for	their	punishment

Hans	et	Mab	pensèrent	que	ceux	qui	se	chargeaient	de	mettre	les
Hans	and	Mab	thought	that	those	who	themselves	charged	of	to put	the

autres	en	prison	devaient	valoir	beaucoup	moins	qu'eux.	Mais	ils
others	in	prison	must	be worth	much	less	than they	But	they

se	contentèrent	d'échanger	leurs	réflexions	en	un	regard.
themselves	contented	of to exchange	their	reflections thoughts	in	a	glance

Le	geôlier	continuait	:
The	gaoler	continued	:

—	Sur	ce	que	gagne	le	prisonnier,	l'administration	s'empare	de	la
—	On	this	that	earns	the	prisoner	the administration	itself empowers grabs	of	the

moitié	si	c'est	la	première	fois	qu'il	est	condamné,	des	trois	et
half	if	it is	the	first	time	that he	is	condemned	of the	three	and

quatre	cinquièmes	dans	les	autres	cas.
four	fifths	in	the	others	cases

Sur	ce	qui	leur	reste,	les	prisonniers	peuvent	en	dépenser	une	autre
On	this	which	them	remains	the	captives	can	of it	spend	an	other

moitié,	le	reliquat	leur	est	remis	à	leur	sortie	de	prison.
half	the	balance	them	is	set back handed over	at	their	exit	of	prison

Ce	que	les	prisonniers	achètent,	ils	sont	forcés	de	l'acheter	dans	la
This	that	the	captives	bought	they	are	forced	of	it to buy	in	the

prison,	à	un	fournisseur	autorisé	pour	cela,	celui	qui	les	fait
prison	at	a	provider	authorized	for	that	the one	who	them	made

travailler	ordinairement	;	autre	source	pour	lui	de	très	grands	bénéfices.
work	usually	;	(an) other	source	for	him	of	very	great	earnings

L'inspection	de	la	salle	terminée,	son	récit	aussi,	il	leur	fit	traverser
The inspection	of	the	room	ended	his	story	as well	he	them	made	cross

un	grand	couloir	sombre	;	puis	s'arrêtant	à	une	porte,	il	fit	signe
a	large	corridor	dark	;	Then	himself halting stopping	at	a	door	he	made	sign

317

à ses visiteurs de venir regarder par un trou percé dedans.
to his visitors of to come look through a hole perforated in there

C'était un cachot. Dans un coin, un prisonnier, un vieillard, était assis
It was a dungeon In a corner a prisoner an old man was seated

d'un air accablé.
with an air stricken

Mab ayant demandé si Nono était dans ce couloir, le geôlier leur
Mab having asked if Nono was in this corridor the gaoler them

désigna une porte. Le cœur de nos amis battait bien fort à la
designated a door The heart of our friends beat well strong at the

pensée de voir enfin celui qu'ils cherchaient depuis si longtemps.
thought of to see finally the one that they were looking for since such (a) long time

L'abattement était passé. De son petit air résolu, Nono se promenait
The dejection was passed With his little air decided Nono himself walked

dans son cachot, un peu comme un ours en cage, car ses chaînes
in his dungeon a bit like a bear in (a) cage because his chains

ne lui permettaient pas de faire grand chemin. Mais les amis durent
not him permitted -not- of to make large way But the friends had to
to move around much

s'arracher de la porte, le geôlier les pressant d'aller plus loin.
themselves tear away from the door the gaoler them pressing of to go more far
farther

Et il les fit pénétrer dans les jardins que les dignitaires de la
And he them made enter in the gardens that the dignitaries of the

prévôté s'étaient réservés, où ils faisaient cultiver pour eux, par
provost themselves were reserved where they made cultivate for them by
for themselves had

les prisonniers, des fleurs et des légumes.
the captives -of the- flowers and -of the- vegetables

Puis, il les entraîna dans une cour où prenaient jour les meurtrières
Then he them dragged in a court where taking day the murderers
loopholes

des cachots, et montra aux visiteurs un espace étroit où on
of the dungeons and showed to the visitors a space narrow where one

permettait aux prisonniers de venir, une heure par jour, prendre l'air.
allowed to the captives of to come one hour by day to take the air

Hans fit quelques questions pour savoir quels étaient les cachots
Hans made some questions for to know what were the dungeons

dont les meurtrières donnaient sur cette cour, car les détours dans
of which the murderers gave on this court because the detours in
loopholes opened

la prison l'avaient désorienté. Et il eut la satisfaction, arrivé au pied
the prison them had confused And he had the satisfaction arrived at the foot

d'une grande tour carrée qui dominait les autres bâtiments, de voir
of a large tower square which dominated the other buildings of to see

une lucarne grillée, à quelques pieds du sol seulement, que lui
a skylight grilled at some feet from the ground only that him

montra le geôlier, en lui affirmant, que c'était celle du cachot du
showed the gaoler in him affirming that it was that of the dungeon of the

jeune prisonnier.
young prisoner

Et Hans remarquait avec joie qu'il était situé au rez-de-chaussée. Il
And Hans noted with joy that it was situated at the level-of-road He
ground floor

se rendit bien compte de sa situation, gravant dans sa mémoire les
himself rendered well account of his situation burning in his memory the

moindres détails, faisant la remarque de signes qui pourraient le
lesser details making the observation of signs which would be able him
smallest

guider, s'assura que la cour où ils se trouvaient n'était
to guide himself assured that the court where they themselves found not was

séparée de l'extérieur que par un mur d'enceinte, garni de
separated from the outdoors (other) than by a wall of enclosure decorated with

sentinelles, il est vrai ; mais cela importait peu...
sentries it is true ; but that mattered little

En montant sur la plate-forme de la tour, le geôlier ayant voulu leur
In climbing on the platform of the tower the gaoler having wanted them

montrer le panorama de la ville, il constata avec joie que la cour
to show the panorama of the city he noted with joy that the court

où donnait le cachot donnait elle-même sur une esplanade plantée
where gave the dungeon gave her self on a esplanade planted
opened

d'arbres, que Hans connaissait bien, et qui était ordinairement déserte.
with trees that Hans knew well and which was usually deserted

Le cœur des amis débordait de joie, car tous les trois, sans
The heart of the friends overflowed with joy because all the three without

s'être rien dit, à cause du geôlier, avaient fait les mêmes
themselves to be nothing said at cause of the gaoler had made the same
to have

remarques ; ils avaient hâte de sortir maintenant pour se
remarks ; they had hurry of to go out now for each other

communiquer leurs impressions.
to communicate their impressions

Il n'y avait plus rien du reste à visiter. L'heure pour le geôlier
It not there had more nothing of the rest to visit The time for the gaoler
for the

de reprendre son service approchait. Les deux jeunes étrangers
of to take again his service approached The two young foreigners

remercièrent leur pseudo-parent, et c'est avec un sentiment de
thanked their pseudo-relative and it is with a feeling of

soulagement qu'ils se retrouvèrent hors de la prison.
relief that they themselves found back outside of the prison

Ils eurent vite fait de se décider. S'ouvrir au geôlier
They had quickly done with themselves decide Themselves open up to the gaoler
were

était très aléatoire. On ne savait comment il prendrait la proposition.
was very unpredictable One not knew how he would take the proposal

Puisque la Taupe avait la facilité de creuser, peut-être pourrait-elle
Since the Mole had the facility of to dig maybe could-she
option

creuser une ouverture assez grande pour permettre au prisonnier de
dig an opening enough large for to allow to the prisoner of

sortir. On la consulterait en rentrant, et si la chose était possible,
to go out One her would consult in returning and if the thing was possible

on enverrait l'Hirondelle avertir Nono, avec une lime pour scier ses
one would send the Swallow to inform Nono with a file for to saw his
{tool}

fers, et on tenterait l'entreprise le soir même.
irons and one would try the enterprise the evening same

Le Réveil

The waking up

Le cœur battait bien fort à nos amis lorsque, accompagnés de
The heart beat well strong to our friends when, accompanied of

Penmoch, ils descendirent de leur mansarde, assez tard dans la soirée.
Penmoch, they descended from their attic enough late in the evening
quite

Ils devaient retrouver l'Insoumis près de l'esplanade.
They must find back The Rebellious near of the esplanade

Consultée, la Taupe s'était fait fort de creuser en peu d'heures
(Once) consulted the Mole itself was made strong of to dig in bit of hours
itself had tasked with a few

un souterrain assez grand pour faciliter la fuite du prisonnier. Aussi,
an underground enough large for to facilitate the flight of the prisoner So
a tunnel

n'avaient-ils pas hésité à donner suite à leurs projets. L'Hirondelle les
they had not -not- hesitated to give suite to their projects The Swallow them
follow up on

suivait voletant.
followed fluttering

Il était près de minuit lorsqu'ils arrivèrent près de l'esplanade où
It was near -of- midnight when they arrived near -of- the esplanade where

les attendait l'Insoumis. Il faisait un clair de lune magnifique. Cela
them awaited The Rebellious It made a clarity of moon splendid That
There was moonlight

gênait bien un peu nos conspirateurs, mais cela permit à Hans de
bothered well a bit our conspirators but that permitted to Hans of

distinguer la lucarne du cachot de Nono, en grimpant à un haut
to distinguish the skylight of the dungeon of Nono in climbing to a high

eucalyptus, et de la désigner à l'Hirondelle en lui remettant la lime
eucalyptus and of it to designate to the Swallow while her handing over the file
{tool}

qu'elle devait lui porter avec un mot d'avertissement.
that she must him carry with a word of warning

Mais le fenêtre était fermée. Il s'agissait d'attirer l'attention du
But the window was closed It itself dealt of to attract the attention of the

prisonnier, de lui donner l'idée de l'ouvrir ; elle se trouvait au-dessus
prisoner of him to give the idea of it open ; she itself found above
it

de sa tête, dans le mur où il était enchaîné. Hans et Mab eurent
of his head in the wall where he was chained Hans and Mab had

l'inspiration de chanter une improvisation sur un de ses airs favoris.
the inspiration of to sing an improvisation on one of his tunes favorite

Toujours par précaution, ils étaient sortis avec leurs instruments,
Always through precaution they were gone out with their instruments
had

poussant la conscience, en venant, jusqu'à aller jouer en quelques
pushing the consciousness in coming up to go play in some
keeping up the pretence

établissements sur leur chemin.
establishments on their way

Assourdissant leurs voix, accordant leurs instruments dans le ton mineur,
Muting their voice giving their instruments in the tone minor

pour que leur chant allât jusqu'aux oreilles de Nono sans trop
for that their song should go up to the ears of Nono without too (much)

éveiller l'attention des sentinelles, ne leur arrivant que comme un écho
wake up the attention of the sentries not them arriving than like an echo

éloigné, ils préludèrent à leur air favori en y adaptant ces paroles
removed they preluded to their air favorite in there adapting these words
far away

de circonstance :
of circumstance :

A l'horizon le soleil fuit,
At the horizon the sun flees

La nuit paraît ;
The night appears ;

Tout est calme ; plus aucun bruit ;
All is calm ; more any noise ;
no more noise

323

L'oiseau se tait.
The bird itself keeps silent

Dans les grands bois, tout repose.
In the great woods all rests

Le cœur transi,
The heart benumbed

Désespéré, seul, je n'ose
Desperate alone I not dare

Dormir aussi.
To sleep as well

Aux premières notes, Nono qui s'assoupissait, rêvant à tous ceux qu'il
To the first notes Nono who dozed dreaming to all those that he
of

aimait, fut aussitôt debout. Haletant, ravi, en extase, il écoutait
loved was immediately upright Breathless delighted in extasy he listened

frémissant, croyant reconnaître les voix des chanteurs.
trembling believing to recognize the voice of the singers

Et l'Espérance, doucement portée par cette musique qui semblait flotter
And the hope softly carried by this music which seemed to float

en l'air, pénétrait jusqu'à lui, le réconfortant de ses douces paroles ;
in the air penetrated up to him the comforting of its sweet words ;

pendant que par un mystérieux effet de son pouvoir magique, elle lui
during that by a mysterious effect of his ability magic she him

rendait la muraille transparente, alors que la lune éclairait le groupe
rendered the wall transparent then that the moon lit the group
so

de ses amis, sous un arbre.
of his friends under a tree

Nono leur envoya des baisers ; mais lorsque leurs voix se
Nono them sent -of the- kisses ; but when their voices themselves

turent, l'Espérance avait disparu, la muraille était redevenue sombre.
silenced the Hope had disappeared the wall was become again dark
had

Anxieux, le prisonnier porta la main à son cœur qui battait avec
Anxious the prisoner carried the hand to his heart which beat with

violence, tendant l'oreille, dans l'espoir d'entendre encore.
violence extending the ear in the hope to hear still

Et la voix des chanteurs reprit, plus douce et plus grave :
And the voice of the singers continued more sweet and more serious :

Insensible à mes larmes,
Insensitive to my tears

Un faux ami,
A false friend

Se riant de mes alarmes
Himself laughing of my alarms

Un jour s'enfuit ;
A day himself fled ;

Et cependant l'Espérance
And However the Hope

Me dit tout bas
Me said all low
soft

Qu'il a gardé souvenance
That he has guarded recollection
kept

Et reviendra.
And will come back

Quand les chanteurs se turent, les yeux du captif étaient baignés
When the singers themselves silenced the eyes of the prisoner were bathed

de larmes. Il avait compris que ses amis étaient près de lui, à sa
of tears. He had understood that his friends were near of him at his

recherche. Imprudemment, il allait crier, les appeler, se faire
search. Imprudently he went cry them call himself make

reconnaître d'eux, lorsqu'un léger frappement sur le carreau de la
to recognize of them when a light knocking on the tile of the
window pane

fenêtre attira son attention. S'aidant des pieds et des mains,
window attracted his attention Himself helping with the feet and with the hands

il atteignit la lucarne et ouvrit le châssis qui la fermait.
he reached the skylight and opened the frame which it closed

Une hirondelle pénétra portant en son bec un petit paquet qu'elle lui
A swallow penetrated carrying in her beak a little package that she him

remit. C'était la lime qu'enveloppait une lettre où Hans lui disait
handed over It was the file that enveloped a letter where Hans him said
{tool}

de limer ses fers et de faire attention à ce qui se passerait
of to file his irons and of to make attention to this which itself would pass

autour de lui, d'écouter au sol, et de soulever, à l'aide de sa
around of him of to hear at the ground and of to raise to the help of his
with

lime, la dalle sous laquelle il entendrait frapper ; de ne pas avoir
file the slab under which he heard knock ; of not -not- to have
{tool} flat stone

peur, et de s'engager sans crainte dans le souterrain qui
fear and of himself to commit without fear in the underground which
tunnel

s'offrirait à lui.
itself would offer to him

Ce ne fut qu'un jeu pour Nono de se débarrasser de ses fers,
It not was (more) than a game for Nono of himself to get rid of his irons

tant la lime mordait bien.
so much the file bit well
{tool}

Puis, après une attente qui lui sembla interminable, trois coups discrets
Then after a wait which him seemed endless three blows discreet

furent frappés à une dalle. Il eut vite fait de la soulever, étant
were struck to a slab He had quickly made of it to raise being
flat stone

animé d'une force inconnue, et il découvrit un sombre boyau, assez
animated with a force unknown and he discovered a dark intestine enough
hole

large cependant pour lui donner passage en marchant à quatre pattes.
wide however for him to give passage in moving at four paws
at hands and feet

Quelques instants après, il était dans les bras de ses amis, riant,
Some moments after he was in the arms of his friends laughing

pleurant tout à la fois. Même Penmoch qui, pas plus que la Taupe, ne
weeping all at the time Even Penmoch who not more that the Mole not

fut oublié dans les embrassades, avait quelque chose comme une larme
was forgotten in the hugs had some thing like a tear

au coin de son œil si malicieux.
at the corner of his eye so mischievous

Mais Hans avait hâte de fuir. Sortant de sa poche le ballon que lui
But Hans had haste of to flee Getting out of his pocket the balloon that him
was in a hurry

avaient remis les vers à soie, il le déploya, et la légère sphère
had handed over the worms to silk he it deployed and the light sphere
silk worms

d'étoffe se gonflant aussitôt présenta à nos amis une ouverture par
of cloth itself inflating immediately presented to our friends an opening by

laquelle ils pénétrèrent à l'intérieur. L'Insoumis, ayant voulu les suivre,
which they penetrated to the interior The Rebellious having wanted them to follow

y monta avec eux, après y avoir auparavant hissé la Taupe et
there went up with them after there to have before hoisted the Mole and

Penmoch. L'Hirondelle avait ses ailes.
Penmoch The swallow had his wings

Et le globe s'éleva joyeusement dans les airs.
And the globe itself rose joyfully in the skies

Mais tant d'émotions avaient tellement brisé Nono, qu'une fois à
But so much of emotions had so much broken Nono that one time at

l'abri il tomba en défaillance. Il lui sembla que l'étoffe se
the shelter he fell in faintness It him seemed that the cloth itself
fainted

dérobait sous eux, qu'il roulait dans le vide.
disappeared under them that he rolled in the empty

L'étoffe, que sa couleur « air du temps » rendait invisible, ne les
The cloth that its color air of the weather rendered invisible not them

empêchait pas de voir autour d'eux, et c'est ce qui donnait à
prevented -not- of to see around of them and this is this which gave to

Nono cette sensation.
Nono this feeling

Tout près, flottait l'étendard royal agité par le vent. Nono crut voir
All near floated the standard royal agitated by the wind Nono believed to see

327

le vampire qui servait d'emblème à Monnaïus prendre son vol et
the vampire which served as emblem to Monnaïus take its flight and

fondre sur lui.
melt on him
itself throw

Il jeta un cri effroyable et tout tremblant, ruisselant de sueur... il
He threw a cry appalling and all trembling streaming of sweat he
uttered

s'éveilla dans les bras de sa mère qui essayait de le consoler, lui
himself awoke in the ars of his mother who tried of him to console him

demandant ce qui avait pu troubler son sommeil.
asking this which had been able to trouble his sleep

Car notre pseudo-voyageur, qui s'était endormi la tête farcie de
Because our pseudo-traveler who himself was fallen asleep the head stuffed with
himself had

ses histoires, vous l'avez sans doute deviné déjà, venait tout simplement
his stories you it have without doubt guessed already came all simply

de rêver les aventures que vous venez de lire.
of to dream the adventures that you come of to read

Encore tout haletant, Nono raconta les phases principales de son rêve.
Still all breathless Nono told the phases main of his dreams

— Gros bêta, lui dit sa mère, tu sais bien qu'il n'y a ni
— Big animal him said his mother you know well that it not there has neither
that there are

fées, ni sorciers, ni animaux parlants, sauf les perroquets et les
fairies nor witches nor animals speaking except the parrots and the

pies qui ne font que répéter les quelques mots qu'on leur
magpies which not do (other) than repeat the few words that one them

apprend.
teaches

Tu te casses la tête avec tes lectures, et c'est ce qui te
You yourself break the head with your readings and it is this which you

donne le cauchemar.
gives the nightmare

Allons ! grand serin, rendors-toi, et ne pense plus à toutes ces
Go ! large canary resleep-yourself and not think (any)more to all these
you go back to sleep

niaiseries. Et en même temps, elle le caressait de bons gros baisers.
sillinesses / And / in / (the) same / time / she / him / carressed / with / good / big / kisses

Mais le père, qui était survenu et avait écouté le récit du rêve
But / the / father / who / was / come up / and / had / listened to / the / story / of the / dreams

d'un air attentif, prit la parole et dit à son fils :
with an / air / attentive / took / the / word / and / said / to / his / son :

— Ta mère a raison. Il n'y a pas de fées, il n'arrive jamais
— Your / mother / has / reason / It / there / has / -not- / of / fairies / it / not arrives / ever
There are no / there never happens

aucun événement sans que l'on puisse en expliquer les causes par
any / event / without / that / it one / can / of it / explain / the / causes / by

des raisons naturelles. Mais tu sais que dans les livres de contes
-of- the / reasons / natural / But / you / know / that / in / the / books / of / (fairy)tales

que l'on te fait lire, sous le récit d'événements merveilleux, on cache
that / it one / you / made / read / under / the / story / of events / wonderful / one / hides

souvent une vérité, — ou que l'on croit telle — une leçon.
often / a / truth / — / or / that / -it- one / believes / such / — / a / lesson

Et ton rêve, pour être d'un petit garçon de ton âge, me semble
And / your / dreams / for / to be / of a / little / boy / of / your / age / me / appear

en contenir un très grand nombre qui échappent peut-être à ton
of them / to contain / a / very / large / number / which / escape / maybe / to / your
{of lessons}

entendement.
mind

Si tu tu le rappelles encore demain, je t'engage à l'écrire, tu
If / you / yourself / it / remember / still / tomorrow / I / you commit / to / it write (down) / you

le reliras plus tard en le méditant. Et sans doute, il t'aidera à
it / will reread / more / late / in / it / meditating / And / without / doubt / it / will help you / to
thinking about

connaître beaucoup d'injustices, beaucoup d'erreurs, que tu n'apercevrais
know / a lot / of injustices / a lot / of errors / that / you / would not perceive
recognize

peut-être pas autrement.
perhaps / -not- / otherwise

www.ingramcontent.com/pod-product-compliance
Lightning Source LLC
Chambersburg PA
CBHW030910090426
42737CB00007B/154